Records of
North American
Whitetail Deer

Records of North American Whitetail Deer

A book of the Boone and Crockett Club Containing Tabulations of Whitetail Deer of North America as Compiled from Data In the Club's Big Game Records Archives.

Edited by Wm. H. Nesbitt and Jack Reneau

First Edition
1987
The Boone and Crockett Club
Dumfries, Virginia

Records of North American Whitetail Deer

Copyright © 1987 by the Boone and Crockett Club.
All rights reserved, including the right to reproduce this book or portions thereof in any form or by any means, electronic or mechanical, including photocopying, recording, or by an information storage and retrieval system, without permission in writing from the Boone and Crockett Club.
Library of Congress Catalog Card Number: 87–072474
ISBN Number: 0-940864-12-6
Published November 1987

Published in the United States of America by the
Boone and Crockett Club
241 South Fraley Boulevard
Dumfries, Virginia 22026

Foreword

I must confess that I have had the idea for this book for more than a decade, but the idea had to wait until the physical basis necessary to produce it was ready. A great deal of this book is formed from the data on score charts accepted during the early days of the records keeping, the days of largely volunteer work and very little in-depth scrutiny of both the data and the other conditions of entry. All that has been changed in recent years, as professionally trained staff in the Club office carefully review the submitted score charts, and the associated conditions of the hunt. The measurements on the score chart are reviewed against the required photos of the trophy, to make sure that the correct scoring interpretation has been made by the Official Measurer. Kill locations are checked on maps and against the state/provincial regulations to ensure compliance with all applicable regulations. Finally, the measurements recorded on the score chart are put into a computer data base. The computer then computes the final score, with any deductions taken into account. Thus, recent entries (roughly the last decade) are as above reproach as humanly possible. But what about the earlier entries?

For the past several years, Club staff has worked long and hard to transfer the data from the early files into the computer data base. Not only were the measurements entered, all the other factors such as kill location were carefully verified before they were added. Then, the computer re-computed the scores for these trophies that have long been published in the all-time records books. The results were surprising. For whitetail deer, about five percent of the older trophy records were found to have mathematical and/or scoring errors. In some cases, this resulted in some rather spectacular changes in ranking, even to the point of trophies falling below minimum score. You'll find several such examples in this book, if you are familiar with the older published records. In no case did the errors seem to be deliberate; rather, they were simply the kind humans seem cursed to make in their normal work.

The extensive review of older trophy records mentioned above was necessary to provide the basis for assembly of the ninth edition of the all-time records book (*Records of North American Big Game*) that will be published in late 1988, the Centennial year of the Club. With that review of the whitetail data files completed, we finally had the necessary framework to publish this whitetail-only records book, with its unique features and value for the whitetail hunter.

This book, for the first time, recognizes state and provincial records. In many hunting camps and sportsman's homes, these are almost mystical standards, having that special and practical appeal as next season's hunts are being planned. To many deer hunters, the "World's Record" doesn't really matter; what counts is the "record" for their own state or province, since that is where they hunt. It is really for this type of hunter that this book was prepared.

My co-editor, Jack Reneau, joins me in wishing you good hunting for your favorite game animal, the whitetail.

>
> Wm. H. Nesbitt
> Executive Director
> Boone and Crockett Club

Contents

Foreword. v
List of Illustrations ix
Introduction 1
Tabulations of Recorded Whitetail Deer 11
   Alabama—Typical 13   Non-Typical 15
   Arkansas—Typical 17   Non-Typical 19
   Colorado—Typical 21
   Connecticut—Typical. 23
   Georgia—Typical 25   Non-Typical 29
   Idaho—Typical. 31   Non-Typical 33
   Illinois—Typical 35   Non-Typical 39
   Indiana—Typical. 43   Non-Typical 45
   Iowa—Typical 47   Non-Typical 51
   Kansas—Typical. 55   Non-Typical 59
   Kentucky—Typical 63   Non-Typical 67
   Louisiana—Typical 69   Non-Typical 71
   Maine—Typical 73   Non-Typical 77
   Maryland—Typical 79   Non-Typical 81
   Michigan—Typical. 83   Non-Typical 87
   Minnesota—Typical 89   Non-Typical 95
   Mississippi—Typical. 101   Non-Typical 103
   Missouri—Typical 105   Non-Typical 109
   Montana—Typical 111   Non-Typical 115
   Nebraska—Typical. 119   Non-Typical 123
   New York—Typical 127   Non-Typical 131
   North Dakota—Typical . . .133   Non-Typical 135

Ohio—Typical	137	Non-Typical	141
Oklahoma—Typical	145	Non-Typical	147
Oregon—Typical			149
Pennsylvania—Typical	151	Non-Typical	153
South Carolina—Non-Typical			155
South Dakota—Typical	157	Non-Typical	161
Tennessee—Typical	163	Non-Typical	165
Texas—Typical	167	Non-Typical	173
Virginia—Typical	177	Non-Typical	179
Washington—Typical	181	Non-Typical	183
West Virginia—Typical	187	Non-Typical	189
Wisconsin—Typical	191	Non-Typical	197
Wyoming—Typical	203	Non-Typical	205
Alberta—Typical	207	Non-Typical	211
British Columbia—Typical	215	Non-Typical	217
Manitoba—Typical	219	Non-Typical	223
New Brunswick—Typical	225	Non-Typical	227
Nova Scotia—Non-Typical			229
Ontario—Typical			231
Saskatchewan—Typical	233	Non-Typical	239
Mexico—Typical	243	Non-Typical	245

Illustrations

Score Chart—Typical	6	Non-Typical	8
Alabama Record—Typical	12	Non-Typical	14
Arkansas Record—Typical	16	Non-Typical	18
Colorado Record—Typical			20
Connecticut Record—Typical			22
Georgia Record—Typical	24	Non-Typical	28
C. W. Shelton's Typical Trophy			27
Idaho Record—Typical	30	Non-Typical	32
Illinois Record—Typical	34	Non-Typical	38
2nd NABG Competition			37
Jessie Byer's Typical Trophy			41
Indiana Record—Typical	42	Non-Typical	44
Iowa Record—Typical	46	Non-Typical	50
Maurice Robinette's Typical Trophy			49
Claude Feathers' Typical Trophy			53
Kansas Record—Typical	54	Non-Typical	58
Gary Littlejohn's Typical Trophy			57
5th NABG Competition			61
Kentucky Record—Typical	62	Non-Typical	66
Al Prouty's Non-Typical Trophy			65
Louisiana Record—Typical	68	Non-Typical	70
Maine Record—Typical	72	Non-Typical	76
Richard E. Johndrow's Typical Trophy			75
Maryland Record—Typical	78	Non-Typical	80
Michigan Record—Typical	82	Non-Typical	86
Janice K. Beranek's Non-Typical Trophy			85
Minnesota Record—Typical	88	Non-Typical	94
Mississippi Record—Typical	100	Non-Typical	102
Missouri Record—Typical	104	Non-Typical	108
Ray Sadler's Typical Trophy			107

ix

Montana Record—Typical . . . 110   Non-Typical 114
Hugh Cox's Non-Typical Trophy 113
Raymond Cowan's Non-Typical Trophy 117
Nebraska Record—Typical . . . 118   Non-Typical 122
Jack Hammond's Typical Trophy 125
New York Record—Typical. . . . 126   Non-Typical 130
13th NABG Competition 129
North Dakota Record—Typical . . 132   Non-Typical 134
Ohio Record—Typical 136   Non-Typical 140
Ken W. Koenig's Typical Trophy 139
Thelma Martens' Non-Typical Trophy 143
Oklahoma Record—Typical. . . . 144   Non-Typical 146
Oregon Record—Typical 148
Pennsylvania Record—Typical . . 150   Non-Typical 152
South Carolina Record—Non-Typical 154
South Dakota Record—Typical . . 156   Non-Typical 160
Rudy C. Grecar's Non-Typical Trophy 159
Tennessee Record—Typical. . . . 162   Non-Typical 164
Texas Record—Typical 166   Non-Typical 172
Ralph Klimek's Non-Typical Trophy 171
John Batten Measuring Trophy 175
Virginia Record—Typical. 176   Non-Typical 178
Washington Record—Typical . . . 180   Non-Typical 182
Dorsey O. Breeden's Non-Typical Trophy 185
West Virginia Record—Typical . . 186   Non-Typical 188
Wisconsin Record—Typical . . . 190   Non-Typical 196
11th NABG Competition 201
Wyoming Record—Typical. . . . 202   Non-Typical 204
Alberta Record—Typical 206   Non-Typical 210
Mark T. Hathcock's Non-Typical Trophy. 213
British Columbia Record—
Typical 214   Non-Typical (2nd). . . 216
Manitoba Record—Typical 218   Non-Typical 222
Gary E. Landry's Typical Trophy 221
New Brunswick Record—
Typical (2nd). 224   Non-Typical 226
Nova Scotia Record—Non-Typical 228
Ontario Record—Typical 230
Saskatchewan Record—Typical . . 232   Non-Typical 238
Mark D. Holmes' Non-Typical Trophy. 237
Mexico Record—Typical 242   Non-Typical 244

Introduction

The Story of This Book

As nearly every sportsman knows, the Boone and Crockett Club publishes what is universally recognized as "the" records book for North American big game. Those records books (the all-time records) have been published on a fairly regular schedule (roughly six-year intervals) since the current scoring system was adopted in 1950. Then, in 1984, the first "awards period" records book was published, summarizing the three years of the 18th Awards entry period, 1980–1982. With both of these records books available, sportsmen can consult each of them for different information. To find the world's records, the greatest expression of trophy character for the category, and the areas traditionally producing the greatest numbers of record-class trophies, one should look to the all-time records. To determine the trophy quality currently available across the continent, and also enjoy the hunting stories and photos for the top trophies receiving awards, one would open the latest Awards records book. Why then is there a need for yet another records book, devoted entirely to the whitetail deer?

This special records book for whitetails allows us to incorporate a couple of data items not found in the traditional records books, but widely used in the hunting world. The total of lengths of all abnormal points is included for *both* typical and non-typical categories, to better indicate the exact conformation of the listed trophies. Although greatest spread is *not* one of the measurements summed up to give the final score for a trophy (it is a "supplementary measurement" to show confirmation), it is easily the most widely used comparison figure, other than final score and main beam length. It was therefore a "natural" for inclusion in this book, once the necessary data had been entered into the computer.

Even the format of this book is different. This is the first records book to be offered in paperback, and it is a much smaller size than the Awards and all-time records books. In part this size difference is to help distinguish this book from the other records books offered. A larger reason is to make it more easily carried in a backpack, a glove compartment, or tossed onto the table at a deer-hunting camp. This is a book to be read and enjoyed in camp, settling some arguments, while no doubt starting some new ones.

Scoring of Trophies

The current scoring system dates from 1950, when a special committee of the Boone and Crockett Club completed its work in developing a fair system of trophy evaluation that would recognize symmetry, be based upon measurements that the average hunter could understand and make, and that would result in a final score that would allow for natural ranking of trophies. That the committee's labors were a success is shown both by the universal acceptance of the system and also by the fact that *no* major changes have been made to the system since its adoption. The great strength of the system is in the repeatability of the measurements. Should someone question either an individual measurement or the entire scoring of a trophy, the measurements and scoring can be repeated to show their correctness, even years after the original measurement. This is, of course, possible only because the enduring characters of skull (for cat and bear), horns, and antlers were chosen as the measured characters. Had body length or weight (or some combination of such factors) been chosen, there could be no such repeating of the measurements.

The first whitetail scoring charts developed in 1950 included both a typical and non-typical version, just as we have today. In 1950, the minimum entry score for typical was 140, while that for non-typical was 160. Today, the minimum entry for the all-time records book (and this edition of the deer records book) is 170 for typical and 195 for non-typical. For the Awards program records book only, the minimums are slightly lower (160 and 185), with these lower scoring trophies being listed only the single time in the

Awards records book. The non-typical category differs from the typical in the recording of the abnormal points (points beyond the "usual" pattern for a typical whitetail). In the typical category they are subtracted as a penalty from the final score, while in the non-typical category they are added into the final score. This is the reason for the minimum entry score being higher for the non-typical category.

Scoring of a whitetail begins with careful reading of the Official Score Chart, then following its instructions to record the measurements that form the basis of the final score. Both of the score charts (typical and non-typical) are reproduced in this chapter so that you can fill them in to see how your favorite trophy stacks up against those trophies published in this book. For detailed instructions and discussion of scoring *all* categories of acceptable big game, you should get a copy of the Club's book, *Measuring and Scoring North American Big Game Trophies*. This extensively illustrated book gives a step-by-step approach to measuring and scoring a trophy, and it is the basic reference for the Official Measurers in scoring trophies for entry.

Entry of Trophies

When a trophy has been determined to be above or very near the necessary minimum entry score by proper use of the score chart, it is then time to consider having an official measurement performed. Only an Official Measurer (specially trained and appointed by the Club) can measure a trophy for official entry into the records keeping and for publication in the Awards and/or (depending upon final score) all-time records book(s). An official measurement cannot be made until the trophy has dried for at least 60 days, under normal atmospheric conditions, after kill. This is necessary to allow for the normal shrinkage that occurs in all trophies. The standard drying period makes sure that shrinkage will be relatively the same for all trophies, a condition that could not be met if green scores were allowed and some trophies were, because of the extended hunt or other conditions, not measured for some time after kill. Should the trophy be in velvet, the velvet must be removed before an official measurement can be made, as the velvet obviously increases the measurements. If the velvet is *not* removed at the time of kill, the 60-day drying period will be dated from the date of velvet removal.

Official Measurers are supplied with all necessary materials for trophy entry, including the score charts for recording the entry measurements. Official Measurers donate their time to measure trophies as a public service, and there is no charge for a measurement. But, the trophy must be taken to them, and it must be at their convenience since they are donating their time. The Official Measurer will notify the trophy owner of any materials beyond the completed score chart and entry fee that are required to complete a trophy entry.

The Awards Programs

For the top-ranking trophies in each three-year program of trophy entry, there is the possibility of being invited to the tri-annual Awards program where a select panel of Official Measurers re-measure and certify the invited trophies for possible awards of the Boone and Crockett Club Medal and/or Certificate. Should an invited trophy not be sent to the Awards Judging, an asterisk will be added to its listing in the various records books and it will be shown without rank until such time as the asterisk is removed by the submission of additional verifying measurements that the Club's Records Committee decides to accept as a substitute for the trophy appearing before the Awards Judges Panel. In the case of a potential World's Record, the trophy *must* come before a Judges Panel in order to be certified as a World's Record; there is *no* alternate path for a potential World's Record.

The invited trophies of an Awards program are put on public display for an extended period that precedes the Awards banquet. These displays are quite popular, with tens of thousands of people viewing the display at each Awards. Awards, as determined by the Judges Panel, are made at the Awards Banquet that closes the Awards events.

The Awards entry periods are on a three-year basis, with the Awards events being held during mid-year of the year following the close of the entry period. Thus, the 20th Awards will be held in 1989, with the three years of the 20th Awards entry period ending on 31 December 1988. You will notice the word "Competition" used in this book. The Club began formal recognition of North American big game in 1947 with the "First North American Big

Game Competition". These programs were held on an annual basis until 1952 when they became biennial. In 1968, they were put on a three-year basis, and in 1971 the term "Awards" was substituted for "Competition" in order to better describe basic objectives of the programs.

Trophies acknowledged with an award at an Awards program will be profiled in the records book for that period by use of a photo and the hunting story, in addition to the listing of the trophy in its rightful place in the trophy rankings.

The Future

The whitetail is easily the most popular big-game animal of North America. Each fall, well over 20 million North American hunters set forth for the woods, a great many of them in quest of a whitetail. It is estimated that more than two million whitetails (both sexes) are harvested in an average year.

It is interesting to note the kill dates for trophies published in this book. The number of large trophies being taken today across the entire range of the whitetail certainly points to the effectiveness of the management programs and the generally good health of the populations. This success story is even more obvious when you examine the three plus decades of the records keeping. Of the 1292 deer recorded in this book (trophies entered and accepted by 31 December 1985), 178 were killed prior to 1950; 165 were killed during 1950–59; 363 were killed during 1960–69; 306 were killed during 1970–79; and a whopping 280 were killed during the *six-years only* of 1980–85. Of course, some of the reasons for the greater numbers of deer (and, by the way, most other categories) being entered are the greatly increased number of Official Measurers (about 30 percent more than in previous decades), better publicity about the records keeping and the records books, and just plain increased interest in the whitetail by today's hunters.

OFFICIAL SCORING SYSTEM FOR NORTH AMERICAN BIG GAME TROPHIES

Records of North American
Big Game

BOONE AND CROCKETT CLUB

241 South Fraley Boulevard
Dumfries, Virginia 22026

Minimum Score:
whitetail 170
Coues' 110

**TYPICAL
WHITETAIL AND COUES' DEER**

Kind of Deer _____

DETAIL OF POINT MEASUREMENT

	Abnormal Points	
	Right	Left

			Total to E			
SEE OTHER SIDE FOR INSTRUCTIONS			Column 1	Column 2	Column 3	Column 4
A. Number of Points on Each Antler	R.	L.	Spread Credit	Right Antler	Left Antler	Difference
B. Tip to Tip Spread						
C. Greatest Spread						
D. Inside Spread of Main Beams	Credit may equal but not exceed length of longer antler					
IF Spread exceeds longer antler, enter difference.						
E. Total of Lengths of all Abnormal Points						
F. Length of Main Beam						
G-1. Length of First Point, if present						
G-2. Length of Second Point						
G-3. Length of Third Point						
G-4. Length of Fourth Point, if present						
G-5. Length of Fifth Point, if present						
G-6. Length of Sixth Point, if present						
G-7. Length of Seventh Point, if present						
H-1. Circumference at Smallest Place Between Burr and First Point						
H-2. Circumference at Smallest Place Between First and Second Points						
H-3. Circumference at Smallest Place Between Second and Third Points						
H-4. Circumference at Smallest Place between Third and Fourth Points (see back if G-4 is missing)						
TOTALS						

ADD	Column 1		Exact locality where killed
	Column 2		Date killed By whom killed
	Column 3		Present owner
	Total		Address
SUBTRACT Column 4			Guide's Name and Address
FINAL SCORE			Remarks: (Mention any abnormalities or unique qualities)

I certify that I have measured the above trophy on _____ 19_____
at (address) _____ City _____ State _____
and that these measurements and data are, to the best of my knowledge and belief, made in accordance
with the instructions given.
Witness: _____ Signature: _____
                                                              OFFICIAL MEASURER [ ][ ][ ]

INSTRUCTIONS FOR MEASURING WHITETAIL AND COUES' DEER

All measurements must be made with a ¼-inch flexible steel tape to the nearest one-eighth of an inch. Wherever it is necessary to change direction of measurement, mark a control point and swing tape at this point. Enter fractional figures in eighths, without reduction. Official measurements cannot be taken for at least sixty days after the animal was killed.

A. Number of Points on Each Antler. To be counted a point, a projection must be at least one inch long and its length must exceed the width of its base. All points are measured from tip of point to nearest edge of beam as illustrated. Beam tip is counted as a point but not measured as a point.

B. Tip to Tip Spread is measured between tips of main beams.

C. Greatest Spread is measured between perpendiculars at a right angle to the center line of the skull at widest part whether across main beams or points.

D. Inside Spread of Main Beams is measured at a right angle to the center line of the skull at widest point between main beams. Enter this measurement again in Spread Credit column if it is less than or equal to the length of longer antler; if longer, enter longer antler length for Spread Credit.

E. Total of lengths of all Abnormal Points. Abnormal points are those nontypical in location (points originating from points or from sides or bottom of main beam) or extra points beyond the normal pattern of up to eight normal points, including beam tip, per antler. Measure in usual manner and enter in appropriate blanks.

F. Length of Main Beam is measured from lowest outside edge of burr over outer curve to the most distant point of what is, or appears to be, the main beam. The point of beginning is that point on the burr where the center line along the outer curve of the beam intersects the burr, then following generally the line of the illustration.

G-1-2-3-4-5-6-7. Length of Normal Points. Normal points project from the top of the main beam. They are measured from nearest edge of main beam over outer curve to tip. Lay the tape along the outer curve of the beam so that the top edge of the tape coincides with the top edge of the beam on both sides of the point to determine baseline for point measurements. Record point lengths in appropriate blanks.

H-1-2-3-4. Circumferences are taken as detailed for each measurement. If brow point is missing, take H-1 and H-2 at smallest place between burr and G-2. If G-4 is missing, take H-4 halfway between G-3 and tip of main beam.

* * * * * * * * * * *

FAIR CHASE STATEMENT FOR ALL HUNTER-TAKEN TROPHIES

To make use of the following methods shall be deemed as UNFAIR CHASE and unsportsmanlike, and any trophy obtained by use of such means is disqualified from entry for Awards.
  I. Spotting or herding game from the air, followed by landing in its vicinity for pursuit;
  II. Herding or pursuing game with motor-powered vehicles;
  III. Use of electronic communications for attracting, locating or observing game, or guiding the hunter to such game;
  IV. Hunting game confined by artificial barriers, including escape-proof fencing; or hunting game transplanted solely for the purpose of commercial shooting.
****

I certify that the trophy scored on this chart was not taken in UNFAIR CHASE as defined above by the Boone and Crockett Club. I further certify that it was taken in full compliance with local game laws of the state, province, or territory.

Date_____Signature of Hunter_____ _____
(Have signature notarized by a Notary Public)

                    Copyright © 1981 by Boone and Crockett Club
              (Reproduction strictly forbidden without express, written consent)

OFFICIAL SCORING SYSTEM FOR NORTH AMERICAN BIG GAME TROPHIES

Records of North American Big Game

BOONE AND CROCKETT CLUB

241 South Fraley Boulevard
Dumfries, Virginia 22026

Minimum Score:
whitetail 195
Coues' 120

NON-TYPICAL
WHITETAIL AND COUES' DEER

Kind of Deer _____

Abnormal Points	
Right	Left
Total to E	

	SEE OTHER SIDE FOR INSTRUCTIONS				Column 1	Column 2	Column 3	Column 4
A.	Number of Points on Each Antler	R.		L.	Spread Credit	Right Antler	Left Antler	Difference
B.	Tip to Tip Spread							
C.	Greatest Spread							
D.	Inside Spread of Main Beams	Credit may equal but not exceed length of longer antler						
	IF Spread exceeds longer antler, enter difference.							
E.	Total of Lengths of Abnormal Points							
F.	Length of Main Beam							
G-1.	Length of First Point, if present							
G-2.	Length of Second Point							
G-3.	Length of Third Point							
G-4.	Length of Fourth Point, if present							
G-5.	Length of Fifth Point, if present							
G-6.	Length of Sixth Point, if present							
G-7.	Length of Seventh Point, if present							
H-1.	Circumference at Smallest Place Between Burr and First Point							
H-2.	Circumference at Smallest Place Between First and Second Points							
H-3.	Circumference at Smallest Place Between Second and Third Points							
H-4.	Circumference at Smallest Place Between Third and Fourth Points							
	TOTALS							

ADD	Column 1		Exact locality where killed
	Column 2		Date killed By whom killed
	Column 3		Present owner
	Total		Address
SUBTRACT	Column 4		
	Result		Guide's Name and Address
Add line E Total			Remarks: (Mention any abnormalities or unique qualities)
FINAL SCORE			

8

I certify that I have measured the above trophy on _____ 19_____
at (address) _____ City _____ State_____
and that these measurements and data are, to the best of my knowledge and belief, made in accordance
with the instructions given.
Witness: _____ Signature: _____
                                                              OFFICIAL MEASURER |__|__|__|__|

INSTRUCTIONS FOR MEASURING NON-TYPICAL WHITETAIL AND COUES' DEER

All measurements must be made with a ¼-inch flexible steel tape to the nearest one-eighth of an inch. Wherever it is necessary to change direction of measurement, mark a control point and swing tape at this point. Enter fractional figures in eighths, without reduction. Official measurements cannot be taken for at least sixty days after the animal was killed.

A. Number of Points on Each Antler. To be counted a point, a projection must be at least one inch long and its length must exceed the width of its base. All points are measured from tip of point to nearest edge of beam as illustrated. Beam tip is counted as a point but not measured as a point.

B. Tip to Tip Spread is measured between tips of main beams.

C. Greatest Spread is measured between perpendiculars at a right angle to the center line of the skull at widest part whether across main beams or points.

D. Inside Spread of Main Beams is measured at a right angle to the center line of the skull at widest point between main beams. Enter this measurement again in Spread Credit column if it is less than or equal to the length of longer antler; if longer, enter longer antler length for Spread Credit.

E. Total of Lengths of all Abnormal Points. Abnormal points are those nontypical in location (points originating from points or from sides or bottom of main beam) or extra points beyond the normal pattern of up to eight normal points, including beam tip, per antler. Measure in usual manner and enter in appropriate blanks.

F. Length of Main Beam is measured from lowest outside edge of burr over outer curve to the most distant point of what is, or appears to be, the main beam. The point of beginning is that point on the burr where the center line along the outer curve of the beam intersects the burr, then following generally the line of the illustration.

G-1-2-3-4-5-6-7. Length of Normal Points. Normal points project from the top of the main beam. They are measured from nearest edge of main beam over outer curve to tip. Lay the tape along the outer curve of the beam so that the top edge of the tape coincides with the beam on both sides of the point to determine baseline for point measurement. Record point lengths in appropriate blanks.

H-1-2-3-4. Circumferences are taken as detailed for each measurement. If brow point is missing, take H-1 and H-2 at smallest place between burr and G-2. If G-4 is missing, take H-4 halfway between G-3 and tip of main beam.

* * * * * * * * * * *

FAIR CHASE STATEMENT FOR ALL HUNTER-TAKEN TROPHIES

To make use of the following methods shall be deemed as UNFAIR CHASE and unsportsmanlike, and any trophy obtained by use of such means is disqualified from entry for Awards.
  I. Spotting or herding game from the air, followed by landing in its vicinity for pursuit;
  II. Herding or pursuing game with motor-powered vehicles;
  III. Use of electronic communications for attracting, locating or observing game, or guiding the hunter to such game;
  IV. Hunting game confined by artificial barriers, including escape-proof fencing; or hunting game transplanted solely for the purpose of commercial shooting.
****
I certify that the trophy scored on this chart was not taken in UNFAIR CHASE as defined above by the Boone and Crockett Club. I further certify that it was taken in full compliance with local game laws of the state, province, or territory.
Date_____Signature of Hunter_____
(Have signature notarized by a Notary Public)

Copyright © 1981 by Boone and Crockett Club
(Reproduction strictly forbidden without express, written consent)

Tabulations of Recorded Whitetails

The trophy data shown herein have been taken from score charts in the Records Archives of the Boone and Crockett Club. Trophies listed are those that meet minimum score and other stated requirements of trophy entry through the end of the 19th Awards entry period (1983–1985).

The final scores and rank shown are official, except for trophies shown with an asterisk. The asterisk is assigned to trophies whose entry scores are subject to certification by an Awards Panel of Judges. The asterisk can be removed (except in the case of a potential World's Record) by the submission of two additional, independent scorings by Official Measurers of the Boone and Crockett Club. The Records Committee of the Club will review the three scorings available (original plus two additional) and determine which, if any, will be accepted in lieu of the Judges Panel measurement. When the score has been accepted as final by the Records Committee, the asterisk will be removed in future editions of the all-time records book, *Records of North American Big Game*, and other publications. In the case of a potential World's Record, the trophy *must* come before a Judges Panel at the end of an entry period. Only a Judges Panel can certify a World's Record and finalize its score.

Asterisked trophies are shown at the end of their category. They are *not* ranked, as their final score is subject to revision by a Judges Panel or by the submission of additional, official scorings, as described above.

Photo Courtesy of James C. Bailey

ALABAMA STATE RECORD
TYPICAL ANTLERS
SCORE: 182 7/8

Locality: Hale Co.   Date: January 1974
Hunter: James C. Bailey

ALABAMA

TYPICAL WHITETAILS

Score	Length of Main Beam R	L	Inside Spread	Greatest Spread	Circumference at Smallest Place Between Burr and First Point R	L	Number of Points R	L	Total of Lengths Abnormal Points	Date Killed	Rank
\<small\>Locality Killed / By Whom Killed / Owner\</small\>											
182 7/8	27 4/8	28 2/8	19 3/8	21 4/8	5 5/8	5 5/8	6	5	2 2/8	1974	1
■ Hale County / James C. Bailey / James C. Bailey											
173 4/8	27 6/8	28	26 1/8	28	5 5/8	5 5/8	7	9	8 7/8	1960	2
■ Marengo County / Picked Up / L. M. Cabiniss											
172 1/8	26 3/8	26 4/8	21 5/8	23 7/8	5 1/8	5 3/8	5	5	0	1968	3
■ Pickens County / Walter Jaynes / Walter Jaynes											
170 2/8	27 1/8	27 2/8	21	22 6/8	5 3/8	5 3/8	4	4	0	1980	4
■ Lee County / George P. Mann / George P. Mann											

Photo Courtesy of James L. Spidle, Sr.

ALABAMA STATE RECORD
NON-TYPICAL ANTLERS
SCORE: 230 7/8

Locality: Sumter Co.   Date: Prior 1942
Hunter: James L. Spidle, Sr.

ALABAMA

NON-TYPICAL WHITETAILS

Score	Length of Main Beam R	L	Inside Spread	Greatest Spread	Circumference at Smallest Place Between Burr and First Point R	L	Number of Points R	L	Total of Lengths Abnormal Points	Date Killed	Rank
230 7/8	24 5/8	24 6/8	15 1/8	19 6/8	6 2/8	5 4/8	24	13	92 2/8	PR 1942	1
■ Sumter County / James L. Spidle, Sr. / James L. Spidle, Sr.												
224 5/8	24 6/8	27 1/8	25 1/8	27 4/8	5 7/8	5 4/8	15	7	70	1976	2
■ Perry County / Robert E. Royster / Robert E. Royster												
218 3/8	23 4/8	22 7/8	15 7/8	25 4/8	5 1/8	5 5/8	11	17	56 4/8	PR 1952	3
■ Sumter County / Josh Jones / Harrison H. Perry												
199 4/8	25 6/8	25 4/8	21 2/8	23 3/8	5 6/8	5 5/8	9	9	24 4/8	1975	4
■ Wilcox County / Billy W. Morton / Billy W. Morton												
199 2/8	28 7/8	27 3/8	23 5/8	27 5/8	5 2/8	5 2/8	7	9	19 1/8	1973	5
■ Winston County / James W. Huckbay / James W. Huckbay												

Photo Courtesy of Walter Spears

ARKANSAS STATE RECORD
TYPICAL ANTLERS
SCORE: 186 7/8

Locality: Arkansas Co.   Date: 1952
Hunter: Walter Spears

ARKANSAS

TYPICAL WHITETAILS

Score	Length of Main Beam R	L	Inside Spread	Greatest Spread	Circumference at Smallest Place Between Burr and First Point R	L	Number of Points R	L	Total of Lengths Abnormal Points	Date Killed	Rank
186 7/8	25 5/8	25 3/8	20 1/8	21 4/8	4 7/8	5	5	5	0	1952	1
■ Arkansas County / Walter Spears / Walter Spears
184 6/8	26 7/8	27	24 4/8	0	5 3/8	5 3/8	8	9	12 2/8	1961	2
■ Desha County / Lee Perry / Walter Brock
183	27 1/8	27 7/8	18 6/8	20 4/8	4 6/8	4 6/8	5	5	0	1954	3
■ Desha County / R. J. Diekhoff / Franzen Bros.
180	26 6/8	26 5/8	19 6/8	23	4 4/8	4 4/8	7	5	1 4/8	1962	4
■ Desha County / Turner Neal / Turner Neal
179 2/8	27 2/8	27 1/8	23 3/8	28 4/8	5	5 2/8	9	11	11 7/8	1962	5
■ Prairie County / Charles Newsom / Charles Newsom
177 7/8	27	28 4/8	20	24 1/8	4 6/8	5	6	6	3 7/8	1923	6
■ Chicot County / George Matthews / W. T. Haynes
173 3/8	26 3/8	26 3/8	19 1/8	22 1/8	5 3/8	5 3/8	7	7	6 6/8	1948	7
■ Arkansas County / Jimmy Hanson / Jimmy Hanson
173 2/8	30 3/8	29 6/8	21 1/8	23 5/8	5	5 7/8	6	8	3 3/8	1951	8
■ Chicot County / Yan Sturdivant / Bruce Sturdivant
172	26 1/8	25	24 2/8	26 2/8	4 5/8	4 4/8	5	5	0	1962	9
■ Bearden / Buddy Wise / Buddy Wise
171 2/8	29 2/8	28 6/8	19 2/8	21 6/8	4 6/8	4 4/8	6	5	0	1953	10
■ Arkansas County / Wilbur Stephens / Wilbur Stephens
170 6/8	27 4/8	26 4/8	18	21	5	5 2/8	6	7	4 2/8	1960	11
■ Chicot County / Mrs. L. M. Hamilton / Mrs. L. M. Hamilton
170 4/8	27	27 2/8	20 6/8	22 7/8	5 2/8	5 2/8	6	5	0	1948	12
■ Desha County / Bob Norris / Bob Norris
170 3/8	26	26	19 1/8	21 1/8	5 3/8	5 3/8	6	5	1	1960	13
■ Woodruff County / R. L. Taylor / R. L. Taylor

■ Locality Killed / By Whom Killed / Owner

Photo Courtesy of Clem Billgisher

ARKANSAS STATE RECORD
NON-TYPICAL ANTLERS
SCORE: 206 1/8

Locality: Boydel   Date: Picked Up in 1959
Owner: Clem Billgisher

ARKANSAS

NON-TYPICAL WHITETAILS

Score	Length of Main Beam R	Length of Main Beam L	Inside Spread	Greatest Spread	Circumference at Smallest Place Between Burr and First Point R	Circumference at Smallest Place Between Burr and First Point L	Number of Points R	Number of Points L	Total of Lengths Abnormal Points	Date Killed	Rank
					■ Locality Killed / By Whom Killed / Owner						
206 1/8	24 4/8	22 6/8	18	23 7/8	4 3/8	4 3/8	14	13	42 7/8	1959	1
	■ Boydel / Picked Up / Clem Billgisher										
201 1/8	28 2/8	27 3/8	16 5/8	21 6/8	5 1/8	5 2/8	8	9	24 4/8	1953	2
	■ Arkansas County / Daniel Boone Bullock / Daniel Boone Bullock										
196 4/8	26 6/8	28 5/8	19	21 6/8	5	4 7/8	8	8	20	1955	3
	■ Desha County / Turner Neal / Turner Neal										

Photo Courtesy of Ivan W. Rhodes

COLORADO STATE RECORD
TYPICAL ANTLERS
SCORE: 182 5/8

Locality: Yuma Co.   Date: October 1978
Hunter: Ivan W. Rhodes

COLORADO

TYPICAL WHITETAILS

Score	Length of Main Beam R	L	Inside Spread	Greatest Spread	Circumference at Smallest Place Between Burr and First Point R	L	Number of Points R	L	Total of Lengths Abnormal Points	Date Killed	Rank
182 5/8	23 6/8	24 3/8	19 4/8	22 1/8	5 5/8	5 7/8	6	8	4 5/8	1978	1
■ Yuma County / Ivan W. Rhodes / Ivan W. Rhodes											
175 7/8	24 6/8	25 6/8	17 1/8	19 5/8	4 5/8	4 4/8	4	4	0	1971	2
■ Logan County / Picked Up / Marvin Gardner											

21

Photo Courtesy of Rickey A. Vincent

CONNECTICUT STATE RECORD
TYPICAL ANTLERS
SCORE: 177 2/8

Locality: Litchfield Co.   Date: Picked Up in 1984
Owner: Rickey A. Vincent

CONNECTICUT

TYPICAL WHITETAILS

Score	Length of Main Beam R	Length of Main Beam L	Inside Spread	Greatest Spread	Circumference at Smallest Place Between Burr and First Point R	Circumference at Smallest Place Between Burr and First Point L	Number of Points R	Number of Points L	Total of Lengths Abnormal Points	Date Killed	Rank
177 2/8	27 5/8	29	21 7/8	24 3/8	6	6	5	6	5 5/8	1984	1

■ Litchfield County / Picked Up / Rickey A. Vincent

Photo Courtesy of Floyd Benson

GEORGIA STATE RECORD
TYPICAL ANTLERS
SCORE: 184 3/8

Locality: Paulding Co.   Date: November 1962
Hunter: Floyd Benson

GEORGIA

TYPICAL WHITETAILS

Score	Length of Main Beam R	Length of Main Beam L	Inside Spread	Greatest Spread	Circumference at Smallest Place Between Burr and First Point R	Circumference at Smallest Place Between Burr and First Point L	Number of Points R	Number of Points L	Total of Lengths Abnormal Points	Date Killed	Rank
	▪ *Locality Killed / By Whom Killed / Owner*										
184 3/8	26	26 6/8	20 6/8	23 4/8	5 3/8	5 6/8	5	6	2 1/8	1962	1
	▪ *Paulding County / Floyd Benson / Floyd Benson*										
184	27 4/8	29 1/8	18 4/8	20 5/8	5	4 7/8	5	6	0	1966	2
	▪ *Newton County / Gene Almand / Gene Almand*										
180 7/8	29	29 6/8	20 4/8	23 1/8	5 2/8	5 2/8	7	6	5 5/8	1957	3
	▪ *Jones County / James H. C. Kitchens / James H. C. Kitchens*										
180 2/8	28 1/8	28 4/8	18 4/8	21 4/8	4 6/8	4 6/8	5	5	0	1972	4
	▪ *Newton County / David Moon / David Moon*										
179 2/8	25 4/8	24 6/8	21 3/8	23 2/8	4 5/8	4 6/8	7	7	1 3/8	1968	5
	▪ *Lamar County / Gary Littlejohn / Gary Littlejohn*										
179 1/8	28 6/8	27 1/8	18 2/8	20 2/8	4 4/8	4 4/8	6	6	2 1/8	1970	6
	▪ *Twiggs County / Cy Smith / Duncan A. Dobie*										
179	28 4/8	28 5/8	20 6/8	15 2/8	4 5/8	4 7/8	5	5	0	1981	7
	▪ *Dooley County / Shannon Akin / Shannon Akin*										
179	26 6/8	26 2/8	21 4/8	23 2/8	4 4/8	4 6/8	5	6	0	1957	7
	▪ *Jasper County / Hubert R. Moody / Hubert R. Moody*										
177 5/8	25	24 3/8	17 6/8	19 6/8	4 1/8	4 1/8	6	8	2 7/8	1976	9
	▪ *Macon County / James W. Athon / Mike's Gun Shop*										
176 2/8	24 7/8	25 4/8	20 6/8	22 5/8	4 5/8	4 7/8	6	6	0	1984	10
	▪ *Troup County / James E. Lasater / James E. Lasater*										
176 2/8	28	26 4/8	21	23 3/8	5 4/8	5 4/8	8	7	7 2/8	1981	10
	▪ *Macon County / Charles M. Wilson / Charles M. Wilson*										
173 6/8	25 2/8	25 3/8	18 2/8	20 3/8	4 3/8	4 4/8	7	7	0	1983	12
	▪ *Carroll County / Ken Yearta / Ken Yearta*										
172 7/8	26	27 3/8	22 5/8	24 6/8	4 4/8	4 6/8	7	10	10 4/8	1982	13
	▪ *Heard County / Keith McCullough / Keith McCullough*										

GEORGIA TYPICAL WHITETAILS *(continued)*

Score	Length of Main Beam R	L	Inside Spread	Greatest Spread	Circumference at Smallest Place Between Burr and First Point R	L	Number of Points R	L	Total of Lengths Abnormal Points	Date Killed	Rank
* Locality Killed / By Whom Killed / Owner											
172 7/8	26 1/8	27	18	20 4/8	5 3/8	5 3/8	6	7	5 1/8	1967	13
■ Newton County / L. W. Shirley, Jr. / L. W. Shirley, Jr.											
172 4/8	26 7/8	25 2/8	19	13 1/8	4 6/8	4 5/8	5	5	0	1979	15
■ Randolph County / Robert D. Bell / Robert D. Bell											
172	24	25 7/8	18	19 7/8	4 2/8	4 2/8	6	5	0	1982	16
■ Tift County / Mayo Tucker / Mayo Tucker											
172	24 1/8	24 1/8	20 2/8	22 3/8	6 5/8	6 5/8	8	7	8 2/8	1963	16
■ Butts County / Jack Hammond / Jack Hammond											
171 5/8	25 1/8	26 1/8	16 7/8	19 2/8	4	4	6	7	6	1977	18
■ Baldwin County / Picked Up / E. Donald Graham											
170 6/8	24 4/8	24 1/8	16 4/8	18 4/8	4	4	7	7	2 4/8	1983	19
■ Harris County / Gorman S. Riley / Gorman S. Riley											
170 5/8	27 1/8	26 1/8	19 3/8	21 1/8	4 6/8	4 5/8	6	5	0	1961	20
■ Jasper County / Gordon W. Cown / Gordon W. Cown											
170 3/8	25 2/8	25 4/8	18 6/8	20 4/8	5 2/8	4 7/8	6	6	2 1/8	1982	21
■ Wilkinson County / James W. Whitaker / James W. Whitaker											
170 3/8	23 6/8	24 3/8	15 7/8	18 2/8	4 4/8	4 4/8	5	6	0	1981	21
■ Wilcox County / Scott H. Urguhart / Scott H. Urguhart											
170 2/8	23 6/8	26 4/8	18 2/8	21	5 2/8	5 1/8	5	5	0	1971	23
■ Oglethorpe County / H. D. Cannon / H. D. Cannon											

Photo Courtesy of C. W. Shelton

C. W. Shelton with his 185 point typical whitetail taken in Todd County, Kentucky, in 1964. Entered in the 12th Competition (1964-1965), Shelton's buck received the Third Place Award. This is the second finest whitetail ever taken in the Bluegrass State.

Photo Courtesy of John L. Hatton, Jr.

GEORGIA STATE RECORD
NON-TYPICAL ANTLERS
SCORE: 240 3/8

Locality: Monroe Co.   Date: November 1973
Hunter: John L. Hatton, Jr.

GEORGIA

NON-TYPICAL WHITETAILS

Score	Length of Main Beam R	L	Inside Spread	Greatest Spread	Circumference at Smallest Place Between Burr and First Point R	L	Number of Points R	L	Total of Lengths Abnormal Points	Date Killed	Rank
240 3/8	24 2/8	24 6/8	18 5/8	24 2/8	7 2/8	7 2/8	18	20	70 4/8	1973	1
■ Monroe County / John L. Hatton, Jr. / John L. Hatton, Jr.												
215 7/8	29 6/8	27 7/8	16 7/8	22 5/8	6 1/8	6 4/8	13	13	46	1974	2
■ Putnam County / Thomas H. Cooper / Thomas H. Cooper												
198 4/8	22 6/8	26	21 1/8	25 4/8	5 2/8	4 5/8	12	8	51 1/8	1983	3
■ Wheeler County / David Frost / David Frost												
197 4/8	26 3/8	27 3/8	18	23	4 6/8	4 5/8	10	12	36 6/8	1984	4
■ Dooly County / Wayne Griffin / Wayne Griffin												
197 3/8	24	26 5/8	16 4/8	19 1/8	5 6/8	5 6/8	9	10	35 5/8	1969	5
■ Newton County / R. H. Bumbalough / R. H. Bumbalough												
195 3/8	27 3/8	29 7/8	20 5/8	23 5/8	6	5 4/8	6	7	14	1976	6
■ Colquitt County / Olen P. Ross / Olen P. Ross												

Photo Courtesy of Carl Groth

IDAHO STATE RECORD
TYPICAL ANTLERS
SCORE: 175 5/8

Locality: Benewah Co.   Date: November 1982
Hunter: Carl Groth

IDAHO

TYPICAL WHITETAILS

Score	Length of Main Beam R	L	Inside Spread	Greatest Spread	Circumference at Smallest Place Between Burr and First Point R	L	Number of Points R	L	Total of Lengths Abnormal Points	Date Killed	Rank
175 5/8	25 5/8	25	17 7/8	23 3/8	4 5/8	4 5/8	6	7	0	1982	1
■ Benewah County / Carl Groth / Carl Groth											
173 6/8	26 6/8	27 6/8	20 3/8	22 7/8	5 7/8	5 4/8	9	6	8 1/8	1967	2
■ Bonner County / Robert L. Campbell / Robert L. Campbell											
172	24 6/8	24 6/8	17 2/8	21 5/8	4 3/8	4 4/8	6	5	0	1965	3
■ Joseph Plains / Jim Felton / Jim Felton											

Photo Courtesy of Zeke West

IDAHO STATE RECORD
NON-TYPICAL ANTLERS
SCORE: 245 5/8

Locality: Nez Perce Co.   Date: October 1983
Hunter: John D. Powers, Jr.
Owner: Zeke West

IDAHO

NON-TYPICAL WHITETAILS

Score	Length of Main Beam R	L	Inside Spread	Greatest Spread	Circumference at Smallest Place Between Burr and First Point R	L	Number of Points R	L	Total of Lengths Abnormal Points	Date Killed	Rank
	■ Locality Killed / By Whom Killed / Owner										
245 5/8	22 1/8	22 2/8	24 6/8	29	5 2/8	6 6/8	9	17	86 1/8	1983	1
	■ Nez Perce County / John D. Powers, Jr. / Zeke West										
226 3/8	25 7/8	27 3/8	18 2/8	20 2/8	5 5/8	5 3/8	10	8	22 3/8	1964	2
	■ Nez Perce County / Mrs. Ralph Bond / Mrs. Ralph Bond										
213 5/8	27 1/8	24 6/8	23 6/8	27 5/8	5 4/8	7	9	9	52 1/8	1968	3
	■ Bonner County / Rodney Thurlow / Rodney Thurlow										
201 3/8	21 1/8	21 6/8	21 3/8	23 4/8	5 2/8	4 6/8	16	11	33	1960	4
	■ Bonner County / Leroy Coleman / Leroy Coleman										
198 1/8	24 6/8	24 3/8	19 6/8	23 3/8	5 5/8	5 4/8	10	9	23 1/8	1967	5
	■ Kootenai County / Frank J. Cheney / Idaho Dept. Fish & Game										
197	24 2/8	26 4/8	25 3/8	28 7/8	5	5 1/8	8	9	18 3/8	1980	6
	■ Kootenai County / D. Whatcott & R. Carlson / D. Whatcott & R. Carlson										

Photo Courtesy of M. J. Johnson

ILLINOIS STATE RECORD
TYPICAL ANTLERS
SCORE: 204 4/8

Locality: Peoria Co.   Date: October 1965
Hunter: M. J. Johnson

ILLINOIS

TYPICAL WHITETAILS

Score	Length of Main Beam R	L	Inside Spread	Greatest Spread	Circumference at Smallest Place Between Burr and First Point R	L	Number of Points R	L	Total of Lengths Abnormal Points	Date Killed	Rank
204 4/8	27 5/8	26 6/8	23 5/8	26 1/8	6 1/8	6 2/8	7	6	1 1/8	1965	1
■ Peoria County / M. J. Johnson / M. J. Johnson											
181 1/8	26	28 5/8	18 6/8	26 5/8	5 2/8	5 2/8	9	7	10 4/8	1968	2
■ Canton / Arnold C. Hegele / Arnold C. Hegele											
181 3/8	24 7/8	24 5/8	18 5/8	20 6/8	6 5/8	6 2/8	6	7	1	1963	3
■ Pope County / Jack A. Higgs / Jack A. Higgs											
178 4/8	24 2/8	25 2/8	18 1/8	19 7/8	5 5/8	5 5/8	5	6	1 1/8	1981	4
■ St. Clair County / Emil W. Kromat / Emil W. Kromat											
177 7/8	26 3/8	26 6/8	22 1/8	24 6/8	5 2/8	5 2/8	6	6	3 4/8	1974	5
■ Christian County / Rodney J. Gorden / Rodney J. Gorden											
175 6/8	26 2/8	26 5/8	22 4/8	0	5 1/8	5	5	6	4 6/8	PR1982	6
■ Pope County / Picked Up / James W. Seets											
175 4/8	30 2/8	29	22 3/8	25	5 6/8	5 7/8	8	7	8 7/8	1963	7
■ Jo Daviess County / J. O. Engebretson / J. O. Engebretson											
175 3/8	24 5/8	25 2/8	20 4/8	22 5/8	5 6/8	5 5/8	5	6	2 3/8	1973	8
■ Williamson County / Lewis F. Simon / Lewis F. Simon											
175 2/8	27 1/8	27	19	21 3/8	6	6 1/8	5	5	0	1984	9
■ Union County / Randy Edmonds / Randy Edmonds											
174 7/8	25 5/8	25 6/8	21 3/8	23 6/8	4 7/8	4 6/8	5	6	0	1983	10
■ Jo Daviess County / W. V. Patrick / Jerry Patrick											
173 6/8	25 6/8	25 6/8	19 6/8	21 1/8	4 1/8	4 4/8	5	5	0	1973	11
■ Pulaski County / Rose Marie Blanchard / Rose Marie Blanchard											
173 6/8	26 6/8	27 1/8	19 7/8	22	5 5/8	5 3/8	7	5	6 1/8	1961	11
■ Mercer County / Floyd A. Clark / Floyd A. Clark											
172 4/8	23 5/8	25 2/8	20	22 5/8	6 1/8	5 7/8	6	5	7	1984	13
■ Franklin County / Joseph S. Smothers / Joseph S. Smothers											

ILLINOIS TYPICAL WHITETAILS *(continued)*

Score	Length of Main Beam R	L	Inside Spread	Greatest Spread	Circumference at Smallest Place Between Burr and First Point R	L	Number of Points R	L	Total of Lengths Abnormal Points	Date Killed	Rank
172 2/8	25 5/8	22 4/8	23 3/8	24 3/8	4 7/8	5	7	6	1 1/8	1978	14
■ Perry County / Ralph J. Przygoda, Jr. / Ralph J. Przygoda, Jr.											
172 2/8	31 4/8	30 7/8	23 5/8	26	4 7/8	5 1/8	6	5	1 3/8	1968	14
■ Perry County / Raymond E. Haertling / Raymond E. Haertling											
171 6/8	26 6/8	26 3/8	19 7/8	24 4/8	5 3/8	5 3/8	7	10	12 3/8	1982	16
■ Perry County / Daniel P. Hollenkamp / Daniel P. Hollenkamp											
171 6/8	27 3/8	26 2/8	21	23 1/8	4 5/8	4 4/8	6	5	1 4/8	1975	16
■ Adams County / R. C. Stephens / R. C. Stephens											
170 3/8	28 1/8	25 2/8	25 7/8	28 1/8	4 6/8	5	4	4	0	1966	18
■ Saline County / Jack Crain / Jack Crain											
170 1/8	22 4/8	25 5/8	20 5/8	24 3/8	4 6/8	4 5/8	6	6	1	1979	19
■ Logan County / Gary L. Humbert / Gary L. Humbert											
170	28 3/8	25 6/8	21 1/8	23 5/8	5 2/8	5 3/8	6	7	4 7/8	1973	20
■ Hancock County / Henry F. Collins / Henry F. Collins											
170	23 2/8	26	19 6/8	23	5 1/8	5 2/8	7	6	1	1960	20
■ Henderson County / Donald R. Vaughn / Donald R. Vaughn											

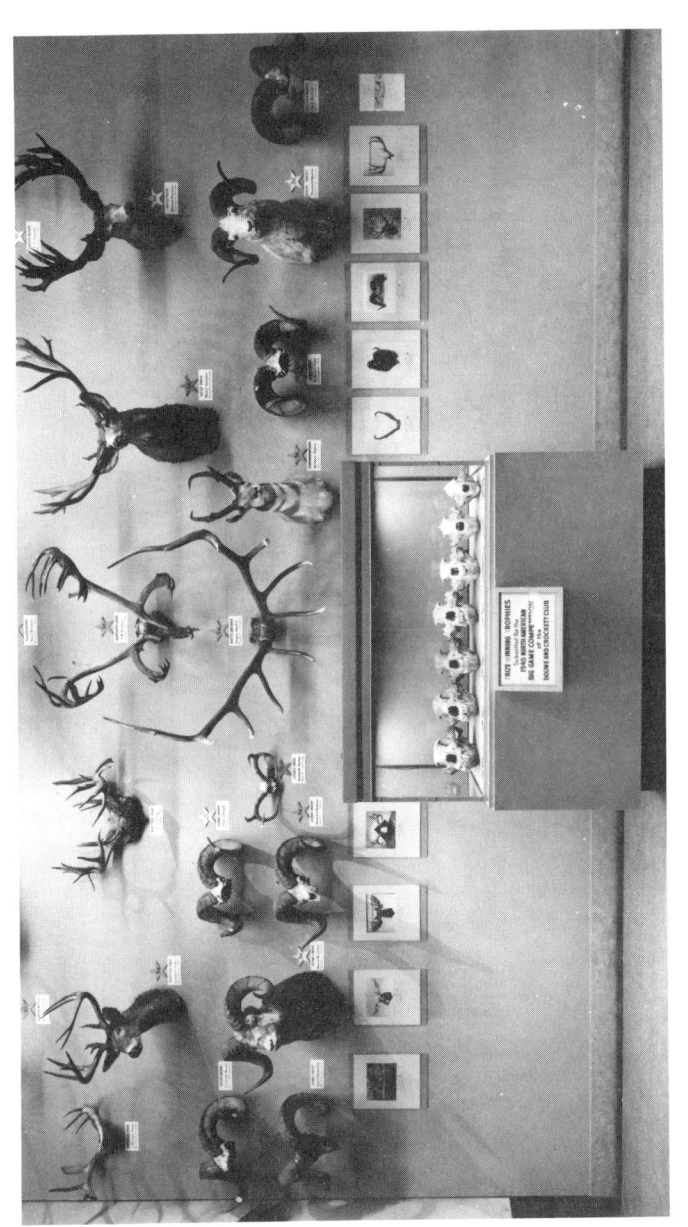

Photo from Boone and Crockett Club Archives

A portion of the trophy display of the Boone and Crockett Club's Second North American Big Game Competition held in 1948 at the Am. Mus. of Nat. History in N. Y. Trophies were then judged and ranked according to the length of the longer antler as the current scoring system had not yet been adopted.

37

Photo by Wm. H. Nesbitt

ILLINOIS STATE RECORD
NON-TYPICAL ANTLERS
SCORE: 267 3/8

Locality: Peoria Co.   Date: November 1983
Hunter: Richard A. Pauli

ILLINOIS

NON-TYPICAL WHITETAILS

Score	Length of Main Beam R	L	Inside Spread	Greatest Spread	Circumference at Smallest Place Between Burr and First Point R	L	Number of Points R	L	Total of Lengths Abnormal Points	Date Killed	Rank
267 3/8	25 4/8	28 2/8	20	29 1/8	6 5/8	6 3/8	18	7	88 1/8	1983	1
■ Peoria County / Richard A. Pauli / Richard A. Pauli
223 6/8	28	28	25 5/8	27 1/8	7 1/8	6 4/8	10	11	43 7/8	1982	2
■ Greene County / Terry L. Walters / Terry L. Walters
220 4/8	30	30 6/8	20 5/8	24 7/8	4 7/8	4 6/8	12	9	26 7/8	1970	3
■ Mercer County / Roger D. Hultgren / Roger D. Hultgren
217 6/8	26 2/8	28 5/8	18 5/8	23 5/8	5 1/8	5	12	12	36 2/8	1966	4
■ Macoupin County / Albert Grichnik / Albert Grichnik
215 1/8	27 1/8	26 5/8	27 7/8	30 1/8	6	5 2/8	9	6	28	1981	5
■ Schuyler County / Donald E. Ziegenbein / Donald E. Ziegenbein
206 4/8	28 4/8	26 7/8	20 5/8	24 7/8	5 1/8	5 3/8	10	9	25 3/8	1976	6
■ Lawrence County / Shirley Lewis / Shirley Lewis
205 4/8	25	25 6/8	19 4/8	26 6/8	6 1/8	5 6/8	11	7	43 4/8	1981	7
■ Adams County / Eldon K. Dagley / Eldon K. Dagley
203	26 2/8	26 1/8	15	17 3/8	5 2/8	5 1/8	9	11	16 4/8	1958	8
■ Hancock County / S. E. Brockschmidt / S. E. Brockschmidt
201	27 1/8	27 6/8	21 4/8	24	5 4/8	5 5/8	11	8	23 6/8	1972	9
■ Mercer County / Gerald L. Olson / Gerald L. Olson
198 5/8	23 6/8	22 2/8	17 7/8	22	4 6/8	5	14	12	58	1977	10
■ Will County / William H. Rutledge / William H. Rutledge
198 4/8	23 7/8	23 5/8	17 7/8	23 5/8	4 6/8	4 7/8	8	9	35 3/8	1974	11
■ Iroquois County / Charles E. Crow / Charles E. Crow
197 5/8	28	28 2/8	21	24 4/8	5 7/8	5 6/8	10	7	19 1/8	1962	12
■ Jo Daviess County / David H. Carpenter / David H. Carpenter
197 4/8	25 6/8	25 6/8	25	28 6/8	5 4/8	5 4/8	10	9	26	1961	13
■ Pope County / Joe C. Schwegman / Joe C. Schwegman

ILLINOIS NON-TYPICAL WHITETAILS *(continued)*

Score	Length of Main Beam R	Length of Main Beam L	Inside Spread	Greatest Spread	Circumference at Smallest Place Between Burr and First Point R	Circumference at Smallest Place Between Burr and First Point L	Number of Points R	Number of Points L	Total of Lengths Abnormal Points	Date Killed	Rank
* *Locality Killed / By Whom Killed / Owner*											
197 1/8	25 3/8	25 2/8	21	25 2/8	5 1/8	5 7/8	10	10	27 7/8	1983	14
■ *Jefferson County / Unknown / Jeff Sartaine*											
196 3/8	24 3/8	18 6/8	24	26 3/8	5 4/8	5 3/8	9	10	7 7/8	1982	15
■ *Clark County / Mary K. LeCrone / Mary K. LeCrone*											
195 6/8	25 6/8	16 2/8	20 6/8	25 4/8	6	6	7	7	47 4/8	1976	16
■ *Bureau County / Picked Up / John Cotter*											
195	22 4/8	23 1/8	20 3/8	25	5 4/8	5 2/8	8	9	41 1/8	1983	17
■ *Calhoun County / Roger F. Becker / Roger F. Becker*											

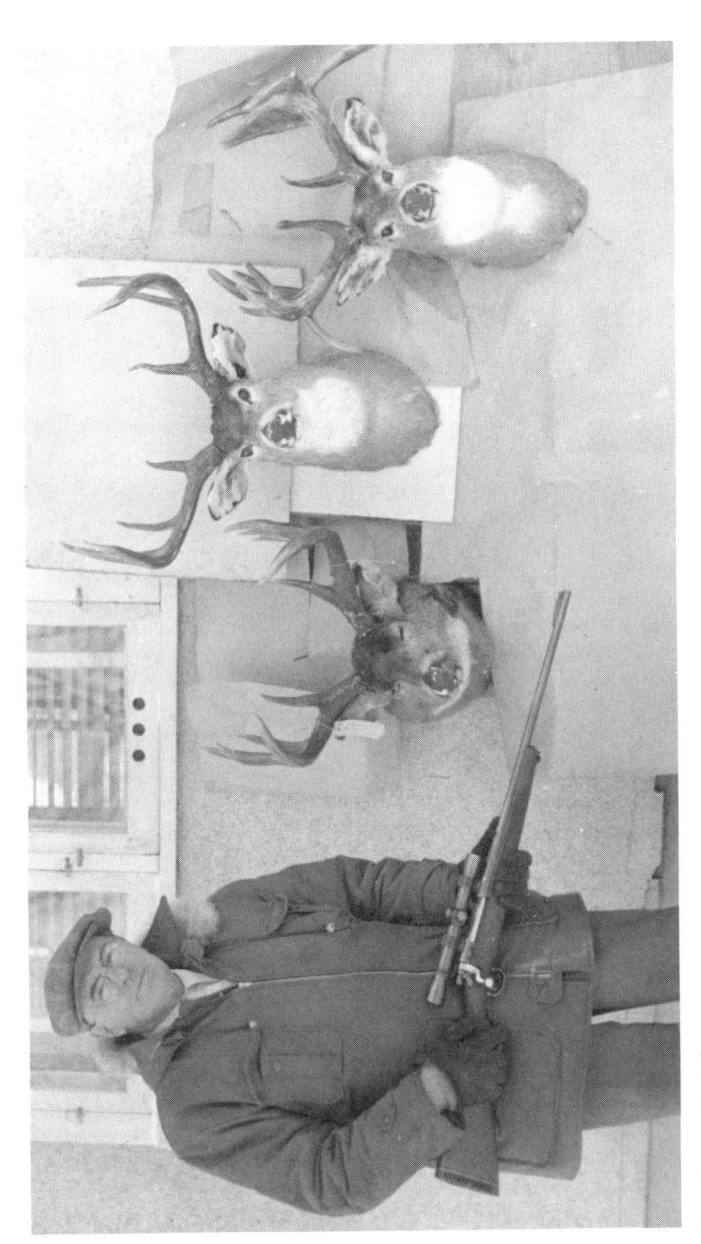

Photo Courtesy of Jessie Byer

Jessie Byer of Brandon, Manitoba, with three of the finest bucks he has ever taken. The typical buck at top center scores 170 points and was taken near Virden, Manitoba, in 1952. This trophy ranked third in the 6th Competition (1952-1953).

41

Photo by Wm. H. Nesbitt

INDIANA STATE RECORD
TYPICAL ANTLERS
SCORE: 194 2/8

Locality: Vigo Co.   Date: November 1983
Hunter: D. Bates & S. Winkler

INDIANA

TYPICAL WHITETAILS

Score	Length of Main Beam R	L	Inside Spread	Greatest Spread	Circumference at Smallest Place Between Burr and First Point R	L	Number of Points R	L	Total of Lengths Abnormal Points	Date Killed	Rank
194 2/8	30 6/8	30 3/8	24 7/8	27 1/8	5 5/8	5 7/8	9	7	12 3/8	1983	1
■ Vigo County / D. Bates & S. Winkler / D. Bates & S. Winkler
185 1/8	26 2/8	27 1/8	23 1/8	25 6/8	4 5/8	5 1/8	6	7	1 4/8	1972	2
■ Franklin County / Gayle Fritsch / Gayle Fritsch
183 6/8	26 6/8	27 6/8	19 2/8	21 1/8	4 3/8	4 4/8	6	6	0	1977	3
■ Clinton County / Stuart C. Snodgrass / Stuart C. Snodgrass
177	26 2/8	27 5/8	18 4/8	21 2/8	4 1/8	4 6/8	5	5	0	1974	4
■ Cass County / Herbert R. Frushour / Herbert R. Frushour
175 2/8	28 2/8	28 3/8	19 6/8	22 1/8	5 1/8	5 2/8	7	5	6 1/8	1984	5
■ Fulton County / Larry A. Croxton / Larry A. Croxton
170 7/8	25 3/8	24 5/8	18 3/8	20 4/8	5 6/8	5 7/8	6	7	5	1976	6
■ Tippecanoe County / Harold A. Anthrop / Harold A. Anthrop
170 4/8	26 1/8	25 4/8	18	20 4/8	4 1/8	4 4/8	5	5	0	1982	7
■ Marshall County / Alan R. Collins / Alan R. Collins
190 5/8	28 4/8	27 7/8	18 5/8	22	5 6/8	6	6	8	8 4/8	1982	*
■ Clinton County / Alan W. Brannan / Alan W. Brannan

43

Photo Courtesy of Paul Graf

INDIANA STATE RECORD
NON-TYPICAL ANTLERS
SCORE: 205 7/8

Locality: Switzerland Co.   Date: November 1981
Hunter: Paul Graf

INDIANA

NON-TYPICAL WHITETAILS

Score	Length of Main Beam R	L	Inside Spread	Greatest Spread	Circumference at Smallest Place Between Burr and First Point R	L	Number of Points R	L	Total of Lengths Abnormal Points	Date Killed	Rank
205 7/8	27 4/8	28 6/8	19 4/8	22 6/8	5	5 1/8	10	8	29 1/8	1981	1
■ Switzerland County / Paul Graf / Paul Graf											
198 7/8	29 2/8	28 3/8	24 6/8	27 4/8	4 6/8	4 7/8	8	7	16 7/8	1982	2
■ Ripley County / William L. Wagner / William L. Wagner											

■ *Locality Killed / By Whom Killed / Owner*

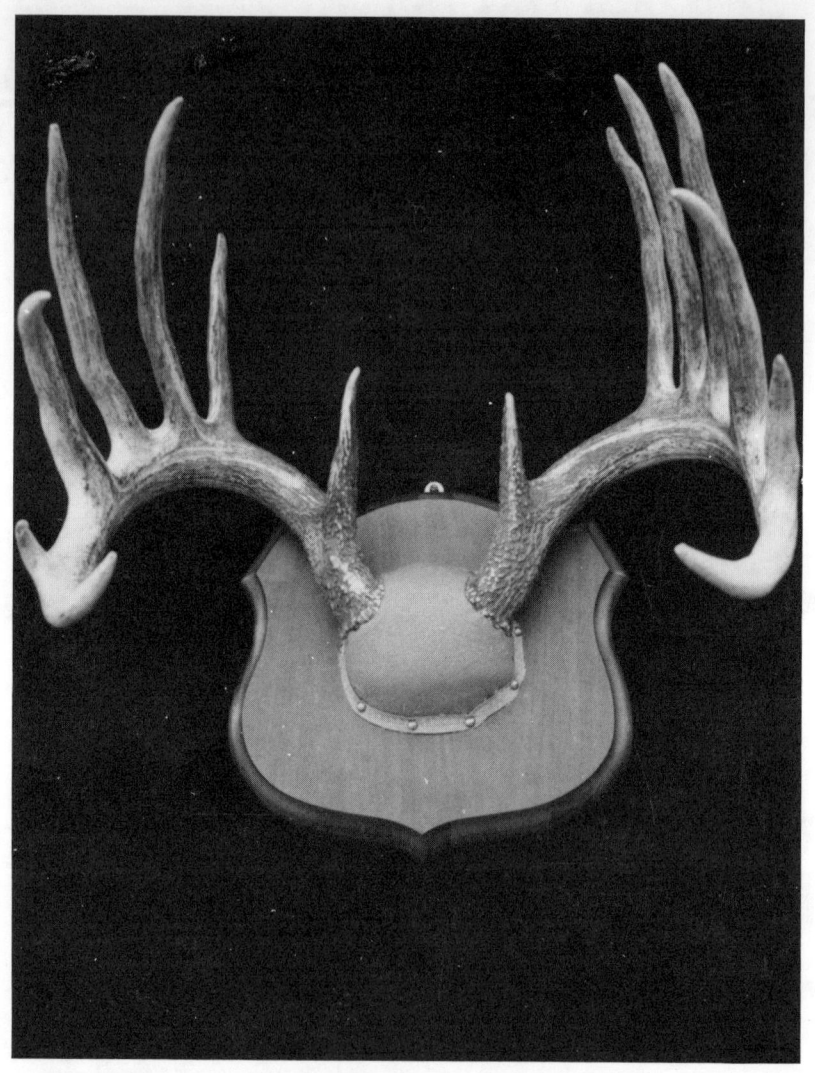

Photo Courtesy of Lloyd Goad

IOWA STATE RECORD
TYPICAL ANTLERS
SCORE: 194 4/8

Locality: Monroe Co.   Date: December 1962
Hunter: Lloyd Goad

IOWA

TYPICAL WHITETAILS

Score	Length of Main Beam R	L	Inside Spread	Greatest Spread	Circumference at Smallest Place Between Burr and First Point R	L	Number of Points R	L	Total of Lengths Abnormal Points	Date Killed	Rank
194 4/8	25 7/8	25 6/8	18 6/8	20 6/8	5 1/8	5 2/8	7	7	0	1962	1
■ Monroe County / Lloyd Goad / Lloyd Goad
187 6/8	25 5/8	26 4/8	19	21 2/8	4 6/8	5 1/8	5	5	0	1983	2
■ Johnson County / Gregg R. Redlin / Gregg R. Redlin
187 5/8	29 2/8	31 1/8	23 1/8	26 2/8	5 2/8	5 1/8	6	6	0	1975	3
■ Cherokee County / Dennis R. Vaudt / Dennis R. Vaudt
187 2/8	31 1/8	30 6/8	30 3/8	32 2/8	4 6/8	4 5/8	7	8	7 5/8	1964	4
■ Warren County / Dwight E. Green / Dwight E. Green
185 1/8	27 7/8	27 4/8	19 1/8	21 6/8	5 2/8	5	6	7	3 4/8	1971	5
■ Harrison County / Marvin E. Tippery / Marvin E. Tippery
184 5/8	26 5/8	26 6/8	27	29	5 7/8	5 6/8	7	7	4 3/8	1953	6
■ Delaware County / R. E. Stewart / R. E. Stewart
183 7/8	27 7/8	28 3/8	20 1/8	22 7/8	6 2/8	6 5/8	6	7	3 4/8	1947	7
■ Taylor County / Wayne Swartz / Spanky Greenville
182 3/8	25 5/8	25 1/8	18 1/8	20 4/8	4 6/8	4 6/8	6	6	0	1967	8
■ Marshall County / Barbara Daniel / Terry Daniel
180 2/8	27 1/8	27 1/8	19 4/8	21 5/8	4 6/8	4 4/8	5	5	0	PR1984	9
■ Iowa / Unknown / Tom Williams
179 2/8	26 5/8	25 5/8	17 7/8	21 3/8	5	4 6/8	7	7	3 7/8	1976	10
■ Worth County / John Janssen / John Janssen
178 7/8	28 1/8	26 2/8	19 5/8	22	4 6/8	4 6/8	6	6	0	1984	11
■ Van Buren County / Noel E. Harlan / Noel E. Harlan
178	25	24 6/8	17 3/8	19 6/8	4 6/8	4 5/8	6	7	3 4/8	1978	12
■ Washington County / Brad Gardner / Vaughn Wilkins
176 5/8	25 5/8	27 1/8	17 3/8	20 1/8	5 1/8	5 3/8	5	5	0	1961	13
■ Montgomery County / Unknown / Chris Hein

IOWA TYPICAL WHITETAILS *(continued)*

Score	Length of Main Beam R	Length of Main Beam L	Inside Spread	Greatest Spread	Circumference at Smallest Place Between Burr and First Point R	Circumference at Smallest Place Between Burr and First Point L	Number of Points R	Number of Points L	Total of Lengths Abnormal Points	Date Killed	Rank
	▪ *Locality Killed / By Whom Killed / Owner*										
176	23 7/8	25 2/8	19 3/8	21 6/8	5 6/8	5 6/8	8	7	7 1/8	1964	14
	▪ *Lyon County / Duane K. Rohde / Duane K. Rohde*										
174 5/8	25 2/8	26 1/8	18 3/8	21 3/8	5 1/8	4 7/8	5	6	2	1972	15
	▪ *Butler County / Vernon Simon / Vernon Simon*										
174 4/8	28 2/8	27 5/8	17	19 4/8	5 2/8	5 3/8	5	7	1	1982	16
	▪ *Boone County / Curtis A. Lind / Curtis A. Lind*										
173 4/8	28	27 4/8	21 6/8	24 4/8	4 7/8	5 1/8	5	5	0	1966	17
	▪ *Union County / Danny E. Abbott / Danny E. Abbott*										
172 6/8	25 1/8	24 3/8	22 2/8	25 7/8	4 7/8	5 2/8	5	6	1 6/8	1976	18
	▪ *Allamakee County / Picked up / Tom Kernat, Sr.*										
172 6/8	24 1/8	24 2/8	20 3/8	23 4/8	6	6	6	5	4 5/8	1975	18
	▪ *Boone County / Lonne L. Tracy / Lonne L. Tracy*										
171 7/8	25 4/8	25 5/8	18 4/8	22 7/8	5	5 3/8	6	7	1 1/8	1973	20
	▪ *Union County / Darrell M. Gutz / Darrell M. Gutz*										
171 6/8	24 4/8	24 3/8	17 1/8	20 2/8	4 1/8	4 1/8	8	8	3 5/8	1967	21
	▪ *Muscatine County / Larry Dipple / Larry Dipple*										
170 7/8	27 2/8	26 5/8	22 2/8	24 1/8	5 2/8	5 2/8	8	6	7 3/8	1981	22
	▪ *Warren County / Gary L. Johnson / Gary L. Johnson*										
170 7/8	30	30	20 2/8	22 4/8	5	5	5	8	10 3/8	1967	22
	▪ *Des Moines County / Craig A. Field / Craig A. Field*										
170 1/8	24 5/8	25 4/8	19	21 4/8	5 5/8	4 4/8	7	5	1 1/8	1975	24
	▪ *Warren County / Arnold J. Hoch / Arnold J. Hoch*										
170	26 2/8	26 6/8	20 2/8	22 4/8	4 7/8	4 5/8	5	7	5 6/8	1984	25
	▪ *Wapello County / George C. Ellis / George C. Ellis*										

Photo Courtesy of Maurice Robinette

Maurice Robinette (left) and Steve Littlefield (right) with the 172-6/8 point typical taken by Robinette in Spokane County, Washington, during the 1968 big-game hunting season. Robinette's trophy was an entry in the 14th Competition (1968-1970).

Photo by Wm. H. Nesbitt

IOWA STATE RECORD
NON-TYPICAL ANTLERS
SCORE: 282

Locality: Clay Co.   Date: December 1973
Hunter: Larry Raveling

IOWA

NON-TYPICAL WHITETAILS

Score	Length of Main Beam R	Length of Main Beam L	Inside Spread	Greatest Spread	Circumference at Smallest Place Between Burr and First Point R	Circumference at Smallest Place Between Burr and First Point L	Number of Points R	Number of Points L	Total of Lengths Abnormal Points	Date Killed	Rank
■ *Locality Killed / By Whom Killed / Owner*											
282	26 1/8	27	24 3/8	26 6/8	6 5/8	6 2/8	15	14	96 7/8	1973	1
■ *Clay County / Larry Raveling / Larry Raveling*											
256 2/8	28 7/8	28 1/8	20 4/8	24 7/8	6 5/8	6 4/8	11	16	64	1968	2
■ *Monona County / Carroll E. Johnson / Carroll E. Johnson*											
221 4/8	30	29 2/8	23 3/8	27 2/8	6 2/8	6 2/8	12	12	36 1/8	1971	3
■ *Humboldt County / Donald Crossley / Donald Crossley*											
220 2/8	25	26 4/8	19 1/8	24 1/8	5 4/8	5 4/8	11	12	31 1/8	1968	4
■ *Union County / George Foster / George Foster*											
216 3/8	26	25 5/8	17 4/8	24 5/8	5 4/8	5 4/8	10	9	29 7/8	1970	5
■ *Clay County / Blaine Salzkorn / Blaine Salzkorn*											
212 1/8	28 1/8	28 1/8	21 6/8	28 6/8	5 3/8	6	8	10	25 7/8	1965	6
■ *Woodbury County / Harold M. Leonard / Harold M. Leonard*											
209 1/8	26	26 2/8	19 3/8	30 1/8	5	4 7/8	8	8	33	1963	7
■ *Clinton County / Gregory Stewart / Gregory Stewart*											
209	26 7/8	28 2/8	23 6/8	25 4/8	5 4/8	5 4/8	8	9	17 6/8	1984	8
■ *Lee County / Glenn L. Carter II / Glenn L. Carter II*											
208 2/8	24 3/8	23 4/8	19	26 6/8	5	5	7	11	30 4/8	1984	9
■ *Monona County / Rob L. Cadwallader / Rob L. Cadwallader*											
201 5/8	27	26	18 3/8	20 7/8	5 5/8	5 6/8	7	10	17 2/8	1981	10
■ *Johnson County / Duane E. Papke / Duane E. Papke*											
200 6/8	24 7/8	25 7/8	25 1/8	26 7/8	6 4/8	6 6/8	9	11	54 1/8	1983	11
■ *Wapello County / Rod A. McKelvey / Rod A. McKelvey*											
197 4/8	25	23 7/8	22 2/8	24 3/8	5 3/8	5 4/8	7	7	15 4/8	1971	12
■ *Johnson County / Dennis R. Ballard / Dennis R. Ballard*											
197	28 2/8	26 5/8	22 1/8	25 2/8	5 5/8	6	6	9	18 1/8	1973	13
■ *Fayette County / Stanley E. Harrison / Stanley E. Harrison*											

IOWA NON-TYPICAL WHITETAILS *(continued)*

Score	Length of Main Beam R	L	Inside Spread	Greatest Spread	Circumference at Smallest Place Between Burr and First Point R	L	Number of Points R	L	Total of Lengths Abnormal Points	Date Killed	Rank
196 5/8	25 6/8	25 1/8	20 6/8	23	5 7/8	5 5/8	9	8	37 3/8	1984	14
■ *Van Buren County / Kenneth R. Barker / Kenneth R. Barker*
195 5/8	26 2/8	26 1/8	21 3/8	27 3/8	5 3/8	5 2/8	8	7	13 6/8	1983	15
■ *Story County / Jordan L. Larson / Jordan L. Larson*
195 2/8	25	23 4/8	18 4/8	22	5 4/8	5 3/8	11	11	30 6/8	1968	16
■ *Pottawattmie County / Ted Houser / Ted Houser*

Photo Courtesy of Claude Feathers

Blair County, Pennsylvania, yielded this once-in-a-lifetime, 20-point buck to Claude Feathers in 1943. With 12 normal points and eight abnormal points, it scores 170 points in the typical category. It was an entry in the 11th Competition (1962-1963).

Photo by Wm. H. Nesbitt

KANSAS STATE RECORD
TYPICAL ANTLERS
SCORE: 198 2/8

Locality: Nemaha Co.   Date: December 1974
Hunter: Dennis P. Finger

KANSAS

TYPICAL WHITETAILS

Score	Length of Main Beam R	L	Inside Spread	Greatest Spread	Circumference at Smallest Place Between Burr and First Point R	L	Number of Points R	L	Total of Lengths Abnormal Points	Date Killed	Rank
* Locality Killed / By Whom Killed / Owner											
198 2/8	27 5/8	26 7/8	20 2/8	22 4/8	5	5	6	8	4 6/8	1974	1
■ Nemaha County / Dennis P. Finger / Dennis P. Finger											
191 4/8	26 5/8	27 4/8	20	22 2/8	4 7/8	5	6	7	1 4/8	1973	2
■ Chautauqua County / Michael A. Young / Michael A. Young											
186 3/8	27 5/8	27 1/8	20 4/8	22 7/8	6 1/8	5 5/8	7	6	4 1/8	1969	3
■ Morris County / Garold D. Miller / Garold D. Miller											
184 4/8	30 3/8	30 4/8	20 4/8	25	5	5 1/8	7	7	17 6/8	1984	4
■ Chase County / Thomas D. Mosher / Thomas D. Mosher											
182 3/8	27	26 5/8	23 1/8	26	5 7/8	5 7/8	6	5	1	1966	5
■ Waubausee County / Norman Anderson / Norman Anderson											
181 6/8	23 6/8	23 3/8	20 6/8	23 7/8	5 3/8	5 2/8	5	5	0	1969	6
■ Lyon County / Kenneth C. Haynes / Kenneth C. Haynes											
179 4/8	27 5/8	27 3/8	19 7/8	23 5/8	5	5	6	6	3 7/8	1973	7
■ Elk County / Lowell E. Howell / Lowell E. Howell											
178 6/8	26	26 5/8	21 7/8	23 6/8	5 2/8	5 2/8	6	8	5 4/8	1967	8
■ McPherson County / Larry D. Daniel / Larry D. Daniel											
177 2/8	29 4/8	30 2/8	18 2/8	21	6 5/8	6 3/8	6	6	4 6/8	1982	9
■ Geary County / Kelly D. Gulker / Kelly D. Gulker											
176 7/8	25 2/8	25 5/8	22 1/8	23 5/8	4 6/8	5	5	5	0	1982	10
■ Butler County / Craig D. Waltman / Craig D. Waltman											
176 6/8	25 2/8	25	23 4/8	26 4/8	4 4/8	4 6/8	6	6	2 4/8	1966	11
■ Frankfort / Ray A. Mosher / Ray A. Mosher											
176	24 5/8	25 6/8	21 1/8	24	4 7/8	4 7/8	5	5	0	1981	12
■ Russell County / Don Mai / Don Mai											
174 5/8	22 4/8	21 4/8	17 1/8	19	5	5	7	6	0	1973	13
■ Jefferson County / Keith D. Hendrix / Keith D. Hendrix											

KANSAS TYPICAL WHITETAILS *(continued)*

Score	Length of Main Beam R	L	Inside Spread	Greatest Spread	Circumference at Smallest Place Between Burr and First Point R	L	Number of Points R	L	Total of Lengths Abnormal Points	Date Killed	Rank
174 1/8	23 7/8	24 5/8	20 6/8	23	5 1/8	5 2/8	5	5	1 5/8	1984	14
■ Johnson County / Ralph E. Schlagel / Ralph E. Schlagel
173 3/8	27 4/8	27 4/8	17 1/8	19 6/8	4 5/8	4 4/8	7	5	3 6/8	1984	15
■ Clay County / Charles A. Hammons / Charles A. Hammons
173 1/8	28 5/8	28 6/8	22 2/8	25 1/8	5 4/8	5 7/8	6	6	7 5/8	1970	16
■ Wabaunsee County / James D. Downey / James D. Downey
173	27	27 7/8	23 5/8	25 4/8	5 7/8	6 1/8	6	7	4 7/8	1983	17
■ Doniphan County / Charles A. Staudenmier / Charles A. Staudenmier
172	24 6/8	25 6/8	22 6/8	25 6/8	5 3/8	5 3/8	5	6	2 2/8	1982	18
■ Miami County / Dan R. Moore / Dan R. Moore
171 5/8	27 3/8	27 4/8	18 3/8	21 2/8	5	4 6/8	6	5	0	1980	19
■ Riley County / Mick McCallister / Mick McCallister
171 3/8	27 2/8	28 2/8	18 1/8	20 1/8	4 4/8	4 4/8	5	5	0	1984	20
■ Sumner County / Jeff D. Ehlers / Jeff D. Ehlers
170 5/8	26 5/8	27 2/8	21	23 6/8	6	5 3/8	6	7	9 3/8	1984	21
■ Lyon County / Bill D. Hollond / Bill D. Hollond
170 3/8	27 4/8	25 4/8	21 1/8	23 6/8	6 1/8	6 4/8	4	4	0	1981	22
■ Franklin County / Judy E. Wiederholt / Fran E. Wiederholt
170 2/8	26 6/8	26 7/8	22 2/8	25 2/8	5 6/8	5 6/8	5	6	2	1983	23
■ Riley County / Paul K. Byarlay / Paul K. Byarlay
188 4/8	27 6/8	28 7/8	20 1/8	22	5	4 7/8	8	8	9 5/8	1984	*
■ Riley County / Robert E. Luke / Robert E. Luke

Photo Courtesy of Gary Littlejohn

Gary Littlejohn (left) and Jack Crockford (long-time Official Measurer) with the typical whitetail taken by Littlejohn in Lamar County, Georgia, in 1968. Littlejohn's buck scores 179-2/8 points and was an entry in the 14th Competition (1968-1970).

Photo Courtesy of John O. Band

KANSAS STATE RECORD
NON-TYPICAL ANTLERS
SCORE: 258 6/8

Locality: Republic Co.   Date: December 1965
Hunter: John O. Band

KANSAS

NON-TYPICAL WHITETAILS

Score	Length of Main Beam R	L	Inside Spread	Greatest Spread	Circumference at Smallest Place Between Burr and First Point R	L	Number of Points R	L	Total of Lengths Abnormal Points	Date Killed	Rank
258⁶/₈	22¹/₈	26²/₈	23⁵/₈	28	6⁴/₈	6	17	15	106⁴/₈	1965	1
■ Republic County / John O. Band / John O. Band
251¹/₈	28²/₈	28	19	22⁷/₈	5⁵/₈	5⁶/₈	12	13	59¹/₈	1974	2
■ Mitchell County / Theron E. Wilson / Theron E. Wilson
248⁷/₈	27⁵/₈	27²/₈	20¹/₈	22⁴/₈	5⁷/₈	5⁷/₈	8	10	61²/₈	1968	3
■ Greenwood County / Clifford G. Pickell / Clifford G. Pickell
229²/₈	27	28⁵/₈	21¹/₈	25⁷/₈	6²/₈	7	8	15	55⁷/₈	1984	4
■ Linn County / Merle C. Beckman / Merle C. Beckman
227	25⁷/₈	26⁶/₈	24¹/₈	28⁵/₈	7²/₈	7⁴/₈	12	10	62¹/₈	1970	5
■ Miami County / Gary A. Smith / Gary A. Smith
216⁶/₈	25¹/₈	25⁴/₈	18²/₈	25¹/₈	6³/₈	6⁴/₈	10	13	38²/₈	1972	6
■ Barber County / Robert L. Rose / Robert L. Rose
209⁶/₈	23²/₈	24¹/₈	22⁶/₈	24⁵/₈	4⁴/₈	4⁶/₈	8	10	18	1984	7
■ Edwards County / Tim C. Schaller / Tim C. Schaller
206⁵/₈	26	24²/₈	19⁶/₈	22⁶/₈	5³/₈	5²/₈	7	12	23⁷/₈	1983	8
■ Chase County / Jay A. Talkington / Jay A. Talkington
205⁶/₈	23⁵/₈	23	20³/₈	27³/₈	5⁴/₈	5³/₈	8	10	39³/₈	1982	9
■ Cloud County / Gary G. Pingel / Gary G. Pingel
204⁶/₈	26²/₈	26³/₈	18⁵/₈	21	5¹/₈	5	9	7	20⁴/₈	PR1985	10
■ Nemaha County / Unknown / John L. Stein
203	26¹/₈	27⁵/₈	17⁴/₈	23²/₈	4⁵/₈	4⁵/₈	9	8	12⁴/₈	1982	11
■ Jefferson County / Dale Heston / Dale Heston
201⁴/₈	22	29²/₈	23⁵/₈	0	6⁷/₈	6	9	8	23²/₈	1975	12
■ Barber County / Joe Ash / Joe Ash
198	25⁵/₈	25²/₈	17⁵/₈	20³/₈	6²/₈	6⁴/₈	9	10	19⁷/₈	1977	13
■ Osage County / Joe A. Rose, Jr. / Joe A. Rose, Jr.

KANSAS NON-TYPICAL WHITETAILS *(continued)*

Score	Length of Main Beam R	Length of Main Beam L	Inside Spread	Greatest Spread	Circumference at Smallest Place Between Burr and First Point R	Circumference at Smallest Place Between Burr and First Point L	Number of Points R	Number of Points L	Total of Lengths Abnormal Points	Date Killed	Rank
	■ *Locality Killed / By Whom Killed / Owner*										
197 4/8	25 3/8	26 3/8	16 7/8	19	5 1/8	5 3/8	6	8	19 5/8	1984	14
	■ *Lyon County / John R. Clifton / John R. Clifton*										
197 3/8	22 7/8	23 7/8	21 6/8	27 1/8	5 6/8	5 1/8	14	10	42 1/8	1983	15
	■ *Marshall County / Lloyd Wenzl / Lloyd Wenzl*										

Photo from Boone and Crockett Club Archives

The Boone and Crockett Club's 5th Competition (1951) exhibit at the Am. Mus. of Nat. History, N. Y. Whitetails displayed include: (from top, l-r) D. Mitchell's typical 174-1/8 taken in Essex County, N. Y., in 1933; L. E. Vandal's typical 178-1/8 taken near Concrete, N. D., in 1947; L. Eldridge's typical 168-2/8 taken near Ossipee, N. H., in 1938; R. R. Henderson's non-typical 187-5/8 taken near Caucomgomoc Lake, Maine, in 1931; and Thelma Martens' non-typical 198-4/8 taken near Cow Creek, Wyo., in 1951.

61

Photo Courtesy of Scott Abbott

KENTUCKY STATE RECORD
TYPICAL ANTLERS
SCORE: 187 1/8

Locality: Pulaski Co.   Date: November 1982
Hunter: Scott Abbott

KENTUCKY

TYPICAL WHITETAILS

Score	Length of Main Beam R	L	Inside Spread	Greatest Spread	Circumference at Smallest Place Between Burr and First Point R	L	Number of Points R	L	Total of Lengths Abnormal Points	Date Killed	Rank
187 1/8	26 6/8	26 4/8	18 7/8	21	4 6/8	4 7/8	6	6	0	1982	1
■ Pulaski County / Scott Abbott / Scott Abbott											
185	30	29 2/8	30 2/8	34 4/8	5 2/8	5 2/8	8	8	10 6/8	1964	2
■ Todd County / C. W. Shelton / McLean Bowman											
181 2/8	25 2/8	25 7/8	25 7/8	27 3/8	5 1/8	5 4/8	5	6	3 5/8	1963	3
■ Hardin County / Thomas L. House / Thomas L. House											
181	27 7/8	27	20 3/8	22 2/8	5 2/8	5 1/8	8	7	13 1/8	1979	4
■ Gallatin County / Kenneth D. Hoffman / Kenneth D. Hoffman											
178	25 1/8	26 2/8	22 6/8	24 6/8	6	6	5	5	4	1983	5
■ Union County / Gary L. Gibson / Gary L. Gibson											
175 3/8	29 6/8	28	22 3/8	24 7/8	4 6/8	4 4/8	6	5	3 6/8	1981	6
■ Todd County / Gary W. Crafton / Gary W. Crafton											
173 4/8	30 5/8	29 6/8	20 7/8	23 2/8	5 2/8	5 3/8	7	5	1 7/8	1965	7
■ Todd County / Troy L. Harris / Troy L. Harris											
173 3/8	27	27 2/8	21 4/8	24	5 2/8	5 4/8	5	5	2 5/8	1968	8
■ Lewis County / Darrell Tully / Darrell Tully											
173 2/8	28	28 4/8	20 5/8	24 5/8	5 2/8	5 2/8	9	8	9 1/8	1979	9
■ Allen County / Terry Wayne Sims / Terry Wayne Sims											
172 5/8	24 7/8	25 7/8	25 1/8	28 1/8	4 7/8	4 7/8	5	5	0	1984	10
■ Barren County / Billy N. Short / Billy N. Short											
172 4/8	24 3/8	25 2/8	23 4/8	30	5 6/8	5 4/8	8	7	12	1982	11
■ Muhlenberg County / Dennis Nolen / Dennis Nolen											
172 4/8	26 4/8	27 2/8	24	26 1/8	4 3/8	5 3/8	5	5	0	1966	11
■ Fort Knox / E. G. Christian / E. G. Christian											
172 2/8	26 2/8	25 1/8	22	23 4/8	5	5	7	5	0	1983	13
■ Pendleton County / Kevin L. Galloway / Kevin L. Galloway											

KENTUCKY TYPICAL WHITETAILS *(continued)*

Score	Length of Main Beam R	Length of Main Beam L	Inside Spread	Greatest Spread	Circumference at Smallest Place Between Burr and First Point R	Circumference at Smallest Place Between Burr and First Point L	Number of Points R	Number of Points L	Total of Lengths Abnormal Points	Date Killed	Rank
170 2/8	23 7/8	22 4/8	17 4/8	20 2/8	4 4/8	4 6/8	5	5	0	1977	14
■ *Locality Killed / By Whom Killed / Owner*											
■ *Hopkins County / Michael E. Dillingham / Michael E. Dillingham*											
170	25 3/8	25 2/8	18	20	4 5/8	4 5/8	7	6	1 2/8	1977	15
■ *Ballard County / Rudolf Koranchan, Jr. / Rudolf Koranchan, Jr.*											

Photo Courtesy of Al Prouty

Al Prouty of Montgomery, Pennsylvania, took this exceptional non-typical whitetail that scores 207 points in Lycoming County, Pennsylvania, during the 1949 deer season. Prouty's buck was an entry in the 6th Competition (1952-1953).

Photo Courtesy of Wilbur E. Buchanan

KENTUCKY STATE RECORD
NON-TYPICAL ANTLERS
SCORE: 236 3/8

Locality: Union Co.   Date: November 1970
Hunter: Wilbur E. Buchanan

KENTUCKY

NON-TYPICAL WHITETAILS

Score	Length of Main Beam R	L	Inside Spread	Greatest Spread	Circ. R	L	Points R	L	Total Abnormal Points	Date Killed	Rank
236 3/8	25 7/8	23 6/8	20 3/8	27 2/8	5 4/8	5 4/8	14	16	93 6/8	1970	1
■ Union County / Wilbur E. Buchanan / Wilbur E. Buchanan
226 5/8	26 6/8	26	18 7/8	21 4/8	6	5 6/8	7	9	32	1984	2
■ Pulaski County / H. C. Sumpter / H. C. Sumpter
221 7/8	25 4/8	26 4/8	16 4/8	23 6/8	5 6/8	5 4/8	12	14	37 3/8	1982	3
■ Trigg County / Bill McWhirter / Bill McWhirter
215	28 6/8	27 2/8	14 6/8	24 7/8	6	6	12	15	52 6/8	1980	4
■ Hardin County / Michael F. Meredith / Michael F. Meredith
210 3/8	24 3/8	25	19 2/8	21 2/8	5	5	13	12	43 1/8	1975	5
■ Lyon County / Roy D. Lee / Roy D. Lee
209 5/8	24 1/8	25 3/8	22 4/8	24	4 6/8	5	10	11	26 5/8	1979	6
■ Butler County / Dean A. Hannold / Dean A. Hannold
208 6/8	24	24 2/8	19 2/8	27	5	5 1/8	13	12	56 4/8	1968	7
■ Daniel Boone Natl. For. / Richard G. Lohre / Richard G. Lohre
204	26 1/8	27 1/8	21 7/8	24 4/8	5 1/8	5 4/8	9	11	28 7/8	1982	8
■ Webster County / Jeff Robinson / Jeff Robinson
202	26 7/8	27	23 4/8	28 1/8	5 2/8	5 2/8	13	10	41	1980	9
■ Powell County / Hershel Ingram / Hershel Ingram
195 4/8	21 3/8	22 4/8	17 3/8	19 6/8	5	5	10	8	29 4/8	1979	10
■ Carlisle County / William H. Deane IV / William H. Deane IV

Photo Courtesy of Johnny M. Hollier

LOUISIANA STATE RECORD
TYPICAL ANTLERS
SCORE: 189 5/8

Locality: St. Landry Parish   Date: November 1965
Hunter: Leonce Mallet
Owner: Johnny M. Hollier

LOUISIANA

TYPICAL WHITETAILS

Score	Length of Main Beam R	L	Inside Spread	Greatest Spread	Circumference at Smallest Place Between Burr and First Point R	L	Number of Points R	L	Total of Lengths Abnormal Points	Date Killed	Rank
\- Locality Killed / By Whom Killed / Owner											
189 5/8	28 7/8	27 6/8	21 3/8	23 2/8	4 7/8	4 6/8	5	5	0	1965	1
■ St. Landry Parish / Leonce Mallet / Johnny M. Hollier											
184 4/8	26 5/8	28 3/8	22 4/8	26 6/8	5 3/8	5 1/8	6	5	0	1961	2
■ Bossier Parish / Earnest O. McCoy / Lucille McCoy											
184 2/8	28 2/8	27 6/8	24	26 4/8	5	5 1/8	5	6	1 2/8	1914	3
■ Franklin Parish / H. B. Womble / Carey B. McCoy											
180 5/8	25	28 3/8	18 7/8	21 5/8	4 7/8	5	8	5	11	1975	4
■ St. Landry Parish / Shawn Paul Ortego / Shawn Paul Ortego											
180 3/8	25 4/8	25 2/8	23 6/8	26 1/8	4 6/8	4 7/8	6	5	1 1/8	1963	5
■ Union Parish / Picked Up / Johnny M. Hollier											
176 5/8	26 6/8	26	20 6/8	23 3/8	4 4/8	4 4/8	6	6	3 3/8	1974	6
■ Tensas Parish / Sam Barber / Johnny M. Hollier											
176 2/8	28 4/8	29 2/8	20 6/8	23	5 4/8	5 4/8	5	5	0	1968	7
■ Richland Parish / Willard Roberson / Willard Roberson											
175 2/8	26 7/8	26 3/8	20 4/8	22 5/8	4 3/8	4 3/8	5	6	0	PR 1985	8
■ Claiborne Parish / Picked Up / Johnny M. Hollier											
171 7/8	27 6/8	27 2/8	20 1/8	23 5/8	5	5	5	5	0	1941	9
■ Madison Parish / M. L. Arnold / David D. Arnold											
171 5/8	22 1/8	23	19	21 1/8	5 2/8	5 4/8	5	6	2 3/8	1960	10
■ Tensas Parish / Jim Keahey / Gerald P. Begnaud, Jr.											
170 6/8	23 7/8	23 4/8	19 2/8	21 3/8	4 6/8	4 6/8	5	5	0	1980	11
■ Winn Parish / William Charles Erwin / William Charles Erwin											
170 1/8	22 3/8	24 3/8	16 1/8	18 2/8	4 7/8	4 7/8	7	6	3 6/8	1979	12
■ Morehouse Parish / Johnnie Kovac, Jr. / Johnnie Kovac, Jr.											
170	26 2/8	25 7/8	21	22 7/8	5 1/8	5 1/8	5	5	0	1960	13
■ Cat Island / Jerry Loper / Jerry Loper											

Photo Courtesy of Gary S. Crnko

LOUISIANA STATE RECORD NON-TYPICAL ANTLERS
SCORE: 218 4/8

Locality: St. Martin Parish　　Date: 1941
Hunter: Drew Ware
Owner: Gary S. Crnko

LOUISIANA

NON-TYPICAL WHITETAILS

Score	Length of Main Beam R	L	Inside Spread	Greatest Spread	Circumference at Smallest Place Between Burr and First Point R	L	Number of Points R	L	Total of Lengths Abnormal Points	Date Killed	Rank
218 4/8	26 2/8	26 3/8	17 2/8	22 3/8	5 5/8	5 3/8	8	8	33 2/8	1941	1
■ St. Martin Parish / Drew Ware / Gary S. Crnko
206 7/8	28 6/8	30 3/8	23 4/8	32 1/8	6 1/8	5 6/8	11	10	26 1/8	1970	2
■ Claiborne Parish / J. H. Thurmon / J. H. Thurmon
206 6/8	25 4/8	26 4/8	17 2/8	22	5 4/8	5 4/8	8	10	43 4/8	1969	3
■ Grant Parish / Richard D. Ellison, Jr. / Richard D. Ellison, Jr.
201 3/8	26 4/8	27	18 5/8	23 5/8	4 6/8	4 7/8	9	10	37 2/8	1963	4
■ Concordia Parish / G. O. McGuffee / G. O. McGuffee
198 5/8	26 4/8	27 5/8	22 2/8	25	6 7/8	5 5/8	6	11	24 1/8	1961	5
■ Concordia Parish / Raymond Cowan / Raymond Cowan

Photo Courtesy of Dick Arsenault

MAINE STATE RECORD
TYPICAL ANTLERS
SCORE: 192 7/8

Locality: York Co.   Date: November 1920
Hunter: Alphonse Chase
Owner: Earl Taylor

MAINE

TYPICAL WHITETAILS

Score	Length of Main Beam R	L	Inside Spread	Greatest Spread	Circumference at Smallest Place Between Burr and First Point R	L	Number of Points R	L	Total of Lengths Abnormal Points	Date Killed	Rank
192⁷⁄₈	27⁴⁄₈	27²⁄₈	19³⁄₈	21⁴⁄₈	4³⁄₈	4⁵⁄₈	8	9	0	1920	1
■ York County / Alphonse Chase / Earl Taylor											
186²⁄₈	28⁶⁄₈	29¹⁄₈	19	22²⁄₈	5²⁄₈	5¹⁄₈	8	5	7²⁄₈	1984	2
■ Hancock County / Gerald C. Murray / Gerald C. Murray											
181⁴⁄₈	29	28⁵⁄₈	23⁵⁄₈	25⁶⁄₈	4⁶⁄₈	4⁵⁄₈	7	5	3⁵⁄₈	1953	3
■ Oxford County / Dean W. Peaco / Dean W. Peaco											
181¹⁄₈	27⁶⁄₈	26²⁄₈	17³⁄₈	20⁷⁄₈	5⁴⁄₈	5⁴⁄₈	5	5	0	1946	4
■ Waldo County / Clarendon Pomeroy / Larry C. Pomeroy											
180⁶⁄₈	30	29⁴⁄₈	23⁴⁄₈	27	5⁶⁄₈	5⁶⁄₈	5	6	2⁴⁄₈	1912	5
■ Hancock County / Cyrus H. Whitaker / Orrin W. Whitaker											
179⁷⁄₈	25³⁄₈	27¹⁄₈	19	21⁴⁄₈	5	5¹⁄₈	9	6	3⁵⁄₈	1930	6
■ Hancock County / Butler B. Dunn / Butler B. Dunn											
179⁶⁄₈	25⁶⁄₈	26⁶⁄₈	21⁵⁄₈	25	5²⁄₈	5³⁄₈	6	5	1⁵⁄₈	1984	7
■ Penobscot County / Dale Rustin / Dale Rustin											
178⁶⁄₈	26²⁄₈	27²⁄₈	20⁶⁄₈	23	5	5	6	6	0	1983	8
■ Aroostook County / John R. Hardy / John R. Hardy											
178⁴⁄₈	27³⁄₈	27³⁄₈	18⁶⁄₈	21¹⁄₈	4⁷⁄₈	4⁵⁄₈	6	6	0	1980	9
■ Cumberland County / Patrick D. Wescott / Patrick D. Wescott											
175¹⁄₈	28	27⁶⁄₈	25	27⁵⁄₈	4⁷⁄₈	4⁶⁄₈	8	7	7¹⁄₈	1924	10
■ Waldo County / Unknown / Kenneth T. Winters											
174⁶⁄₈	28³⁄₈	27⁶⁄₈	21	24	4⁶⁄₈	4⁵⁄₈	5	6	0	PR 1977	11
■ Maine / Unknown / Warren H. Delaware											
174⁴⁄₈	27⁴⁄₈	27³⁄₈	21	23¹⁄₈	4²⁄₈	4	6	6	0	1979	12
■ Knox County / Robert E. Young / Robert E. Young											
174¹⁄₈	27	26¹⁄₈	21¹⁄₈	23²⁄₈	5²⁄₈	5⁵⁄₈	7	6	4⁴⁄₈	1930	13
■ Aroostook County / Unkown / Vern Black											

MAINE TYPICAL WHITETAILS *(continued)*

Score	Length of Main Beam R	L	Inside Spread	Greatest Spread	Circumference at Smallest Place Between Burr and First Point R	L	Number of Points R	L	Total of Lengths Abnormal Points	Date Killed	Rank
* Locality Killed / By Whom Killed / Owner
173	26	26	21	23 2/8	4 5/8	4 6/8	6	6	0	1981	14
■ Somerset County / Charles A. Moulton / Charles A. Moulton
172 6/8	27 3/8	27 5/8	24	25 7/8	5	5	5	5	0	1963	15
■ Waldo County / Wallace Humphrey / Arthur Humphrey
172 5/8	26 6/8	25	17 3/8	21 3/8	4 5/8	4 7/8	9	6	4 7/8	1974	16
■ Knox County / Willis A. Moody, Jr. / Willis A. Moody, Jr.
171 7/8	25 2/8	26 1/8	21 1/8	24	4 2/8	4 4/8	5	5	0	1980	17
■ Oxford County / Picked Up / Francis Ontengco
171 7/8	26 1/8	25 5/8	20 1/8	25	5 1/8	5 2/8	7	6	5 6/8	1962	17
■ Aroostook County / Julian B. Perry / Julian B. Perry
171 3/8	27	26 4/8	21 4/8	23 7/8	5 3/8	5 2/8	6	6	1	1957	19
■ Waldo County / Paul K. Nickerson / Paul K. Nickerson
171 1/8	24 7/8	25	20 6/8	23 4/8	6	6	5	5	1 1/8	1960	20
■ Penobscot County / Kenneth Scott / Kenneth W. Bennett
171	26	26	20	22 4/8	5	4 6/8	5	5	0	1983	21
■ Aroostook County / Roland L. Demers / Roland L. Demers
170 7/8	25 7/8	25 5/8	17 5/8	19 5/8	5 4/8	5 4/8	5	5	0	1979	22
■ Washington County / Merle G. Michaud / Merle G. Michaud
170	28 3/8	27 4/8	21	22 6/8	4 6/8	5	4	6	5 4/8	1981	23
■ Androscoggin County / Ricky D. Cavers / Ricky D. Cavers
170	26 4/8	25 5/8	19 5/8	23 2/8	4 5/8	4 4/8	6	6	3 1/8	1973	23
■ York County / Aubin Huertas / Aubin Huertas
187 5/8	29 6/8	28 4/8	21 1/8	23 4/8	5 5/8	5 5/8	5	5	0	1981	*
■ Somerset County / M. Dana Goodwin / M. Dana Goodwin

Photo Courtesy of Richard E. Johndrow

A very pleased Richard E. Johndrow displays the NRA's Silver Bullet Award plaque that he received for his typical whitetail taken near Schroon Lake, N. Y., in 1968. Scoring 171-4/8 points, Johndrow's buck was an entry in the 14th Competition (1968-1970).

Photo Courtesy of Fred Goodwin

MAINE STATE RECORD
NON-TYPICAL ANTLERS
SCORE: 228 7/8
Locality: Cherryfield   Date: November 1953
Hunter: Flora Campbell
Owner: Fred Goodwin

MAINE

NON-TYPICAL WHITETAILS

Score	Length of Main Beam R	L	Inside Spread	Greatest Spread	Circumference at Smallest Place Between Burr and First Point R	L	Number of Points R	L	Total of Lengths Abnormal Points	Date Killed	Rank
228⁷⁄₈	28²⁄₈	27⁷⁄₈	18⁵⁄₈	25³⁄₈	5⁷⁄₈	6	11	10	54⁴⁄₈	1953	1
■ Cherryfield / Flora Campbell / Fred Goodwin												
228¹⁄₈	28⁷⁄₈	29	20¹⁄₈	28²⁄₈	5⁶⁄₈	6	13	14	49⁴⁄₈	PR1911	2
■ Maine / Henry A. Caesar / National Collection												
224	29²⁄₈	29²⁄₈	27	34⁴⁄₈	5²⁄₈	5³⁄₈	7	14	34	PR1975	3
■ Hancock County / Picked Up / Wesley B. Starn												
219²⁄₈	24⁶⁄₈	24⁶⁄₈	21⁶⁄₈	27	5⁴⁄₈	5⁴⁄₈	9	11	55²⁄₈	1973	4
■ Aroostook County / Harold C. Kitchin / Harold C. Kitchin												
218⁷⁄₈	29²⁄₈	28⁶⁄₈	21	23⁴⁄₈	5⁴⁄₈	5⁴⁄₈	6	8	21⁷⁄₈	1957	5
■ Waldo County / Roy C. Guse / J. Bruce Probert												
207⁶⁄₈	27	27⁵⁄₈	25⁴⁄₈	30	6⁶⁄₈	6⁴⁄₈	9	9	17⁴⁄₈	1945	6
■ Aroostook County / Alfred Wardwell / Alfred Wardwell												
206⁶⁄₈	25⁶⁄₈	23³⁄₈	23⁷⁄₈	30²⁄₈	5⁴⁄₈	5⁵⁄₈	12	9	49¹⁄₈	1979	7
■ Somerset County / Mark T. Lary / Mark T. Lary												
206²⁄₈	31¹⁄₈	31	22⁷⁄₈	25⁵⁄₈	6	5³⁄₈	9	7	18⁵⁄₈	1964	8
■ Piscataquis County / Ralph E. Dow / Ralph E. Dow												
202	26⁶⁄₈	28⁶⁄₈	26⁶⁄₈	28⁵⁄₈	5	5	8	7	15⁶⁄₈	1981	9
■ Knox County / Skip Black / Skip Black												
201⁵⁄₈	26¹⁄₈	23¹⁄₈	26⁶⁄₈	28⁷⁄₈	5²⁄₈	5²⁄₈	8	9	38¹⁄₈	1959	10
■ Waldo County / James A. Tripp, Sr. / James A. Tripp, Sr.												
197²⁄₈	27¹⁄₈	26⁵⁄₈	21	24	5	5	8	9	18⁴⁄₈	PR1950	11
■ Hancock County / Hollis Patterson / Reginald R. Clark												
195¹⁄₈	23²⁄₈	28⁶⁄₈	15	19²⁄₈	5	5¹⁄₈	15	14	51³⁄₈	1963	12
■ Washington County / M. Chandler Stith / M. Chandler Stith												
259	25⁴⁄₈	26⁷⁄₈	19⁵⁄₈	28¹⁄₈	6¹⁄₈	5⁷⁄₈	15	16	66¹⁄₈	1910	*
■ Washington County / Hill Gould / Charles T. Arnold												
248¹⁄₈	31¹⁄₈	32¹⁄₈	22⁶⁄₈	25²⁄₈	5²⁄₈	5⁴⁄₈	15	15	42⁵⁄₈	1945	*
■ Penobscot County / Unknown / James L. Mason, Sr.												

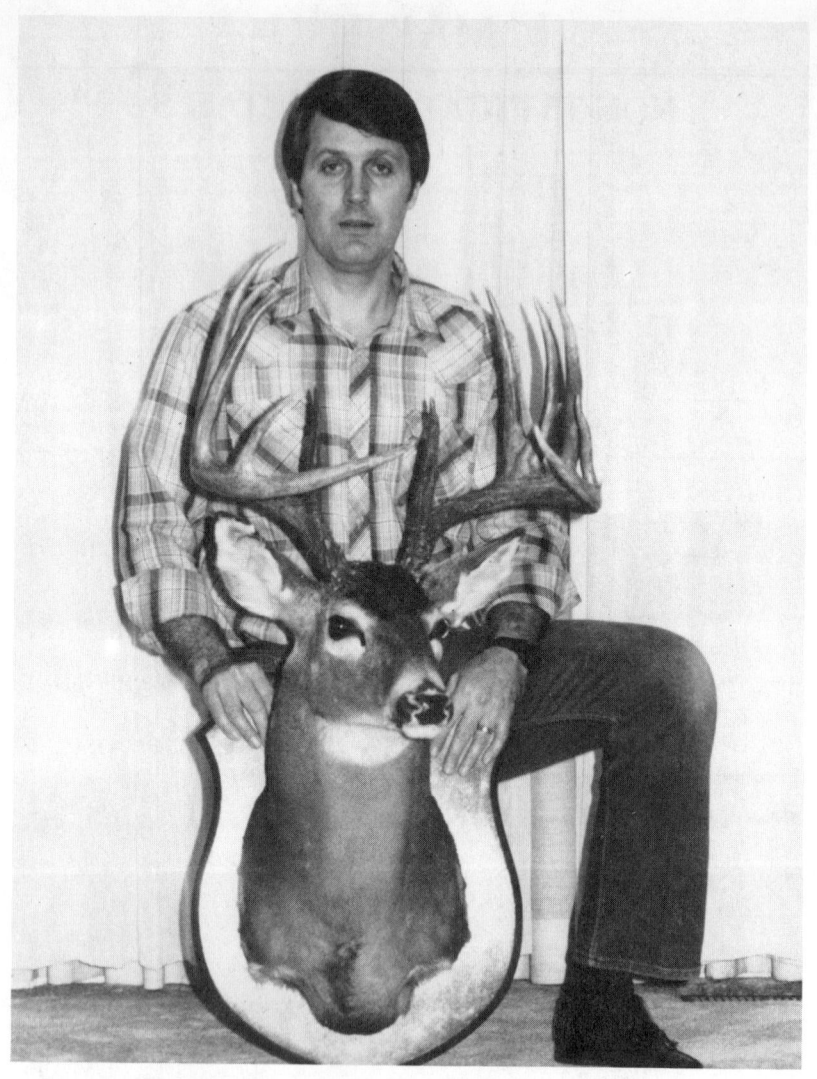

Photo Courtesy of John R. Seifert, Jr.

MARYLAND STATE RECORD
TYPICAL ANTLERS
SCORE: 183 3/8
Locality: Dorchester Co.   Date: November 1973
Hunter: John R. Seifert, Jr.

MARYLAND

TYPICAL WHITETAILS

Score	Length of Main Beam R	L	Inside Spread	Greatest Spread	Circumference at Smallest Place Between Burr and First Point R	L	Number of Points R	L	Total of Lengths Abnormal Points	Date Killed	Rank
183 3/8	27 1/8	26 4/8	18 5/8	21 1/8	4 3/8	4 4/8	8	9	6 2/8	1973	1
■ Dorchester County / John R. Seifert, Jr. / John R. Seifert, Jr.
172 1/8	27 2/8	26 5/8	18 6/8	20 7/8	4 6/8	4 6/8	6	5	1 5/8	1976	2
■ Queen Annes County / James R. Spies, Jr. / James R. Spies, Jr.
170 6/8	25 7/8	25 6/8	20	22 1/8	4 6/8	4 6/8	5	5	0	1971	3
■ Carroll County / Wes McKenzie / Wes McKenzie
170 5/8	24 3/8	26 4/8	17 3/8	0	5 1/8	4 7/8	5	5	0	1980	4
■ St. Marys County / Brian M. Boteler / Brian M. Boteler

■ Locality Killed / By Whom Killed / Owner

Photo Courtesy of Vincent Lee Jordan, Sr.

MARYLAND STATE RECORD
NON-TYPICAL ANTLERS
SCORE: 217 2/8
Locality: Talbot Co.   Date: December 1974
Hunter: Vincent Lee Jordan, Sr.

MARYLAND

NON-TYPICAL WHITETAILS

Score	Length of Main Beam R	L	Inside Spread	Greatest Spread	Circumference at Smallest Place Between Burr and First Point R	L	Number of Points R	L	Total of Lengths Abnormal Points	Date Killed	Rank
217 2/8	22	20	20	29 6/8	4 5/8	4 5/8	13	12	51 4/8	1974	1
■ Talbot County / Vincent Lee Jordan, Sr. / Vincent Lee Jordan, Sr.
208 7/8	26 7/8	26 7/8	26 6/8	30 2/8	5 3/8	5 3/8	10	8	52 7/8	1984	2
■ Charles County / Robert A. Boarman / Robert A. Boarman
201 3/8	24 7/8	25 1/8	19	0	5 2/8	5 3/8	12	10	49 3/8	1978	3
■ Queen Annes County / Franklin E. Jewell / Franklin E. Jewell
196 2/8	27	25 1/8	27	31	6	6	7	14	21 2/8	1979	4
■ Dorchester County / Kevin R. Coulbourne / Kevin R. Coulbourne

Photo Courtesy of Mac's Taxidermy

MICHIGAN STATE RECORD
TYPICAL ANTLERS
SCORE: 186 3/8

Locality: Ontonagon Co.   Date: 1980
Hunter: Unknown
Owner: Mac's Taxidermy

MICHIGAN

TYPICAL WHITETAILS

Score	Length of Main Beam R	L	Inside Spread	Greatest Spread	Circumference at Smallest Place Between Burr and First Point R	L	Number of Points R	L	Total of Lengths Abnormal Points	Date Killed	Rank
* Locality Killed / By Whom Killed / Owner												
186 3/8	26 2/8	27 2/8	20 4/8	23 1/8	5 2/8	5 2/8	8	7	5 7/8	1980	1
■ Ontonagon County / Unknown / Mac's Taxidermy												
181 5/8	27 6/8	27 6/8	21 5/8	23 5/8	5 2/8	5 2/8	6	6	8	1947	2
■ Ionia County / Lester Bowen / Richard Bowen												
180 4/8	29 2/8	28 4/8	20 6/8	23 4/8	4 7/8	4 6/8	6	5	1 6/8	1927	3
■ Iron County / John Schmidt / Bob Schmidt												
177 7/8	28	27 4/8	20 3/8	22 7/8	5 6/8	5 6/8	5	5	0	1939	4
■ Iron County / Felix Brzoznowski / Joseph Brzoznowski												
176 6/8	25 5/8	27 3/8	20 6/8	23 3/8	5 7/8	5 1/8	12	11	17	1963	5
■ Clinton County / Ray Sadler / Ray Sadler												
176 3/8	26	26 5/8	20 5/8	23	5 4/8	5 6/8	7	5	0	1945	6
■ Baraga County / Paul Korhonen / Paul Korhonen												
175 1/8	26 2/8	27 2/8	19 5/8	22	4 4/8	4 7/8	5	5	0	1936	7
■ Alger County / Warren Beebe / Donald J. Docking												
173 6/8	25 6/8	25 6/8	18 4/8	20 6/8	4 3/8	4 3/8	6	6	0	1979	8
■ Livingston County / Terry J. Kemp / Terry J. Kemp												
172 5/8	26 7/8	25 5/8	18 4/8	20 7/8	5 4/8	5 3/8	6	5	1 1/8	1971	9
■ Cass County / Ben R. Williams / Ben R. Williams												
171 6/8	26 3/8	26 3/8	20 4/8	22 5/8	4 5/8	4 6/8	4	5	0	1983	10
■ Van Buren County / Ronald E. Eldred / Ronald E. Eldred												
171 3/8	28	27 1/8	18 4/8	20 4/8	4 4/8	4 7/8	5	6	1 1/8	1984	11
■ Kalamazoo County / Harvey B. Braden / Harvey B. Braden												
171 3/8	25 2/8	25 2/8	19 3/8	23 3/8	4 2/8	4 3/8	6	7	4 4/8	1967	11
■ Oceana County / Delos Highland / Delos Highland												
171 1/8	27 2/8	27 1/8	18	20 3/8	4 4/8	4 4/8	8	7	3 5/8	1963	13
■ Alger County / Shirley L. Robare / Shirley L. Robare												

MICHIGAN TYPICAL WHITETAILS *(continued)*

Score	Length of Main Beam R	L	Inside Spread	Greatest Spread	Circumference at Smallest Place Between Burr and First Point R	L	Number of Points R	L	Total of Lengths Abnormal Points	Date Killed	Rank
171 1/8	27 4/8	27 4/8	21 1/8	23 2/8	4 2/8	4 2/8	5	5	0	1957	13
■ Charlevoix County / Noel Thomson / Ivan Thomson											
170 5/8	25 5/8	26	20 3/8	22 4/8	4 4/8	4 5/8	5	6	5 4/8	1982	15
■ Berrien County / G. Steven Abdoe / G. Steven Abdoe											
170 5/8	21 5/8	21 7/8	15 3/8	17 3/8	4 5/8	4 5/8	6	6	0	1948	15
■ Allegan County / William Caywood / William Caywood											
170 4/8	24 7/8	24 1/8	21	22 7/8	4 7/8	5	5	5	0	1984	17
■ Chippewa County / Paul Slawski / Paul Slawski											
170 3/8	25 5/8	26 1/8	18 5/8	21	4 7/8	5	5	5	0	1978	18
■ Newago County / Dennis Carlson / Dennis Carlson											

Photo Courtesy of Janice K. Beranek

Janice K. Beranek with the non-typical whitetail she took in Richland County, Wisconsin, in 1983. Ms. Beranek's buck scores 222-4/8 points and is the 12th largest whitetail ever taken in the Dairy State.

Photo by Wm. H. Nesbitt

MICHIGAN STATE RECORD
NON-TYPICAL ANTLERS
SCORE: 238 2/8

Locality: Bay Co.   Date: November 1976
Hunter: Paul M. Mickey

MICHIGAN

NON-TYPICAL WHITETAILS

Score	Length of Main Beam R	L	Inside Spread	Greatest Spread	Circumference at Smallest Place Between Burr and First Point R	L	Number of Points R	L	Total of Lengths Abnormal Points	Date Killed	Rank
\# Locality Killed / By Whom Killed / Owner												
238 2/8	27 1/8	26 2/8	21 4/8	0	5 5/8	5 7/8	12	17	65 2/8	1976	1
■ Bay County / Paul M. Mickey / Paul M. Mickey												
218 3/8	24 7/8	25 5/8	23 2/8	28 1/8	5 2/8	5 2/8	10	11	48 1/8	1980	2
■ Keweenaw County / Bernard J. Murn / Bernard J. Murn												
215 5/8	26	25 6/8	20	23 3/8	5 5/8	5 6/8	16	12	34 1/8	1970	3
■ Iron County / Chuck & Robert Lester / Chuck & Robert Lester												
212	29	27 4/8	23 6/8	26 5/8	6 7/8	6 5/8	8	9	22 6/8	1942	4
■ Iron County / Ben Komblevicz / Duaine K. Wenzel												
201 5/8	25 1/8	24 7/8	19 7/8	22 6/8	6 3/8	6 1/8	7	8	23 4/8	1981	5
■ Baraga County / Dennis D. Bess / Dennis D. Bess												
201 5/8	27	26 6/8	18	23 7/8	5 6/8	5 6/8	15	16	40 7/8	1973	5
■ Charlevoix County / Robert V. Doerr / Robert V. Doerr												
201	22 4/8	22 7/8	15 2/8	20 1/8	5 3/8	5 3/8	14	12	43	1953	7
■ Delta County / Ernest B. Fosterling / Ernest B. Fosterling												
198 5/8	26 7/8	26 1/8	18 3/8	22 2/8	5 4/8	5 5/8	11	13	19 2/8	1930	8
■ Iron County / Eino Macki / J. D. Andrews												
197 5/8	20	24	18	24 2/8	8 4/8	4 7/8	12	8	68 5/8	1917	9
■ Luce County / Sid Jones / Jim Deavereaux												

Photo Courtesy of Charles T. Arnold

MINNESOTA STATE RECORD
TYPICAL ANTLERS
SCORE: 202

Locality: Beltrami Co.   Date: November 1918
Hunter: John A. Breen
Owner: Charles T. Arnold

MINNESOTA

TYPICAL WHITETAILS

Score	Length of Main Beam R	L	Inside Spread	Greatest Spread	Circumference at Smallest Place Between Burr and First Point R	L	Number of Points R	L	Total of Lengths Abnormal Points	Date Killed	Rank
202	31²⁄₈	31	23⁵⁄₈	26⁷⁄₈	5⁷⁄₈	6	8	8	8³⁄₈	1918	1
■ Beltrami County / John A. Breen / Charles T. Arnold
195⁵⁄₈	28⁴⁄₈	27⁶⁄₈	22¹⁄₈	24⁵⁄₈	5⁶⁄₈	5⁷⁄₈	6	7	2	1960	2
■ Marshall County / Robert Sands / Robert Sands
193²⁄₈	28⁶⁄₈	28⁶⁄₈	21²⁄₈	23⁶⁄₈	4⁴⁄₈	4⁴⁄₈	5	7	2⁴⁄₈	1935	3
■ Itasca County / Picked Up / Paul M. Shaw
189³⁄₈	25⁷⁄₈	24¹⁄₈	23¹⁄₈	26⁴⁄₈	6²⁄₈	6²⁄₈	6	7	1²⁄₈	1975	4
■ Fillmore County / Tom Norby / Tom Norby
187⁵⁄₈	25²⁄₈	25⁵⁄₈	19²⁄₈	22³⁄₈	5²⁄₈	5³⁄₈	6	8	3³⁄₈	1976	5
■ Winona County / Ken W. Koenig / Ken W. Koenig
187⁴⁄₈	28³⁄₈	27	24⁶⁄₈	28⁶⁄₈	5³⁄₈	5³⁄₈	8	5	6²⁄₈	1974	6
■ Winona County / Dan Groebner / Dan Groebner
187²⁄₈	29	28⁵⁄₈	26⁴⁄₈	28⁴⁄₈	5²⁄₈	5³⁄₈	5	5	0	1967	7
■ Lyon County / Lynn Jackson / J. D. Andrews
186	30⁵⁄₈	31³⁄₈	26³⁄₈	30⁶⁄₈	5¹⁄₈	5	5	9	10¹⁄₈	1955	8
■ Itasca County / Knud W. Jensen / Wayne Williamson
185⁴⁄₈	26⁶⁄₈	27¹⁄₈	22	24³⁄₈	4⁵⁄₈	4⁵⁄₈	6	6	0	1972	9
■ Otter Tail County / Orris T. Neirby / Orris T. Neirby
185³⁄₈	26⁴⁄₈	27	19⁴⁄₈	22⁴⁄₈	5¹⁄₈	5²⁄₈	7	10	1¹⁄₈	1973	10
■ Marshall County / Donald W. Wilkens / Donald W. Wilkens
184¹⁄₈	26⁷⁄₈	27⁶⁄₈	21	23⁶⁄₈	5	5	8	7	4⁵⁄₈	1953	11
■ Marshall County / Alvin C. Westerlund / Alvin C. Westerlund
182⁴⁄₈	28³⁄₈	27¹⁄₈	23⁴⁄₈	26³⁄₈	5⁵⁄₈	5⁵⁄₈	7	7	10	1973	12
■ Kanabec County / Steven R. Berg / Steven R. Berg
182³⁄₈	25⁴⁄₈	25⁶⁄₈	21³⁄₈	24¹⁄₈	6	5⁵⁄₈	5	6	2⁴⁄₈	1969	13
■ Freeborn County / Robert H. Dowd / Robert H. Dowd

MINNESOTA TYPICAL WHITETAILS *(continued)*

Score	Length of Main Beam R	Length of Main Beam L	Inside Spread	Greatest Spread	Circumference at Smallest Place Between Burr and First Point R	Circumference at Smallest Place Between Burr and First Point L	Number of Points R	Number of Points L	Total of Lengths Abnormal Points	Date Killed	Rank
▪ *Locality Killed / By Whom Killed / Owner*											
181 7/8	26 7/8	27 1/8	23 3/8	25 5/8	5 4/8	5 3/8	8	7	10 6/8	1963	14
▪ *Cottonwood County / Picked Up / Minn. Game & Fish Dept.*											
181 6/8	26 1/8	26 4/8	17 6/8	19 6/8	6	6 1/8	5	5	0	1971	15
▪ *Wabasha County / Lee G. Partington / Lee G. Partington*											
181 4/8	28 4/8	27 7/8	22	24 5/8	5 1/8	5 3/8	5	5	0	1962	16
▪ *Wadena County / Lester Zentner, Jr. / E. E. Patson*											
181 3/8	26	25	17 5/8	19 6/8	4 5/8	4 5/8	6	6	0	1980	17
▪ *Winona County / Kenneth W. Schreiber / Kenneth W. Schreiber*											
181	26 5/8	26 2/8	21 2/8	26	6 2/8	6 3/8	7	8	5 6/8	1978	18
▪ *Lac qui Parle County / Mary A. Barvels / Mary A. Barvels*											
181	25 7/8	24 6/8	22 3/8	24 3/8	4 7/8	5 3/8	6	8	7 3/8	1910	18
▪ *Beltrami County / Robert C. Shaw / Robert C. Shaw*											
180 3/8	30	29 5/8	22 3/8	24 5/8	4 5/8	4 5/8	6	8	5	1981	20
▪ *Meeker County / Stanley M. Messner / Stanley M. Messner*											
180 1/8	24	24 7/8	19 4/8	24 1/8	5 1/8	5	7	5	1 5/8	1984	21
▪ *Hubbard County / Larry D. Dierks / Larry D. Dierks*											
180 1/8	25 1/8	25 1/8	19 1/8	21 6/8	5 2/8	5 2/8	6	6	0	1983	21
▪ *Cottonwood County / Charles C. Burnham / Charles C. Burnham*											
180	25 6/8	25 4/8	19 3/8	21 4/8	5	5 2/8	6	6	2 3/8	1966	23
▪ *Nicollet County / T. J. Merkley / T. J. Merkley*											
179 6/8	28 1/8	26 4/8	22 2/8	25 2/8	4 6/8	4 6/8	6	5	0	1973	24
▪ *Aitkin County / Harland A. Kern / Harland A. Kern*											
179 6/8	27 1/8	29 3/8	21 2/8	23 2/8	4 7/8	5	7	7	2 4/8	1972	24
▪ *Steele County / Elmer Janning / Elmer Janning*											
179	27 1/8	25 5/8	19 4/8	22 3/8	5 5/8	5 4/8	6	7	10 4/8	1956	26
▪ *Sherburne County / Victor Nagel / Victor Nagel*											
178 5/8	25 4/8	25 5/8	22 7/8	25 4/8	4 4/8	4 4/8	5	5	0	1980	27
▪ *Itasca County / Gino P. Maccario / Gino P. Maccario*											
178 3/8	28 4/8	28 7/8	23 7/8	25 7/8	5 1/8	5 2/8	7	8	7 2/8	1976	28
▪ *Lincoln County / Larry Lustfield / Larry Lustfield*											
178 3/8	26 7/8	26 5/8	24 3/8	26 7/8	5 4/8	5 2/8	6	5	2	1969	28
▪ *Aitkin County / George E. Jenks / George E. Jenks*											
177 6/8	26 5/8	27 4/8	23 4/8	27	4 5/8	4 4/8	6	5	1 2/8	1975	30
▪ *Stearns County / Robert G. Schwarz / Robert G. Schwarz*											
177 5/8	26 2/8	26 6/8	22 6/8	24 4/8	4 7/8	4 7/8	7	6	1 3/8	1972	31
▪ *Wabasha County / Bruce J. Hall / Bruce J. Hall*											

MINNESOTA TYPICAL WHITETAILS *(continued)*

Score	Length of Main Beam R	L	Inside Spread	Greatest Spread	Circumference at Smallest Place Between Burr and First Point R	L	Number of Points R	L	Total of Lengths Abnormal Points	Date Killed	Rank
177 4/8	28 2/8	28 3/8	22 4/8	27 5/8	5 6/8	5 6/8	5	6	1	1968	32
■ Beltrami County / Sheldon M. Stockdale / Sheldon M. Stockdale
176 6/8	26 5/8	26 4/8	21 1/8	25 2/8	5 2/8	5 3/8	5	5	0	1977	33
■ Pine County / Kim Shira / Kim Shira
176 4/8	26 6/8	27	26 6/8	29 3/8	4 2/8	4 4/8	6	6	0	1971	34
■ Houston County / James L. Reinhart / James L. Reinhart
176 4/8	23 5/8	23 5/8	17 4/8	20 4/8	5 4/8	5 3/8	5	5	0	1962	34
■ St. Louis County / Michael J. Nielsen / Michael J. Nielsen
176 3/8	26 1/8	25 5/8	22 4/8	25	5 7/8	5 6/8	5	6	2 7/8	1957	36
■ Koochiching County / Picked Up / James R. Smith
176 1/8	25 3/8	24 5/8	19 7/8	22 7/8	6 6/8	6 7/8	7	7	7 4/8	1960	37
■ Goodhue County / David Anderson / David Anderson
175 7/8	26 5/8	27	21 7/8	23 7/8	4 3/8	4 3/8	5	6	0	1982	38
■ Swift County / Kim Manska / Kim Manska
175 6/8	24 6/8	24 5/8	17 7/8	21	6 2/8	6 3/8	8	10	10 1/8	1974	39
■ Marshall County / Ell-Kay B. Foss / Ell-Kay B. Foss
175 4/8	26 7/8	27 7/8	21	23 2/8	5 1/8	5 1/8	5	5	0	1973	40
■ Renville County / Larry D. Youngs / Larry D. Youngs
175 1/8	24 7/8	26 1/8	20 7/8	23	4 4/8	4 4/8	6	7	2	1976	41
■ Lac qui Parle County / Harold Kittelson / Harold Kittelson
175 1/8	27 1/8	25 5/8	18 3/8	20 7/8	5	5	5	5	0	1973	41
■ Houston County / Craig F. Swenson / Craig F. Swenson
175	25 3/8	25 4/8	19 2/8	22	5 4/8	5 4/8	5	5	0	1982	43
■ Itasca County / David A. Frandsen / David A. Frandsen
174 5/8	24	22 5/8	18 3/8	20 4/8	4 5/8	4 4/8	5	5	0	1973	44
■ Meeker County / James L. Mattson / James L. Mattson
173 2/8	26 4/8	26 5/8	19	21 1/8	4 1/8	4	5	5	0	1984	45
■ Chisago County / Roger A. Peterson / Roger A. Peterson
173 1/8	29 3/8	28 7/8	25 1/8	27 3/8	5 2/8	5 1/8	4	4	0	1973	46
■ Fillmore County / Gerry D. Arnold / Gerry D. Arnold
173	27 1/8	27 7/8	21 6/8	24 2/8	4 5/8	4 5/8	5	6	5	1980	47
■ Cook County / Wesley A. Nelson / Wesley A. Nelson
172 7/8	26 4/8	26 1/8	16 7/8	19	4 2/8	4 1/8	6	6	0	1966	48
■ Olmsted County / Wesley W. Holtz / Wesley W. Holtz
172 1/8	25 1/8	25 5/8	16 4/8	19 2/8	4 7/8	4 7/8	6	6	1 1/8	1979	49
■ Winona County / Robert J. Cordie / Robert J. Cordie

MINNESOTA TYPICAL WHITETAILS *(continued)*

Score	Length of Main Beam R	Length of Main Beam L	Inside Spread	Greatest Spread	Circumference at Smallest Place Between Burr and First Point R	Circumference at Smallest Place Between Burr and First Point L	Number of Points R	Number of Points L	Total of Lengths Abnormal Points	Date Killed	Rank
■ *Locality Killed / By Whom Killed / Owner*											
172 1/8	24	24 4/8	20 6/8	22 6/8	5 1/8	5 1/8	8	7	8 3/8	1977	49
■ *Fillmore County / Murrel Mathison / Murrel Mathison*											
171 7/8	26 1/8	27	20 5/8	22 5/8	4 6/8	4 5/8	5	5	0	1958	51
■ *Houston County / Donald R. Sobolik / Donald R. Sobolik*											
171 6/8	26	27	18 4/8	21	6 2/8	6 2/8	5	5	0	1946	52
■ *St. Louis County / Paul S. Paulson / Paul S. Paulson*											
171 5/8	25 3/8	24 7/8	18 3/8	20 6/8	4 6/8	4 5/8	5	5	0	1980	53
■ *Grant County / Gary P. Kollman / Gary P. Kollman*											
171 5/8	27	25 5/8	18 2/8	20 7/8	5 2/8	5 2/8	6	6	3 1/8	1977	53
■ *Otter Tail County / Carl D. Hill / Carl D. Hill*											
171 4/8	27 1/8	26 7/8	18 6/8	20 5/8	4 5/8	4 5/8	5	6	0	1983	55
■ *Becker County / Kraig J. Ketter / Kraig J. Ketter*											
171 4/8	25 6/8	24 5/8	19 6/8	22	4 4/8	4 3/8	5	5	0	1978	55
■ *Clearwater County / Peter Tranby / Peter Tranby*											
171 4/8	26 3/8	27 2/8	23 6/8	27	5 6/8	5 7/8	7	9	9	1965	55
■ *Clay County / Clint Foslien / Clint Foslien*											
171 3/8	25 7/8	26 3/8	21 3/8	26	5 1/8	5 1/8	8	10	12	1984	58
■ *Douglas County / Gregory A. Dropik / Gregory A. Dropik*											
171 3/8	25 2/8	24 5/8	22 5/8	25	5	5	7	6	3	1975	58
■ *Pope County / Corbin G. Corson / Corbin G. Corson*											
171 3/8	23 4/8	24 2/8	23 1/8	25 2/8	4 7/8	4 7/8	5	5	0	1974	58
■ *Kandiyohi County / Werner B. Reining / Werner B. Reining*											
171 1/8	26	26 7/8	16 7/8	19 5/8	5 6/8	5 6/8	5	5	0	1962	61
■ *Douglas County / James M. Bircher / James M. Bircher*											
171	27	26 5/8	26 2/8	28 4/8	5 3/8	5 2/8	7	8	8	1974	62
■ *Otter Tail County / Lawrence J. Anderson / Lawrence J. Anderson*											
170 5/8	27 2/8	27 2/8	21 6/8	23 6/8	5 4/8	5 2/8	5	7	2 5/8	1967	63
■ *Sherburne County / Sylvester Zormeier / Sylvester Zormeier*											
170 5/8	25 6/8	25 5/8	18 3/8	20 4/8	4 5/8	4 6/8	6	6	0	1960	63
■ *Lake County / Unknown / George W. Flaim*											
170 4/8	29 6/8	29 2/8	21 2/8	23 3/8	4 6/8	4 4/8	7	8	6	1981	65
■ *Sherburne County / Curtis G. Nelson / Curtis G. Nelson*											
170 4/8	28 5/8	28	20	23	5	5	8	8	6	1982	65
■ *Todd County / Freddie H. Peterson / Freddie H. Peterson*											
170 4/8	26 1/8	25 4/8	20 4/8	23	4 6/8	4 5/8	6	6	0	1931	65
■ *Beltrami County / Hank Sandland / Hank Sandland*											

MINNESOTA TYPICAL WHITETAILS *(continued)*

Score	Length of Main Beam R	L	Inside Spread	Greatest Spread	Circumference at Smallest Place Between Burr and First Point R	L	Number of Points R	L	Total of Lengths Abnormal Points	Date Killed	Rank
* Locality Killed / By Whom Killed / Owner												
170 4/8	25 2/8	24 5/8	18	20	4 4/8	4 4/8	6	6	0	1946	65
■ Douglas County / August P. J. Nelson / Roger M. Holmes												
170 3/8	25 5/8	25 2/8	22 6/8	25 2/8	5 2/8	5 4/8	7	8	6 1/8	1974	69
■ Lac qui Parle County / Paul W. Hill / Paul W. Hill												
170 2/8	28 6/8	29 1/8	19 5/8	23 1/8	4 5/8	4 4/8	9	5	11 1/8	1967	70
■ Blue Earth County / Roland Bode / Roland Bode												
170 1/8	27	27 1/8	19	22 2/8	4 6/8	4 6/8	7	6	2 3/8	1984	71
■ Cook County / William Bohnen / William Bohnen												
170 1/8	25 6/8	25 2/8	21 3/8	24 3/8	4 4/8	4 5/8	5	5	0	1984	71
■ Mower County / Robert D. Plumb / Robert D. Plumb												
170 1/8	25 4/8	25 7/8	22 2/8	24 1/8	4 5/8	4 3/8	6	7	2 3/8	1980	71
■ Winona County / Roger J. Traxler / Roger J. Traxler												
170 1/8	28 5/8	29	23 3/8	25 7/8	4 2/8	4 3/8	4	5	0	1956	71
■ Faribault County / Harlan Francis / Harlan Francis												
170 1/8	25 3/8	24 6/8	16 5/8	19 4/8	4 7/8	5	6	7	5 2/8	1959	71
■ St. Louis County / Allan Ramstad / Allan Ramstad												

Photo by Wm. H. Nesbitt

MINNESOTA STATE RECORD
NON-TYPICAL ANTLERS
SCORE: 268 5/8

Locality: Norman Co.   Date: November 1974
Hunter: Mitchell A. Vakoch

MINNESOTA

NON-TYPICAL WHITETAILS

Score	Length of Main Beam R	L	Inside Spread	Greatest Spread	Circumference at Smallest Place Between Burr and First Point R	L	Number of Points R	L	Total of Lengths Abnormal Points	Date Killed	Rank
■ Locality Killed / By Whom Killed / Owner												
268 5/8	20 6/8	24 5/8	14 2/8	0	6 4/8	5 3/8	20	21	118 3/8	1974	1
■ Norman County / Mitchell A. Vakoch / Mitchell A. Vakoch												
258 2/8	27	26 6/8	19 5/8	26 3/8	4 7/8	4 6/8	17	17	73 5/8	1973	2
■ Becker County / J. J. Matter / J. J. Matter												
240 6/8	25 5/8	26 2/8	17 2/8	24 3/8	5 2/8	5 1/8	17	20	62	1964	3
■ St. Louis County / John Cesarek / John Cesarek												
236	22 3/8	24 5/8	19 5/8	23 3/8	5 4/8	5 1/8	11	12	71 3/8	1964	4
■ Winona County / Francis A. Pries / Francis A. Pries												
225 2/8	29 1/8	29 2/8	23 4/8	28 6/8	6 2/8	6 1/8	9	8	29 2/8	1938	5
■ St. Louis County / Elmer H. Sellin / Elmer H. Sellin												
224 3/8	26 7/8	27	21 2/8	25 7/8	5 1/8	5 2/8	8	7	31 5/8	1969	6
■ Lac qui Parle County / Mike Unzen / Mike Unzen												
224 2/8	23 2/8	23 2/8	22	26 7/8	5 3/8	5 2/8	18	15	54	1980	7
■ Pine County / Greg S. Blom / Greg S. Blom												
224	29 4/8	29 2/8	20	22 4/8	6 2/8	5 4/8	15	13	29 4/8	1890	8
■ Minnesota / Unknown / Harvard Univ. Mus.												
222 6/8	21 4/8	22 7/8	16 1/8	20 6/8	5 7/8	5 3/8	11	10	45 1/8	1936	9
■ Itasca County / Picked Up / James R. Smith												
222 3/8	25 2/8	25 6/8	19 1/8	26 6/8	5 6/8	5 6/8	14	12	45 2/8	1942	10
■ Itasca County / Lumie Jackson / Rick Ferguson												
221 2/8	22 5/8	23 6/8	17 1/8	26 4/8	4 5/8	4 4/8	16	11	63 5/8	1955	11
■ Itasca County / Richard I. Goble / Richard I. Goble												
220 6/8	26 2/8	25 6/8	19 6/8	25 2/8	6 1/8	6 3/8	12	15	47 4/8	1946	12
■ Anoka County / Donald Torgerson / J. D. Andrews												
220 3/8	25 1/8	25 6/8	18 6/8	22 6/8	5	5	14	13	53 1/8	1963	13
■ Olmstead County / E. E. Comartin III / E. E. Comartin, Jr.												

MINNESOTA NON-TYPICAL WHITETAILS *(continued)*

Score	Length of Main Beam R	Length of Main Beam L	Inside Spread	Greatest Spread	Circumference at Smallest Place Between Burr and First Point R	Circumference at Smallest Place Between Burr and First Point L	Number of Points R	Number of Points L	Total of Lengths Abnormal Points	Date Killed	Rank
▪ *Locality Killed / By Whom Killed / Owner*											
218	25 4/8	25 3/8	19	23 5/8	5 4/8	5 3/8	11	15	48 6/8	1977	14
▪ *Otter Tail County / Dennis A. Pearson / Dennis A. Pearson*											
217 4/8	25 5/8	25	19 4/8	23 2/8	6 2/8	6 3/8	11	12	31 4/8	1973	15
▪ *Aitkin County / Fred C. Melichar / Fred C. Melichar*											
217 3/8	27	28 5/8	18 3/8	24 5/8	5 2/8	5 4/8	12	15	38 6/8	1982	16
▪ *Meeker County / Steven R. Turek / Steven R. Turek*											
216 1/8	23 1/8	19 4/8	15 2/8	26	5 3/8	6 1/8	15	16	48 7/8	1977	17
▪ *Itasca County / Thomas Thurstin / Thomas Thurstin*											
215 6/8	24 4/8	24 4/8	23 3/8	25 3/8	6 2/8	7 4/8	10	12	45 3/8	1974	18
▪ *Chippewa County / Micheal Allickson / Micheal Allickson*											
214 5/8	25 5/8	25 7/8	16 5/8	25 5/8	5	4 7/8	15	14	54	1956	19
▪ *Koochiching County / Unknown / Wilbur Tilander*											
214 4/8	26 6/8	26 4/8	20 1/8	25 2/8	5 2/8	5	11	9	30 7/8	1972	20
▪ *Swift County / Leonard N. Kanuit / Leonard N. Kanuit*											
214	28 7/8	28 6/8	23 1/8	28 2/8	4 5/8	4 4/8	10	9	19 1/8	1984	21
▪ *Clay County / Dean Klemetson / Dean Klemetson*											
213 5/8	24 2/8	24 2/8	17 1/8	20 5/8	5 6/8	5 5/8	12	6	35 4/8	1924	22
▪ *Beltrami County / Unknown / Jim Smith*											
212 2/8	26 6/8	26 1/8	23 6/8	25 4/8	5 4/8	5 3/8	9	7	18 4/8	1977	23
▪ *Houston County / Alfred C. Pieper / Alfred C. Pieper*											
212 1/8	27	27	19 6/8	25 7/8	5 2/8	5 3/8	14	16	41 3/8	1968	24
▪ *St. Louis County / Robert J. LaPine / Robert J. LaPine*											
212	26 7/8	25	16 7/8	21	4 7/8	5 1/8	14	13	35 7/8	1922	25
▪ *Becker County / Unknown / George W. Flaim*											
211 6/8	22 3/8	25 5/8	21	26 3/8	5	5	10	11	24 4/8	1981	26
▪ *Cottonwood County / James A. Sykora / James A. Sykora*											
211 4/8	25 3/8	25	18 3/8	25 4/8	5 1/8	4 7/8	14	17	43 5/8	1963	27
▪ *St. Louis County / John E. Peterson, Jr. / John E. Peterson, Jr.*											
211 2/8	27 7/8	27	19 2/8	23 1/8	6 2/8	6 1/8	8	9	33 4/8	1959	28
▪ *Marshall County / Picked Up / Robert Sands*											
209 7/8	25 6/8	25 4/8	18 1/8	20 6/8	4 5/8	4 5/8	10	15	34 6/8	1980	29
▪ *Pine County / Scott A. Miller / Scott A. Miller*											
209 6/8	27	27 2/8	17 1/8	19 6/8	5 2/8	5 1/8	11	10	29 3/8	1929	30
▪ *Koochiching County / Harry Van Keuren / Louis E. Muench*											
208 2/8	27	26 1/8	20 4/8	23 2/8	4 7/8	4 6/8	11	11	37 2/8	1961	31
▪ *St. Louis County / Walter H. Enzenauer / Walter H. Enzenauer*											

MINNESOTA NON-TYPICAL WHITETAILS *(continued)*

Score	Length of Main Beam R	L	Inside Spread	Greatest Spread	Circumference at Smallest Place Between Burr and First Point R	L	Number of Points R	L	Total of Lengths Abnormal Points	Date Killed	Rank
207 5/8	27 1/8	26 5/8	22 2/8	27 5/8	6 6/8	7	11	9	30 1/8	1961	32
■ Lincoln County / Joe Ness / Joe Ness
206 7/8	26 2/8	29 5/8	27 7/8	30 4/8	5 2/8	5 4/8	11	10	21	1983	33
■ Wright County / Richard A. Erickson / Richard A. Erickson
206 4/8	26	26 1/8	19 2/8	24 2/8	6 3/8	6 1/8	11	6	13 2/8	1974	34
■ Lac qui Parle County / Steven J. Karels / Steven J. Karels
206 4/8	23 2/8	23 1/8	16 4/8	26	5 4/8	5 4/8	14	8	44	1950	34
■ Norman County / Unknown / Tom Williams
205 6/8	25 3/8	26 4/8	18 1/8	21 3/8	4 5/8	4 4/8	11	9	19 3/8	1965	36
■ Minnesota / Unknown / Greg Jensen
205 5/8	26	25 2/8	21 2/8	23 2/8	5 4/8	5 7/8	14	9	32 3/8	1975	37
■ Cottonwood County / Larry G. Gravley / Larry G. Gravley
205 4/8	27 2/8	25 4/8	22 4/8	26 1/8	5 5/8	5 6/8	9	9	29 6/8	1955	38
■ Roseau County / Erwin Klaassen / Erwin Klaassen
205 3/8	22 4/8	23 2/8	17	26	6	6	10	12	46 1/8	1979	39
■ Todd County / Mark A. Miksche / Mark A. Miksche
205	26 3/8	26 4/8	16 7/8	19 4/8	6 1/8	5 7/8	12	9	25 5/8	1964	40
■ St. Louis County / Ed Nelson / George W. Flaim
204	26 1/8	25 5/8	18 6/8	25 3/8	5 3/8	5 2/8	13	10	38 2/8	1977	41
■ Grant County / Douglas S. Olson / Douglas S. Olson
204	26 1/8	27 3/8	16 2/8	18 5/8	5 1/8	5 3/8	10	11	16 2/8	1964	41
■ Carlton County / Erick Zack / Glen Van Guilder
203 5/8	24 3/8	26 3/8	21 7/8	25 5/8	5 5/8	5 7/8	12	11	25 6/8	1981	43
■ St. Louis County / Picked Up / Phillip A. Roalstad
203 3/8	26 2/8	26 1/8	17 6/8	22	5 4/8	5 4/8	8	10	24 5/8	1967	44
■ Olmsted County / Daniel J. Bernard / Daniel J. Bernard
203 3/8	25 1/8	24 1/8	21	23 1/8	5 4/8	5 3/8	8	10	46 5/8	1961	44
■ Olmsted County / Logan Behrens / Logan Behrens
203 1/8	23 5/8	25 5/8	16	22 2/8	4 7/8	4 6/8	11	10	56 1/8	1934	46
■ Koochiching County / Unknown / George W. Flaim
202 3/8	26 1/8	27	20 7/8	23 4/8	5	5 1/8	10	10	23	1960	47
■ Aitkin County / Joe Clarke / Joe Clarke
202 3/8	26	24 5/8	21 2/8	24 6/8	5 4/8	5 4/8	11	12	30 7/8	1955	47
■ Koochiching County / George A. Balaski / George A. Balaski
202 1/8	25 4/8	25 4/8	19 1/8	21 3/8	4 5/8	4 6/8	10	7	22 2/8	1980	49
■ Pennington County / R. Scott Sorvig / R. Scott Sorvig

MINNESOTA NON-TYPICAL WHITETAILS *(continued)*

Score	Length of Main Beam R	L	Inside Spread	Greatest Spread	Circumference at Smallest Place Between Burr and First Point R	L	Number of Points R	L	Total of Lengths Abnormal Points	Date Killed	Rank
	▪ Locality Killed / By Whom Killed / Owner										
201⁷⁄₈	28²⁄₈	27	17²⁄₈	19⁶⁄₈	6	6	11	11	29⁷⁄₈	1981	50
	▪ Itasca County / Picked Up / J. Gorden & G. Dopp										
201⁴⁄₈	29⁷⁄₈	28⁵⁄₈	19⁷⁄₈	23²⁄₈	5²⁄₈	5⁴⁄₈	10	10	23¹⁄₈	1973	51
	▪ Hubbard County / Duane G. Lorsung / Duane G. Lorsung										
201³⁄₈	26³⁄₈	25⁷⁄₈	18⁴⁄₈	21¹⁄₈	5²⁄₈	5¹⁄₈	10	8	28⁷⁄₈	1958	52
	▪ St. Louis County / Andrew G. Groen / Andrew G. Groen										
201²⁄₈	26³⁄₈	27³⁄₈	16⁵⁄₈	18⁵⁄₈	5⁶⁄₈	5⁴⁄₈	10	7	17⁵⁄₈	1976	53
	▪ Itasca County / Cecil L. Johnson / Cecil L. Johnson										
201²⁄₈	26⁷⁄₈	26⁴⁄₈	16	21²⁄₈	5³⁄₈	5⁵⁄₈	17	14	48⁶⁄₈	1940	53
	▪ Pennington County / Glenn Tasa / Glenn Tasa										
201¹⁄₈	25	25¹⁄₈	20⁴⁄₈	23⁷⁄₈	6¹⁄₈	6⁴⁄₈	10	8	29¹⁄₈	1972	55
	▪ Freeborn County / Jim Palmer / Jim Palmer										
201	23²⁄₈	21²⁄₈	19²⁄₈	22	6⁶⁄₈	7²⁄₈	8	11	38²⁄₈	1977	56
	▪ Anoka County / Unknown / John L. Stein										
200³⁄₈	23⁵⁄₈	24	18⁶⁄₈	21³⁄₈	4⁶⁄₈	4⁶⁄₈	8	8	21⁵⁄₈	1974	57
	▪ Lake of the Woods County / Mark H. Hagen / Mark H. Hagen										
200¹⁄₈	27³⁄₈	26⁶⁄₈	21²⁄₈	26¹⁄₈	4⁷⁄₈	5¹⁄₈	12	12	38³⁄₈	1966	58
	▪ Kandiyohi County / Robert J. Custer / Robert J. Custer										
199⁴⁄₈	25²⁄₈	25²⁄₈	20⁶⁄₈	24³⁄₈	5¹⁄₈	5⁴⁄₈	8	8	30²⁄₈	1963	59
	▪ Aitkin County / Sanford Patrick / Sanford Patrick										
199¹⁄₈	25²⁄₈	25⁷⁄₈	17⁴⁄₈	21¹⁄₈	5¹⁄₈	5²⁄₈	10	13	30⁷⁄₈	1978	60
	▪ St. Louis County / Orville Schultz / Orville Schultz										
199	26³⁄₈	25	19¹⁄₈	24	5¹⁄₈	5	10	8	26¹⁄₈	1976	61
	▪ Yellow Medicine County / William A. Botten / William A. Botten										
198⁷⁄₈	26⁷⁄₈	25⁶⁄₈	21¹⁄₈	41¹⁄₈	5⁴⁄₈	5²⁄₈	10	7	23⁵⁄₈	1976	62
	▪ Chippewa County / Ray N. Strand / Ray N. Strand										
198⁶⁄₈	29⁷⁄₈	27¹⁄₈	15⁷⁄₈	19¹⁄₈	5³⁄₈	5³⁄₈	11	7	25⁵⁄₈	1973	63
	▪ Fillmore County / Phillip S. Hansen / Phillip S. Hansen										
198⁴⁄₈	26²⁄₈	24²⁄₈	21⁵⁄₈	24²⁄₈	4⁷⁄₈	4⁶⁄₈	7	8	17³⁄₈	1980	64
	▪ Lincoln County / Dennis G. Geiken / Dennis G. Geiken										
198⁴⁄₈	26⁴⁄₈	22⁵⁄₈	18⁷⁄₈	22	5⁶⁄₈	5⁵⁄₈	9	10	44³⁄₈	1946	64
	▪ Clay County / F. W. Kolle / Kolle Farms, Inc.										
198²⁄₈	23³⁄₈	22⁵⁄₈	21⁶⁄₈	24²⁄₈	5	5	9	12	33	1941	66
	▪ Crow Wing County / Harold B. Stotts / Harold B. Stotts										
197⁵⁄₈	25¹⁄₈	24⁶⁄₈	22⁴⁄₈	25⁵⁄₈	5⁴⁄₈	5¹⁄₈	10	8	26³⁄₈	1981	67
	▪ Blue Earth County / Daniel R. Nelson / Daniel R. Nelson										

MINNESOTA NON-TYPICAL WHITETAILS *(continued)*

Score	Length of Main Beam R	L	Inside Spread	Greatest Spread	Circumference at Smallest Place Between Burr and First Point R	L	Number of Points R	L	Total of Lengths Abnormal Points	Date Killed	Rank
* Locality Killed / By Whom Killed / Owner												
197 4/8	24 4/8	24 5/8	21 6/8	25 2/8	7	6 7/8	8	10	18	1973	68
■ Chippewa County / Dean D. Anspach / Dean D. Anspach										
197 3/8	27 3/8	26 3/8	20 4/8	26 1/8	5 2/8	5 2/8	8	9	22 1/8	1982	69
■ Faribault County / Randy L. Sandt / Randy L. Sandt										
195 7/8	26 3/8	26 5/8	19 2/8	21 5/8	6	6	10	7	14 3/8	1938	70
■ Beltrami County / Ollie Jamtaas / James Gorden										
195 6/8	25 4/8	26 5/8	19 5/8	23 4/8	6 5/8	7	11	12	27 1/8	1984	71
■ Roseau County / George H. Tepley / George H. Tepley										
195 6/8	25 6/8	25	20 2/8	25	5 3/8	5 2/8	10	7	13	1963	71
■ St. Louis County / Mike Desanto / Mike Desanto										
195 4/8	26	25 3/8	16 6/8	21 7/8	4 7/8	4 6/8	10	7	20 4/8	1976	73
■ Winona County / Patrick Bartholomew / Patrick Bartholomew										
195 3/8	20 1/8	22 4/8	16 2/8	19 5/8	7 3/8	7 5/8	10	12	40 3/8	1980	74
■ Beltrami County / John G. Binsfeld / John G. Binsfeld										

Photo Courtesy of R. L. Bobo

MISSISSIPPI STATE RECORD
TYPICAL ANTLERS
SCORE: 182 2/8
Locality: Claiborne Co.   Date: November 1955
Hunter: R. L. Bobo

MISSISSIPPI

TYPICAL WHITETAILS

Score	Length of Main Beam R L	Inside Spread	Greatest Spread	Circumference at Smallest Place Between Burr and First Point R L	Number of Points R L	Total of Lengths Abnormal Points	Date Killed	Rank
182 2/8	27 1/8 26 4/8	19 6/8	21 6/8	5 1/8 5 2/8	5 5	0	1955	1
■ Claiborne County / R. L. Bobo / R. L. Bobo									
181 5/8	25 6/8 25 7/8	19 7/8	21 6/8	5 4/8 5 4/8	6 7	2 4/8	1981	2
■ Wilkinson County / Ronnie P. Whitaker / Ronnie P. Whitaker									
180 4/8	28 27	22 7/8	25 3/8	5 3/8 5 1/8	6 6	1 5/8	1968	3
■ Leflore County / W. F. Smith / W. F. Smith									
178 5/8	25 6/8 27 2/8	20 2/8	23	5 4/8 5 4/8	6 5	3 3/8	1951	4
■ Bolivar County / Grady Robertson / Merigold Hunting Club									
176 5/8	25 4/8 25 4/8	21 7/8	17 4/8	4 5/8 4 7/8	5 5	0	1952	5
■ Bolivar County / Sidney D. Sessions / Sidney D. Sessions									
175 2/8	26 1/8 25 5/8	21 1/8	25 4/8	5 1/8 5 2/8	8 6	3 5/8	1978	6
■ Wilkinson County / Johnnie J. Leake, Jr. / Johnnie J. Leake, Jr.									
174 6/8	27 2/8 29 1/8	21 3/8	24 2/8	5 1/8 5	5 5	0	1960	7
■ Coahoma County / O. P. Gilbert / O. P. Gilbert									
173 5/8	25 25 6/8	22 5/8	24 5/8	4 2/8 4 4/8	6 6	0	1982	8
■ Lowndes County / Geraline Holliman / Geraline Holliman									
172 5/8	28 4/8 28	22	25 2/8	6 2/8 6 3/8	8 8	4 3/8	1983	9
■ Adams County / Adrian L. Stallone / Adrian L. Stallone									
172	25 25 2/8	18 6/8	20 7/8	5 2/8 5 2/8	6 5	0	1977	10
■ Adams County / Nan Foster New / Nan Foster New									
170 7/8	28 1/8 27 1/8	19 2/8	23	5 5	5 4	2 1/8	1920	11
■ Issaquena County / Warren A. Miller / Alford M. Cooley									

Photo by Wm. H. Nesbitt

MISSISSIPPI STATE RECORD
NON-TYPICAL ANTLERS
SCORE: 217 5/8

Locality: Carroll Co.   Date: January 1978
Hunter: Mark T. Hathcock

MISSISSIPPI

NON-TYPICAL WHITETAILS

Score	Length of Main Beam R	L	Inside Spread	Greatest Spread	Circumference at Smallest Place Between Burr and First Point R	L	Number of Points R	L	Total of Lengths Abnormal Points	Date Killed	Rank
\[Locality Killed / By Whom Killed / Owner\]											
217 5/8	27 3/8	24 6/8	23	28	4 6/8	5 3/8	14	14	55 7/8	1978	1
■ Carroll County / Mark T. Hathcock / Mark T. Hathcock											
209 6/8	24 6/8	24 2/8	20 7/8	25 7/8	5 6/8	5 3/8	10	11	48 5/8	1981	2
■ Franklin County / Ronnie Strickland / Ronnie Strickland											
205 6/8	23 1/8	21 4/8	21	25 7/8	4 7/8	4 4/8	12	12	56	1976	3
■ Lowndes County / Joe W. Shurden / Joe W. Shurden											
202 1/8	28 7/8	28 1/8	16 7/8	26 7/8	5 6/8	5 4/8	15	11	44	1983	4
■ Oktibbeha County / Oliver H. Lindig / Oliver H. Lindig											
196 5/8	21 2/8	20 5/8	19 4/8	23 5/8	4 7/8	4 7/8	10	12	74 5/8	1982	5
■ Wilinson County / Robert D. Sullivan / Robert D. Sullivan											
195 5/8	23 7/8	24 2/8	13	23 7/8	5	5 2/8	14	10	71 1/8	1981	6
■ Adams County / Kathleen McGehee / Kathleen McGehee											

Photo by Wm. H. Nesbitt

MISSOURI STATE RECORD
TYPICAL ANTLERS
SCORE: 205
Locality: Randolph Co.   Date: November 1971
Hunter: Larry W. Gibson

MISSOURI

TYPICAL WHITETAILS

Score	Length of Main Beam R	L	Inside Spread	Greatest Spread	Circumference at Smallest Place Between Burr and First Point R	L	Number of Points R	L	Total of Lengths Abnormal Points	Date Killed	Rank
205	26⁶⁄₈	25⁴⁄₈	24²⁄₈	25²⁄₈	4⁶⁄₈	4⁶⁄₈	6	6	0	1971	1
■ Randolph County / Larry W. Gibson / Larry W. Gibson
199⁴⁄₈	27²⁄₈	26²⁄₈	20	22⁴⁄₈	5¹⁄₈	5¹⁄₈	8	5	1¹⁄₈	1969	2
■ Clark County / Jeffrey A. Brunk / Jeffrey A. Brunk
187²⁄₈	26	26²⁄₈	19⁴⁄₈	21⁶⁄₈	4⁶⁄₈	4⁶⁄₈	6	8	4⁶⁄₈	1971	3
■ Scotland County / Robin Berhorst / Robin Berhorst
187¹⁄₈	26⁴⁄₈	26⁵⁄₈	19⁴⁄₈	21¹⁄₈	4⁴⁄₈	4⁵⁄₈	6	7	2⁵⁄₈	1973	4
■ Cooper County / Joe Ditto / Joe Ditto
186⁷⁄₈	27¹⁄₈	27²⁄₈	19¹⁄₈	21²⁄₈	5	5²⁄₈	7	8	5²⁄₈	1968	5
■ Atchison County / Mike Moody / Mike Moody
186²⁄₈	25	25⁴⁄₈	22⁴⁄₈	22	5	5²⁄₈	6	7	1¹⁄₈	1972	6
■ Laclede County / Larry Ogle / Larry Ogle
183⁴⁄₈	26⁵⁄₈	26⁶⁄₈	18²⁄₈	20²⁄₈	5³⁄₈	5⁴⁄₈	5	6	0	1968	7
■ Sumner / Marvin F. Lentz / Marvin F. Lentz
182⁴⁄₈	27	26⁶⁄₈	18⁴⁄₈	21⁵⁄₈	5³⁄₈	5³⁄₈	7	5	1⁶⁄₈	1968	8
■ Warren County / Donald L. Tanner / Donald L. Tanner
180⁴⁄₈	23⁵⁄₈	24⁴⁄₈	17²⁄₈	19	5²⁄₈	5	6	5	1	1967	9
■ Andrew County / Virgil M. Ashley / Virgil M. Ashley
180¹⁄₈	26⁴⁄₈	26⁵⁄₈	20¹⁄₈	22	4⁴⁄₈	4⁵⁄₈	6	6	0	1973	10
■ Phelps County / William A. Hagenhoff / William A. Hagenhoff
178⁴⁄₈	26²⁄₈	25³⁄₈	21	22⁶⁄₈	5³⁄₈	5³⁄₈	5	5	0	1984	11
■ Scotland County / Picked Up / Roland E. Meyer
178	26⁷⁄₈	27²⁄₈	21⁶⁄₈	24²⁄₈	4³⁄₈	4³⁄₈	6	6	0	1966	12
■ Clark County / Allen L. Courtney / Allen L. Courtney
175⁴⁄₈	25⁶⁄₈	25⁴⁄₈	21³⁄₈	23¹⁄₈	5⁵⁄₈	6¹⁄₈	5	5	0	1962	13
■ Corning / Orrie L. Schaeffer / Orrie L. Schaeffer

MISSOURI TYPICAL WHITETAILS *(continued)*

Score	Length of Main Beam R	Length of Main Beam L	Inside Spread	Greatest Spread	Circumference at Smallest Place Between Burr and First Point R	Circumference at Smallest Place Between Burr and First Point L	Number of Points R	Number of Points L	Total of Lengths Abnormal Points	Date Killed	Rank
■ *Locality Killed / By Whom Killed / Owner*											
175	23 2/8	24	19 6/8	22 4/8	5 1/8	5 2/8	5	5	0	1973	14
■ *Harrison County / Carl J. Graham / Carl J. Graham*											
174 3/8	28 1/8	26 7/8	23 5/8	0	5 3/8	5 4/8	6	5	3 2/8	1972	15
■ *Knox County / Jon Simmons / Jon Simmons*											
174 1/8	25	25	16 6/8	18 6/8	4 7/8	4 6/8	8	7	4 1/8	1968	16
■ *Calloway County / Jac LaFon / Jac LaFon*											
173 5/8	25 2/8	25 4/8	18 3/8	20 5/8	5	5	5	8	1 6/8	1969	17
■ *Gentry County / William F. Oberbeck / William F. Oberbeck*											
173 2/8	26 7/8	28 5/8	23 5/8	25 6/8	4 4/8	4 4/8	6	6	4 3/8	1980	18
■ *Warren County / Jerome E. Ley / Jerome E. Ley*											
173 1/8	26 5/8	27 6/8	19 5/8	23 6/8	4 4/8	4 5/8	7	6	3 6/8	1981	19
■ *Shelby County / William A. Light, Jr. / William A. Light, Jr.*											
173	28	28 2/8	21 7/8	23 7/8	5 3/8	5 3/8	7	6	1 1/8	1978	20
■ *Howard County / Thomas R. Banning / Thomas R. Banning*											
172 3/8	26	26 2/8	19 5/8	21 2/8	4 6/8	4 6/8	6	5	1 6/8	1967	21
■ *Monroe County / Clark Ernest Bray / Clark Ernest Bray*											
171 7/8	26 2/8	26 4/8	24 1/8	27 7/8	4 4/8	4 4/8	5	5	0	1984	22
■ *Scotland County / David R. Smith / David R. Smith*											
171	25 2/8	24	15 6/8	18 1/8	5 1/8	5 2/8	5	5	0	1983	23
■ *Christian County / Melba J. Herndon / Melba J. Herndon*											
171	24 4/8	25 2/8	17 2/8	21	4 2/8	4 1/8	6	5	3 6/8	1966	23
■ *Ray County / Darle R. Siegel / Darle R. Siegel*											
170 6/8	27 2/8	26 4/8	20	23	4 4/8	4 4/8	6	6	2 2/8	1974	25
■ *Howell County / Roy W. Woodson / Roy W. Woodson*											
170 5/8	26 7/8	25 4/8	18 2/8	20 5/8	5 4/8	5 2/8	5	7	1 5/8	1980	26
■ *Atchison County / Roy E. Munsey / Roy E. Munsey*											
170 5/8	22 5/8	23 2/8	17 7/8	20	4 7/8	5	5	5	0	1962	26
■ *St. Charles County / Oscar Mallinckrodt / Oscar Mallinckrodt*											
170	24 3/8	23 2/8	20 6/8	22 5/8	4 7/8	4 6/8	5	5	0	1974	28
■ *Scotland County / Chester James Young / Chester James Young*											
170	26 3/8	24 5/8	19 6/8	23	5 2/8	5 1/8	5	5	0	1973	28
■ *Shelby County / Rusty D. Gander / Rusty D. Gander*											
170	26 4/8	26 5/8	17 4/8	20 1/8	4 6/8	4 7/8	7	5	2 4/8	1969	28
■ *Bates County / Gary Rosier / Gary Rosier*											

Photo Courtesy of Ray Sadler

Ray Sadler was hunting in Clinton County, Michigan, in 1963 when he took this 23-point typical whitetail. Scoring an impressive 176-6/8 points, this buck was an entry in the 14th Competition (1968-1970).

Photo by Wm. H. Nesbitt

MISSOURI STATE RECORD
NON-TYPICAL ANTLERS
SCORE: 333 7/8

Locality: St. Louis Co.   Date: Picked Up in 1981
Owner: Missouri Dept. of Cons.

MISSOURI

NON-TYPICAL WHITETAILS

Score	Length of Main Beam R	L	Inside Spread	Greatest Spread	Circ. R	L	Points R	L	Total Abnormal Points	Date Killed	Rank
333 7/8	24 1/8	23 3/8	23 3/8	33 3/8	5 1/8	5 1/8	19	25	184	1981	1
■ St. Louis County / Picked Up / Missouri Dept. of Cons.												
219 5/8	24 5/8	25 1/8	21 1/8	25 4/8	5 7/8	6 3/8	13	12	34 4/8	1959	2
■ Warren County / James E. Williams / James E. Williams												
218 5/8	26 2/8	25 5/8	18 4/8	23 3/8	4 4/8	4 4/8	9	11	36 7/8	1979	3
■ Chariton County / Stanley McSparren / Stanley McSparren												
217 7/8	27 7/8	28 2/8	21 3/8	23 5/8	5 4/8	5 7/8	10	16	30	1974	4
■ Maries County / Gerald R. Dake / Gerald R. Dake												
215 5/8	28	28	20 2/8	23 3/8	5 2/8	5 1/8	10	9	21 1/8	1974	5
■ Worth County / B. Miller & R. Nonneman / B. Miller & R. Nonneman												
208 7/8	25 1/8	26	21 6/8	24 6/8	5	4 7/8	8	11	20 1/8	1964	6
■ Atchison County / Kenneth W. Lee / Kenneth W. Lee												
207 3/8	28 7/8	29 1/8	18 5/8	16 3/8	6 5/8	6 2/8	10	10	44	1955	7
■ Lincoln County / Melvin Zumwalt / Melvin Zumwalt												
205 7/8	23 2/8	23 3/8	17 5/8	24 4/8	5 4/8	5 4/8	9	13	33 4/8	1983	8
■ Clark County / Allen L. Courtney / Allen L. Courtney												
203 5/8	26 6/8	28	15 5/8	19 4/8	6 5/8	6	18	13	56	1953	9
■ Chariton County / Vernon Sower / Vernon Sower												
202	28 5/8	27 3/8	15 5/8	21 2/8	5 5/8	6	12	11	26 1/8	1972	10
■ Nodaway County / Richard L. Stewart / Richard L. Stewart												
199 7/8	20 1/8	20 7/8	14	27 5/8	5 1/8	5	7	14	66 1/8	1971	11
■ Hickory County / Darwin Lee Stogsdill / Darwin Lee Stogsdill												
199 3/8	28	26 4/8	21 6/8	24 5/8	5 5/8	5 5/8	10	8	24 7/8	1973	12
■ Clark County / Bob Arnold / Bob Arnold												
197 1/8	26 1/8	26 3/8	17 3/8	24 2/8	5 2/8	4 6/8	8	7	27	1984	13
■ Jackson County / Jim Martin / Jim Martin												
197 1/8	28 2/8	26 6/8	18 7/8	21 4/8	5	5 1/8	9	11	32	1982	13
■ Worth County / Gary G. Kinder / Gary G. Kinder												

Photo by Wm. H. Nesbitt

MONTANA STATE RECORD
TYPICAL ANTLERS
SCORE: 199 3/8

Locality: Missoula Co.   Date: November 1974
Hunter: Thomas H. Dellwo

MONTANA

TYPICAL WHITETAILS

Score	Length of Main Beam R	L	Inside Spread	Greatest Spread	Circumference at Smallest Place Between Burr and First Point R	L	Number of Points R	L	Total of Lengths Abnormal Points	Date Killed	Rank
\■ Locality Killed / By Whom Killed / Owner											
199 3/8	27 3/8	27 4/8	22 3/8	24 3/8	4 4/8	4 6/8	6	7	1	1974	1
■ Missoula County / Thomas H. Dellwo / Thomas H. Dellwo											
191 5/8	26 5/8	26 2/8	19	21 5/8	5 1/8	5	6	7	1 5/8	1963	2
■ Flathead County / Earl T. McMaster / McLean Bowman											
189 1/8	28	28 1/8	23 5/8	30 1/8	4 4/8	4 5/8	5	7	3 6/8	1959	3
■ Blaine County / Kenneth Morehouse / Kenneth Morehouse											
187 5/8	26 5/8	26 3/8	15 6/8	19 1/8	5 5/8	5 6/8	6	6	1 3/8	PR1984	4
■ Montana / Unknown / Johnny M. Hollier											
186 3/8	30 2/8	29	22 5/8	25 4/8	4 4/8	4 5/8	5	5	0	1973	5
■ Flathead County / Unknown / Wayne D. Williamson											
186	25 1/8	25 3/8	19	22 4/8	4 3/8	4 3/8	6	6	0	1966	6
■ Flathead County / Douglas G. Mefford / Douglas G. Mefford											
183 3/8	21 5/8	23 3/8	19 3/8	22 7/8	5 4/8	5 2/8	7	9	2 2/8	1957	7
■ Flathead County / Unknown / Edwin M. Sager											
182 7/8	27 1/8	26 4/8	24	26 6/8	5 4/8	5 4/8	6	7	6 3/8	PR1983	8
■ Montana / Unknown / Johnny M. Hollier											
182 2/8	26	26 4/8	18 1/8	20 4/8	5 2/8	5 1/8	5	5	1 1/8	1983	9
■ Park County / Jim Whitt / Jim Whitt											
180 5/8	24 7/8	25 1/8	18 3/8	20 7/8	4 7/8	4 6/8	6	7	1 6/8	1958	10
■ Treasure County / Jack Welch / Jack Welch											
180 3/8	24 5/8	24 4/8	19 1/8	21 1/8	5 4/8	5 6/8	8	6	4 4/8	1957	11
■ Orvando / Clinton Berry / Clinton Berry											
180	25 7/8	25 5/8	19 4/8	22 7/8	6 1/8	6 1/8	6	8	7	1967	12
■ Big Horn County / Clair W. Jensen / Clair W. Jensen											
179 4/8	24 1/8	25 3/8	19 5/8	21 5/8	5	4 7/8	7	8	8 3/8	1977	13
■ Chouteau County / Richard L. Charlson / Richard L. Charlson											

111

MONTANA TYPICAL WHITETAILS *(continued)*

Score	Length of Main Beam R	L	Inside Spread	Greatest Spread	Circumference at Smallest Place Between Burr and First Point R	L	Number of Points R	L	Total of Lengths Abnormal Points	Date Killed	Rank
	■ Locality Killed / By Whom Killed / Owner										
177 7/8	26 4/8	27 4/8	23	26 3/8	5 5/8	5	7	9	11 1/8	1983	14
	■ Jefferson County / Tracy Forcella / Tracy Forcella										
177 7/8	25 7/8	25 1/8	24 3/8	24 3/8	5	5 1/8	5	6	0	1967	14
	■ Wibaux County / Dan Amunrud / David Welliever										
176 4/8	27 3/8	28	21 7/8	24	4 3/8	4 4/8	5	5	6	1983	16
	■ Sanders County / Dallas J. C. Nelson / Dallas J. C. Nelson										
175 5/8	24 7/8	25 2/8	25 1/8	28 2/8	4 5/8	4 4/8	7	7	4	1974	17
	■ Lake County / Kenneth D. Johnson / Kenneth D. Johnson										
174 4/8	22 2/8	23 2/8	19 5/8	21 5/8	4 3/8	4 5/8	7	7	5 3/8	1973	18
	■ Powell County / Dave Rittenhouse / Dave Rittenhouse										
173 5/8	28 3/8	28 5/8	20 7/8	25 4/8	5 2/8	5 4/8	6	7	8 4/8	1984	19
	■ Flathead County / Mike J. Beaty / Mike J. Beaty										
173 5/8	22 6/8	21 7/8	20 5/8	23 3/8	4 7/8	4 7/8	6	6	0	1978	19
	■ Valley County / Scott Fossum / Scott Fossum										
173 3/8	24 4/8	25	16 7/8	19	5 1/8	5 1/8	5	5	0	1978	21
	■ Valley County / Steve K. Sukut / Steve K. Sukut										
173 3/8	23 3/8	23 3/8	23 3/8	25 5/8	5 1/8	5 1/8	5	5	0	1975	21
	■ Rosebud County / Ted Millhollin / Ted Millhollin										
173 1/8	26 1/8	24 5/8	21 1/8	23 5/8	4 7/8	4 5/8	5	5	0	1971	23
	■ Lake County / Darrell Brist / Darrell Brist										
172 7/8	24 3/8	25 1/8	21 1/8	24	4 5/8	4 4/8	6	8	9 2/8	1976	24
	■ Cascade County / Skip Halmes / Skip Halmes										
172 2/8	25 4/8	25 2/8	23 3/8	26 7/8	5 1/8	5 1/8	6	7	1 1/8	1963	25
	■ Flathead County / Lonny Hanson / Lonny Hanson										
170 1/8	24 3/8	22 6/8	18 3/8	21 6/8	5	5 1/8	8	6	9	1984	26
	■ Sanders County / Richard Lukes / Richard Lukes										
170	26 1/8	24 5/8	17 7/8	20 2/8	4 4/8	4 4/8	6	6	8 5/8	1966	27
	■ Flathead County / Dave Delap / Dave Delap										

Photo Courtesy of Hugh Cox

Bowhunter Hugh Cox with the non-typical 198-1/8 that he took in Hocking County, Ohio, in 1964. This is the 18th largest non-typical from Ohio, and it was an entry in the 12th Competition (1964-1965).

Photo Courtesy of Frank A. Pleskac

MONTANA STATE RECORD
NON-TYPICAL ANTLERS
SCORE: 252 1/8

Locality: Hill Co.   Date: November 1968
Hunter: Frank A. Pleskac

MONTANA

NON-TYPICAL WHITETAILS

Score	Length of Main Beam R	L	Inside Spread	Greatest Spread	Circumference at Smallest Place Between Burr and First Point R	L	Number of Points R	L	Total of Lengths Abnormal Points	Date Killed	Rank
252 1/8	25 6/8	28 3/8	19 5/8	25 1/8	5 3/8	5 6/8	9	9	60 6/8	1968	1
■ Hill County / Frank A. Pleskac / Frank A. Pleskac
248 5/8	25	24	20 5/8	24 4/8	5 1/8	5 2/8	16	12	79 6/8	PR1980	2
■ Snowy Mts. / Unknown / McLean Bowman
241 7/8	26 1/8	25 2/8	20 1/8	25	4 5/8	5	14	19	61 6/8	1960	3
■ Flathead County / George Woldstad / George Woldstad
234 1/8	25 7/8	27 1/8	17 2/8	22	4 5/8	4 2/8	6	10	41 5/8	PR1968	4
■ Glacier County / Unknown / Larry W. Lander
224	23 1/8	24	17 6/8	32	4 6/8	5	16	12	51 6/8	1935	5
■ Lincoln County / Ray Baenen / Ed Boyes
223 4/8	23 7/8	21 1/8	17	26 5/8	5 1/8	5 3/8	18	13	91 2/8	1960	6
■ Richland County / Verner King / Verner King
219 1/8	27	27	18 2/8	21	5 4/8	5 6/8	9	15	34 1/8	1962	7
■ Flathead County / R. C. Garrett / R. C. Garrett
216 2/8	26 5/8	27 5/8	20 3/8	26 5/8	5 6/8	5 7/8	10	14	40 3/8	1972	8
■ Richland County / Joseph P. Culbertson / Joseph P. Culbertson
215	23 2/8	25 4/8	15 5/8	21 3/8	5 6/8	5 4/8	17	13	66 5/8	1958	9
■ Fergus County / Robert D. Fleherty / Robert D. Fleherty
214 3/8	23 2/8	24	14 2/8	18 2/8	5 1/8	5 2/8	14	10	42 5/8	1962	10
■ Missoula County / Lyle Pettit / Lyle Pettit
213 1/8	22	22	17	22 7/8	5 1/8	5 1/8	12	10	18 7/8	1950	11
■ Havre / Unknown / Frank English
212 6/8	27 1/8	26 7/8	18 1/8	20 3/8	5 2/8	5 2/8	14	16	42 3/8	1952	12
■ Lewis & Clark County / LeFleur / L. S. Kuter
212 5/8	29 1/8	28 2/8	23 7/8	27	5 7/8	5 7/8	10	9	23 6/8	1975	13
■ Lake County / Dennis Courville / Dennis Courville

115

MONTANA NON-TYPICAL WHITETAILS *(continued)*

Score	Length of Main Beam R	Length of Main Beam L	Inside Spread	Greatest Spread	Circumference at Smallest Place Between Burr and First Point R	Circumference at Smallest Place Between Burr and First Point L	Number of Points R	Number of Points L	Total of Lengths Abnormal Points	Date Killed	Rank
212 5/8	25 3/8	25 4/8	23 6/8	27 4/8	4 2/8	4 4/8	11	11	40 1/8	1973	13
■ Lincoln County / Charles F. Woods, Jr. / Charles F. Woods, Jr.												
212 3/8	23 3/8	23 4/8	18 3/8	22 3/8	5	4 7/8	10	10	25 5/8	1979	15
■ Rosebd County / Picked Up / Art F. Hayes III												
210 5/8	26 2/8	28 3/8	23 6/8	25 4/8	5	5	8	9	35 1/8	1934	16
■ Lincoln County / Glen Savage / Patrick W. Savage												
208 1/8	21 6/8	23 7/8	24 1/8	25 5/8	5	4 7/8	8	8	41 2/8	1969	17
■ Prairie County / Charles Danielson / Charles Danielson												
205 7/8	25	23 3/8	20 2/8	22 3/8	6	6	13	12	30 3/8	1973	18
■ Missoula County / Unknown / John L. Stein												
202 4/8	24 4/8	24 6/8	16 4/8	19	5	4 7/8	13	12	19	1962	19
■ Missoula County / Unknown / Robert A. Bracken												
202 2/8	21 6/8	22 4/8	22	23 7/8	5	5 1/8	12	9	20 6/8	1948	20
■ Fergus County / Harold K. Stewart / Harold K. Stewart												
201 4/8	28 5/8	25 6/8	18 3/8	21	6 7/8	6 7/8	7	7	14 3/8	1976	21
■ Flathead County / Barry L. Wensel / Barry L. Wensel												
199 4/8	23	23 5/8	17 6/8	20 5/8	5 4/8	5 4/8	10	10	24 4/8	PR1980	22
■ Flathead County / Unknown / Tom Williams												
197 6/8	25 6/8	26 4/8	17	20	5 3/8	5	9	11	29	1965	23
■ Riceville / James R. Eastman / James R. Eastman												
197	21 1/8	22 1/8	15 4/8	21 2/8	5 4/8	5	11	11	47 2/8	1983	24
■ Rosebud County / Mark D. Holmes / Mark D. Holmes												

Photo Courtesy of Raymond Cowan

Raymond Cowan with the non-typical 198-5/8 that he took in Concordia Parish, Louisiana, in 1961. Cowan's buck is the 5th largest non-typical ever taken in Louisiana, and it was an entry in the 13th Competition (1966-1967).

Photo Courtesy of E. Keith Fahrenholz

NEBRASKA STATE RECORD
TYPICAL ANTLERS
SCORE: 194 1/8
Locality: Dakota Co.   Date: November 1966
Hunter: E. Keith Fahrenholz

NEBRASKA

TYPICAL WHITETAILS

Score	Length of Main Beam R	L	Inside Spread	Greatest Spread	Circumference at Smallest Place Between Burr and First Point R	L	Number of Points R	L	Total of Lengths Abnormal Points	Date Killed	Rank
* Locality Killed / By Whom Killed / Owner											
194 1/8	30	30 1/8	19 4/8	21 6/8	4 6/8	5	6	7	2 7/8	1966	1
■ Dakota County / E. Keith Fahrenholz / E. Keith Fahrenholz											
189 1/8	27 5/8	26 6/8	25 7/8	27 5/8	5 1/8	5 2/8	6	6	0	1968	2
■ Nuckolls County / Van Shotzman / Van Shotzman											
185 5/8	24 3/8	25	19 5/8	21 4/8	4 6/8	4 5/8	6	8	3 2/8	1965	3
■ Nenzel / Richard Kehr / Richard Kehr											
180 7/8	29 6/8	29 2/8	24 1/8	26 4/8	5 2/8	5	6	5	3 6/8	1966	4
■ Keya Paha County / Steve R. Pecsenye / Steve R. Pecsenye											
179 4/8	27 3/8	28 4/8	20 1/8	23 2/8	5 3/8	5 5/8	6	5	4 7/8	1975	5
■ Pawnee County / Kenneth C. Mort / Kenneth C. Mort											
178 5/8	27	26 4/8	20 4/8	22 6/8	4 3/8	4 3/8	6	6	3 3/8	1961	6
■ Harlan County / Don Tripe / Don Tripe											
178 2/8	26 5/8	26 1/8	20 6/8	25 4/8	4 6/8	4 6/8	5	5	0	1960	7
■ Pawnee County / Picked Up / Gale Sup											
178 1/8	29 1/8	28 4/8	18 4/8	23 1/8	4 7/8	4 7/8	7	7	8 5/8	1967	8
■ Harlan County / Duane E. Johnson / Duane E. Johnson											
178 1/8	24 1/8	23 5/8	19 1/8	23 7/8	4 4/8	4 5/8	8	8	6 6/8	PR1925	8
■ Dismal River / Gift of G. B. Grinnell / National Collection											
177 6/8	24 5/8	24 7/8	19	24 2/8	4 5/8	4 6/8	6	6	0	1956	10
■ Paxton / Ole Herstedt / Ole Herstedt											
177 3/8	25 4/8	25 4/8	18	20 5/8	6	6 2/8	5	6	3 5/8	1969	11
■ Hall County / Charles R. Babel / Spanky Greenville											
177	25	26	19 1/8	23 4/8	6	5 7/8	6	5	5 1/8	1968	12
■ Gage County / Art Wallman / Art Wallman											
176 6/8	26 3/8	26 2/8	18 4/8	21 3/8	5	5 3/8	5	5	0	1966	13
■ Knox County / Alvin Zimmerman / Spanky Greenville											

NEBRASKA TYPICAL WHITETAILS *(continued)*

Score	Length of Main Beam R	L	Inside Spread	Greatest Spread	Circumference at Smallest Place Between Burr and First Point R	L	Number of Points R	L	Total of Lengths Abnormal Points	Date Killed	Rank
* Locality Killed / By Whom Killed / Owner											
176²⁄₈	28⁴⁄₈	27⁴⁄₈	25	27⁶⁄₈	5⁴⁄₈	5⁴⁄₈	5	4	3⁶⁄₈	1962	14
■ Washington County / Albert Ohrt / Spanky Greenville											
176	27	25²⁄₈	20⁴⁄₈	23³⁄₈	5²⁄₈	5⁵⁄₈	5	5	0	1957	15
■ Dawson County / Unknown / Spanky Greenville											
175⁵⁄₈	26⁴⁄₈	25³⁄₈	16⁷⁄₈	21²⁄₈	5⁴⁄₈	5⁴⁄₈	8	6	8¹⁄₈	1963	16
■ Cuming County / Herman Blankenau / Herman Blankenau											
175⁴⁄₈	25⁵⁄₈	27	20⁴⁄₈	23	4⁴⁄₈	4⁴⁄₈	5	5	0	1963	17
■ Dodge County / LeRoy W. Ahrndt / LeRoy W. Ahrndt											
175¹⁄₈	25²⁄₈	25¹⁄₈	19	21⁴⁄₈	5⁶⁄₈	5⁶⁄₈	7	6	1¹⁄₈	1970	18
■ Knox County / Paul Klawitter / Paul Klawitter											
174⁶⁄₈	23⁶⁄₈	24⁴⁄₈	17⁵⁄₈	20³⁄₈	6	5⁶⁄₈	6	7	2⁵⁄₈	1960	19
■ Lancaster County / Vaughn Wright / Phillip Wright											
173⁶⁄₈	25¹⁄₈	25⁵⁄₈	18⁶⁄₈	21	5³⁄₈	5⁴⁄₈	7	6	1²⁄₈	1970	20
■ Knox County / Paul H. Klawitter / Paul H. Klawitter											
173⁶⁄₈	26	26	18⁶⁄₈	21⁴⁄₈	5⁷⁄₈	6¹⁄₈	6	5	1²⁄₈	1962	20
■ Colfax County / Leonard Bowman / Leonard Bowman											
173³⁄₈	26¹⁄₈	25⁵⁄₈	18⁶⁄₈	21⁴⁄₈	5	5	5	5	1³⁄₈	1980	22
■ Keya Paha County / Gene F. Pool / Gene F. Pool											
173²⁄₈	29	29⁴⁄₈	20	22⁴⁄₈	5¹⁄₈	5²⁄₈	6	5	3	1969	23
■ Furnas County / Marvin F. Wieland / Marvin F. Wieland											
173	25⁵⁄₈	27²⁄₈	25³⁄₈	27¹⁄₈	5⁷⁄₈	5⁶⁄₈	6	5	7¹⁄₈	1967	24
■ Pawnee County / Gary G. Habegger / Gary G. Habegger											
172	25¹⁄₈	26	19³⁄₈	21¹⁄₈	5²⁄₈	4⁷⁄₈	7	5	2⁷⁄₈	1980	25
■ Furnas County / Marvin A. Briegel / Marvin A. Briegel											
171⁶⁄₈	25¹⁄₈	24⁶⁄₈	18⁴⁄₈	20⁴⁄₈	4⁷⁄₈	4⁷⁄₈	5	5	0	1974	26
■ Dawes County / Tim Morava / Tim Morava											
171³⁄₈	27²⁄₈	27²⁄₈	21²⁄₈	23⁶⁄₈	5	4⁷⁄₈	7	6	4³⁄₈	1982	27
■ Boyd County / Scott A. Sperling / Scott A. Sperling											
171	22⁶⁄₈	20⁴⁄₈	19⁵⁄₈	22⁴⁄₈	5⁷⁄₈	5⁶⁄₈	7	8	4³⁄₈	1964	28
■ Antelope County / Leo M. Beelart / Leo M. Beelart											
170⁵⁄₈	26¹⁄₈	25⁴⁄₈	19³⁄₈	23	4²⁄₈	4²⁄₈	5	6	1⁶⁄₈	1973	29
■ Boyd County / Leonard Reiser / Leonard Reiser											
170³⁄₈	28⁵⁄₈	28²⁄₈	21⁶⁄₈	25²⁄₈	4⁴⁄₈	4⁴⁄₈	6	4	1¹⁄₈	1965	30
■ Hall County / Gust Bergman / Gust Bergman											
170	27⁴⁄₈	27⁶⁄₈	23¹⁄₈	25⁴⁄₈	6⁵⁄₈	6⁷⁄₈	6	6	5³⁄₈	1959	31
■ Fullerton / Truman Lauterback / Truman Lauterback											

NEBRASKA TYPICAL WHITETAILS (continued)

Score	Length of Main Beam R	Length of Main Beam L	Inside Spread	Greatest Spread	Circumference at Smallest Place Between Burr and First Point R	Circumference at Smallest Place Between Burr and First Point L	Number of Points R	Number of Points L	Total of Lengths Abnormal Points	Date Killed	Rank
199 2/8	31 7/8	31 7/8	24 4/8	26 4/8	5 3/8	5 3/8	5	5	0	1983	*
	■ Saunders County / Vernon A. Virka / Vernon A. Virka										
196 4/8	25	25 4/8	21 6/8	23 5/8	4 2/8	4 3/8	6	6	0	1963	*
	■ Antelope County / John R. Harvey / Walter Schreiner										

121

Photo Courtesy of Del Austin

NEBRASKA STATE RECORD
NON-TYPICAL ANTLERS
SCORE: 277 3/8
Locality: Hall Co.   Date: 1962
Hunter: Del Austin

NEBRASKA

NON-TYPICAL WHITETAILS

Score	Length of Main Beam R	L	Inside Spread	Greatest Spread	Circumference at Smallest Place Between Burr and First Point R	L	Number of Points R	L	Total of Lengths Abnormal Points	Date Killed	Rank
277 3/8	28 1/8	28 3/8	21 1/8	29 5/8	6 5/8	6 7/8	19	18	91 4/8	1962	1
■ Hall County / Del Austin / Del Austin
242 5/8	27 2/8	26 1/8	17 2/8	23	6	5 4/8	13	16	56 1/8	1961	2
■ Nance County / Robert E. Snyder / Robert E. Snyder
238	26 4/8	27 6/8	23 5/8	26 4/8	5 6/8	5 7/8	12	8	42 4/8	1969	3
■ Keya Paha County / Donald B. Phipps / Donald B. Phipps
215 7/8	25	24 4/8	24 3/8	27 4/8	6 6/8	6	11	12	48 4/8	1964	4
■ Long Pine / Picked Up / Duane Lotspeich
212 3/8	29	28 4/8	24 3/8	27 6/8	5 5/8	5 6/8	11	10	18	1959	5
■ Hershey / Ray Liles / Spanky Greenville
211 5/8	23 1/8	22 5/8	13 4/8	20	7	5 4/8	18	11	78 5/8	1964	6
■ Alda / Donald Knuth / Donald Knuth
208 4/8	28	27 1/8	23 5/8	26 3/8	6 2/8	6 1/8	11	10	35 1/8	1969	7
■ Dixon County / Dan Greeny / Dan Greeny
208 1/8	28 1/8	30 1/8	24 2/8	28 4/8	6 2/8	5	10	8	43 3/8	1966	8
■ Atkinson Highway / Russell Angus / Russell Angus
208 1/8	24 1/8	25 2/8	20 2/8	23 4/8	4 7/8	4 7/8	13	8	33 1/8	1965	8
■ Antelope County / Leon McCoy / Leon McCoy
207 5/8	25	20 5/8	19 6/8	25 4/8	6	6	10	17	47 1/8	1964	10
■ Seward County / Ladislav Dolezal / Ladislav Dolezal
207 1/8	22	23 7/8	19 2/8	21	8	8 5/8	14	13	50 7/8	1978	11
■ Buffalo County / Unknown / John L. Stein
206 7/8	25	24 1/8	18	22 2/8	5 2/8	5 3/8	10	12	27 1/8	1963	12
■ Loup County / T. A. Brandenburg / J. D. Andrews
203 1/8	28 1/8	27 5/8	21	29 4/8	4 7/8	4 6/8	9	7	21 5/8	1970	13
■ Pawnee County / Virgil J. Fisher / Virgil J. Fisher

NEBRASKA NON-TYPICAL WHITETAILS *(continued)*

Score	Length of Main Beam R	L	Inside Spread	Greatest Spread	Circumference at Smallest Place Between Burr and First Point R	L	Number of Points R	L	Total of Lengths Abnormal Points	Date Killed	Rank
201 4/8	28 5/8	28 1/8	22 1/8	26	5 3/8	5 1/8	8	9	14 5/8	1965	14
■ Brown County / R. L. Tinkham / R. L. Tinkham												
201 1/8	25 3/8	25 4/8	18 2/8	21 6/8	5	4 7/8	8	7	22 7/8	1973	15
■ Butler County / James L. Sklenar / James L. Sklenar												
200 3/8	24 4/8	25 1/8	18	22	5 6/8	5 5/8	10	12	23 3/8	1983	16
■ Butler County / J. L. Novak / J. L. Novak												
200 1/8	24 3/8	24 5/8	20 4/8	23 1/8	5	5	9	8	22 3/8	1983	17
■ Blaine County / Pauline C. Sander / Pauline C. Sander												
198 2/8	23 5/8	23 1/8	19 4/8	23 4/8	5 7/8	5 7/8	8	8	22 6/8	1966	18
■ Rock County / Gerald M. Lewis / Gerald M. Lewis												
198	26 1/8	24 4/8	23	25 5/8	7 4/8	6 2/8	9	7	21 6/8	1961	19
■ Valley / Ivan Masher / Ivan Masher												
197 7/8	27 4/8	28 1/8	25	27 1/8	5 4/8	5 2/8	9	8	22 1/8	1984	20
■ Cheyenne County / Reid Block / Reid Block												
197 2/8	23 3/8	26 1/8	17 1/8	22 1/8	5 4/8	6 1/8	10	9	28 7/8	1963	21
■ Stanton / Peter Bartman III / Peter Bartman III												
196 1/8	24 3/8	24 1/8	19 3/8	25 4/8	5 4/8	5 6/8	8	11	26 6/8	1975	22
■ Nemaha County / Picked Up / Gale Sup												

124

Photo Courtesy of Jack Hammond

Jack Hammond took this impressive typical that scores 172 points on the Tologia River in Butts County, Georgia, in 1963. Hammond's buck was an entry in the 14th Competition (1968-1970).

Photo by Charles J. Alsheimer

NEW YORK STATE RECORD
TYPICAL ANTLERS
SCORE: 198 3/8

Locality: Allegany Co.   Date: 1939
Hunter: Roosevelt Luckey
Owner: N. Y. State Dept. Env. Cons.

NEW YORK

TYPICAL WHITETAILS

Score	Length of Main Beam R	L	Inside Spread	Greatest Spread	Circumference at Smallest Place Between Burr and First Point R	L	Number of Points R	L	Total of Lengths Abnormal Points	Date Killed	Rank
198 3/8	29 5/8	29 4/8	18 1/8	21	4 6/8	4 6/8	6	8	8 4/8	1939	1
■ Allegany County / Roosevelt Luckey / N. Y. State Dept. Env. Cons.
181 3/8	24 7/8	27 4/8	18 1/8	20	5	5	6	7	4 4/8	1960	2
■ Orange County / Roy Vail / Roy Vail
180 3/8	30 2/8	30	23 1/8	26 2/8	5 1/8	5 2/8	8	6	2 4/8	1943	3
■ Livingston County / Edward Beare / Edward Beare
179 3/8	29	29 2/8	19 7/8	23	4 6/8	4 5/8	10	8	12 6/8	1953	4
■ Essex County / Herbert Jaquish / Herbert Jaquish
176 2/8	24 4/8	26 4/8	17 1/8	22 3/8	5 4/8	5 4/8	8	7	6 3/8	1961	5
■ Warren County / Frank Dagles / Frank Dagles
176 2/8	25 6/8	28 6/8	25 4/8	28	4 7/8	5	5	5	0	1944	5
■ Erie County / Wesley H. Iulg / Wesley H. Iulg
175 5/8	26	27 4/8	18 1/8	20 2/8	4 4/8	4 4/8	5	6	0	1981	7
■ Allegany County / William L. Damon / William L. Damon
174 2/8	25 3/8	26 3/8	22	24 4/8	4 5/8	4 4/8	5	5	0	1941	8
■ Livingston County / Kenneth Bowen / Kenneth Bowen
174 1/8	26 3/8	27 3/8	16 7/8	19 3/8	4 3/8	4 2/8	6	7	0	1933	9
■ Essex County / Denny Mitchell / Lewis P. Evans
173 3/8	28 5/8	29 3/8	23 2/8	25 4/8	6 3/8	6 2/8	7	8	10 7/8	1946	10
■ Ontario County / Martin Solway / N. Y. State Dept. Env. Cons.
172 7/8	27 1/8	26 2/8	21 7/8	25	4 6/8	4 7/8	6	5	1 6/8	1968	11
■ Seneca County / Martin J. Way / Martin J. Way
172 2/8	25 7/8	25 6/8	20 3/8	22 5/8	4 4/8	4 4/8	5	5	0	1982	12
■ Cattaraugus County / Thomas J. Hinchey / Thomas J. Hinchey
171 6/8	25 5/8	25 6/8	24 1/8	26 1/8	5 6/8	5 6/8	6	6	3 1/8	1982	13
■ Clinton County / William J. Branch / William J. Branch

NEW YORK TYPICAL WHITETAILS *(continued)*

Score	Length of Main Beam R	L	Inside Spread	Greatest Spread	Circumference at Smallest Place Between Burr and First Point R	L	Number of Points R	L	Total of Lengths Abnormal Points	Date Killed	Rank
171 4/8	26	26	23 2/8	25 2/8	4 7/8	4 3/8	5	7	1 4/8	1968	14
■ Schroon Lake / Richard E. Johndrow / Richard E. Johndrow										
171 3/8	26	26 3/8	17 6/8	20 3/8	4 4/8	4 3/8	6	7	4 1/8	1957	15
■ Herkimer County / John Christie / John Christie										
170 7/8	27	26 5/8	23 1/8	0	4 7/8	5	8	6	5 2/8	1976	16
■ Steuben County / Duane L. Horton / Duane L. Horton										

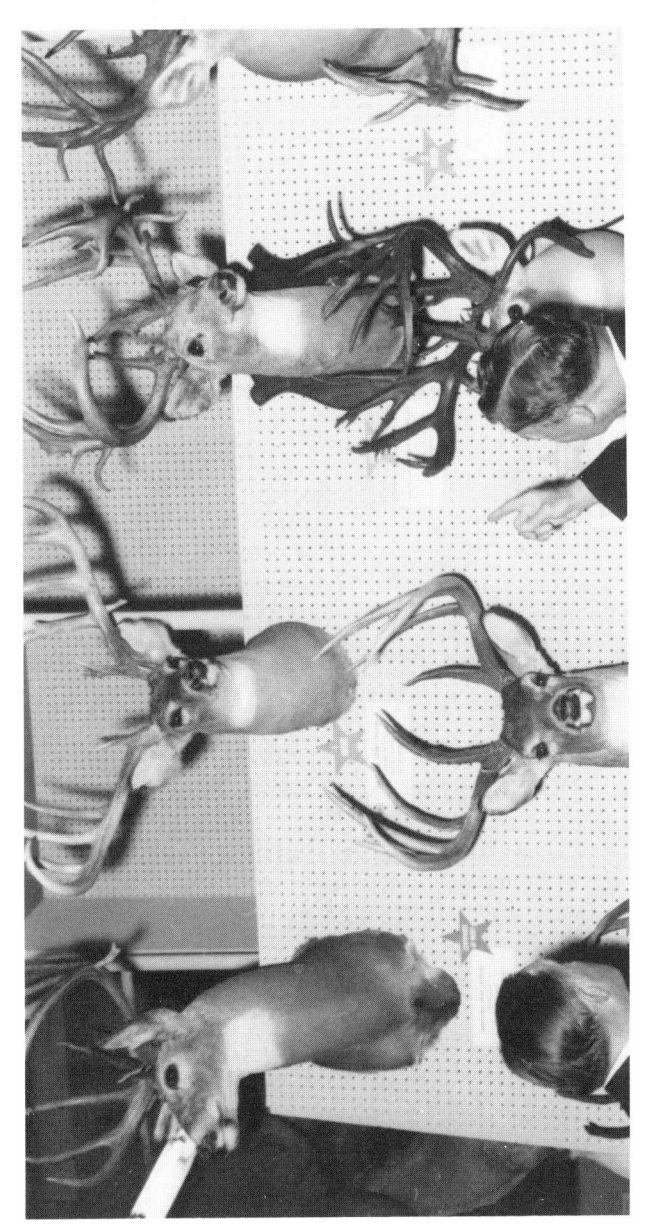

Photo from Boone and Crockett Club Archives

A portion of the trophy display at the 13th Competition (1966-1967), Carnegie Museum, Pittsburgh, Pennsylvania. Deer displayed include: (from top, l-r) B. Weidner's typical 192 taken in Lyman County, S. D., in 1957; D. E. Green's typical 187-2/8 taken in Warren County, Iowa, in 1964; R. E. Snyder's non-typical 242-5/8 taken in Nance County, Nebraska, in 1961; B. Dailey's typical 192-2/8 taken in Frio County, Texas, in 1903; D. F. Allison's typical 184-1/8 taken in Vinton County, Ohio, in 1965; and F. Mudge's non-typical 272 that was picked up near Junction, Texas, in 1925.

129

Photo Courtesy of Harry Boylan

NEW YORK STATE RECORD
NON-TYPICAL ANTLERS
SCORE: 244 2/8

Locality: Allegany Co.   Date: 1939
Hunter: Homer Boylan
Owner: Harry Boylan

NEW YORK

NON-TYPICAL WHITETAILS

Score	Length of Main Beam R	Length of Main Beam L	Inside Spread	Greatest Spread	Circumference at Smallest Place Between Burr and First Point R	Circumference at Smallest Place Between Burr and First Point L	Number of Points R	Number of Points L	Total of Lengths Abnormal Points	Date Killed	Rank
244 2/8	27	27 2/8	16 5/8	23 6/8	5 6/8	5 5/8	13	13	55 3/8	1939	1
■ Allegany County / Homer Boylan / Harry Boylan
224	23 4/8	23 2/8	22 2/8	34 5/8	4 6/8	4 6/8	13	14	87 2/8	PR1983	2
■ New York / Unknown / Johnny M. Hollier
219 7/8	27 2/8	27 6/8	19 7/8	26 5/8	6	6	10	10	38	1944	3
■ Genesee County / Robert Wood / Robert Wood
207 7/8	23 7/8	23 5/8	21 3/8	23 6/8	4 5/8	4 7/8	13	19	40	1950	4
■ Suffolk County / George Hackal / Gary C. Boyer
206 2/8	28 4/8	28 5/8	25	32	5 5/8	5 6/8	9	11	22 6/8	1947	5
■ Cortland County / Hank Hayes / Interlaken Sportsmans Club
205 7/8	28 6/8	27 4/8	17 1/8	19 4/8	5	5 4/8	8	17	28	1938	6
■ Steuben County / Fred J. Kelley / Fred J. Kelley
204 7/8	26 4/8	26 4/8	29 1/8	31	6	6	7	10	22	1959	7
■ Portageville / Howard W. Smith / Howard W. Smith

Photo Courtesy of McLean Bowman

NORTH DAKOTA STATE RECORD
TYPICAL ANTLERS
SCORE: 189 3/8

Locality: McKenzie Co.   Date: 1972
Hunter: Gene Veeder
Owner: McLean Bowman

NORTH DAKOTA

TYPICAL WHITETAILS

Score	Length of Main Beam R	L	Inside Spread	Greatest Spread	Circumference at Smallest Place Between Burr and First Point R	L	Number of Points R	L	Total of Lengths Abnormal Points	Date Killed	Rank
■ Locality Killed / By Whom Killed / Owner												
189 3/8	28 2/8	27 2/8	20 1/8	22 4/8	4 1/8	4 1/8	5	5	0	1972	1
■ McKenzie County / Gene Veeder / McLean Bowman												
187 5/8	25	25 2/8	20 1/8	23 2/8	5 2/8	5 2/8	6	6	4	1959	2
■ Emmons County / Joseph F. Bosch / Joseph F. Bosch												
182	24 4/8	25	23	25 2/8	4 3/8	4	7	7	0	1962	3
■ Zap / Wally Duckwitz / Sioux Sporting Goods												
178 1/8	28 2/8	26 7/8	18 7/8	21 2/8	4 7/8	5	5	7	1 2/8	1947	4
■ Concrete / Lawrence E. Vandal / Lawrence E. Vandal												
177 2/8	25 3/8	24 3/8	21 5/8	23 2/8	4 1/8	4 1/8	8	9	11 7/8	1964	5
■ Golden Valley County / Allen Goltz / Allen Goltz												
175 5/8	22 5/8	24 5/8	20	23 1/8	5	5	6	6	0	1963	6
■ Burleigh County / Earl Haakenson / Earl Haakenson												
175	25 5/8	25 1/8	21	23	4 4/8	3 7/8	5	5	0	1957	7
■ New Salem / John T. Cartwright / John T. Cartwright												
174 4/8	22 5/8	23 3/8	18	21	5	5 2/8	6	6	0	1976	8
■ McKenzie County / Ben Dekker / Ben Dekker												
173 1/8	23 3/8	23 5/8	18 3/8	20 4/8	4	4	6	6	0	1967	9
■ Slope County / Robert L. Stroup / Robert L. Stroup												
172 7/8	25 3/8	25	20 2/8	22 5/8	4 3/8	4 2/8	7	7	2 1/8	1959	10
■ McHenry County / David Medalen / David Medalen												
171 5/8	24 5/8	24 5/8	19 4/8	23 4/8	5	5	9	10	9 3/8	1955	11
■ Morton County / Dick Eastman / Sioux Sporting Goods												
171	26 4/8	26 5/8	19 1/8	22	4 7/8	5	7	6	2 3/8	1947	12
■ Sherwood / Roy Foss / Roy Foss												
170 7/8	25 5/8	24 5/8	22 5/8	25	5	5 7/8	6	7	8 6/8	1982	13
■ Burleigh County / Ronald C. Wagner / Ronald C. Wagner												

Photo Courtesy of Roger Ritchie

NORTH DAKOTA STATE RECORD
NON-TYPICAL ANTLERS
SCORE: 254 6/8

Locality: Stanley   Date: November 1968
Hunter: Roger Ritchie

NORTH DAKOTA

NON-TYPICAL WHITETAILS

Score	Length of Main Beam R	L	Inside Spread	Greatest Spread	Circumference at Smallest Place Between Burr and First Point R	L	Number of Points R	L	Total of Lengths Abnormal Points	Date Killed	Rank
254⁶⁄₈	28³⁄₈	27	20²⁄₈	26	5²⁄₈	5	14	17	77⁶⁄₈	1968	1
■ Stanley / Roger Ritchie / Roger Ritchie
232¹⁄₈	24⁵⁄₈	24⁵⁄₈	16⁴⁄₈	24⁵⁄₈	4⁷⁄₈	4⁶⁄₈	11	11	41⁷⁄₈	1886	2
■ McLean County / Olaf P. Anderson / Burton L. Anderson
216⁶⁄₈	26	24⁴⁄₈	22³⁄₈	26¹⁄₈	5²⁄₈	5¹⁄₈	11	13	43¹⁄₈	1963	3
■ Kathryn / Gerald R. Elsner / Gerald R. Elsner
210⁵⁄₈	24⁷⁄₈	25⁷⁄₈	18⁶⁄₈	25⁴⁄₈	5⁶⁄₈	5⁵⁄₈	14	10	28³⁄₈	1978	4
■ Renville County / Glen Southam / Glen Southam
206¹⁄₈	25⁴⁄₈	25³⁄₈	18¹⁄₈	24⁷⁄₈	5²⁄₈	5¹⁄₈	8	9	31²⁄₈	1982	5
■ Dunn County / Kenneth E. DeLap / Kenneth E. DeLap
203⁵⁄₈	23²⁄₈	25²⁄₈	17³⁄₈	25⁵⁄₈	6	5⁶⁄₈	10	9	32²⁄₈	1975	6
■ Grand Forks County / Thomas G. Bernotas / Thomas G. Bernotas
202⁶⁄₈	22³⁄₈	22	18	20⁵⁄₈	5⁶⁄₈	5¹⁄₈	7	8	21²⁄₈	1961	7
■ Garrison / Clarence Hummel / Clarence Hummel
201¹⁄₈	21⁶⁄₈	22³⁄₈	16³⁄₈	21²⁄₈	5²⁄₈	5²⁄₈	9	11	52²⁄₈	1961	8
■ Slope County / Arthur Hegge / J. D. Andrews
200⁷⁄₈	23⁴⁄₈	24⁵⁄₈	20¹⁄₈	23⁴⁄₈	5³⁄₈	5²⁄₈	9	8	24⁴⁄₈	1957	9
■ Mandan / Virgil Chadwick / Peter Voigt
195³⁄₈	26²⁄₈	26	19⁴⁄₈	24³⁄₈	5²⁄₈	5⁵⁄₈	7	10	24⁷⁄₈	1955	10
■ Valley City / William F. Cruff / William F. Cruff

Photo Courtesy of Dale Hartberger

OHIO STATE RECORD
TYPICAL ANTLERS
SCORE: 184 2/8
Locality: Muskingum Co.   Date: December 1981
Hunter: Dale Hartberger

OHIO

TYPICAL WHITETAILS

Score	Length of Main Beam R	Length of Main Beam L	Inside Spread	Greatest Spread	Circumference at Smallest Place Between Burr and First Point R	Circumference at Smallest Place Between Burr and First Point L	Number of Points R	Number of Points L	Total of Lengths Abnormal Points	Date Killed	Rank
184 2/8	27	26	27 4/8	29	6	6 1/8	6	5	1 4/8	1981	1
■ Muskingum County / Dale Hartberger / Dale Hartberger
184 1/8	29	31	20 5/8	23	5 5/8	4 4/8	6	5	2 2/8	1965	2
■ Vinton County / Dan F. Allison / Dan F. Allison
183	26 2/8	25	19 6/8	22 6/8	5	5	8	9	9 6/8	1958	3
■ Piedmont Lake / J. Rumbaugh & J. Ruyan / J. Rumbaugh & J. Ruyan
182 7/8	28 5/8	28 5/8	19	24 1/8	5 5/8	6	6	6	4 3/8	1975	4
■ Wayne County / Gary E. Landry / Gary E. Landry
181 4/8	25 2/8	25 5/8	22 7/8	24 4/8	5 5/8	5 7/8	7	7	2 5/8	1962	5
■ Licking County / Arlee McCullough / Arlee McCullough
181 3/8	27 4/8	27 5/8	20 6/8	23 4/8	4 4/8	4 4/8	7	6	4 5/8	1953	6
■ Portage County / Robert M. Smith / Robert M. Smith
179	27 4/8	29 4/8	20 2/8	23 7/8	4 6/8	4 6/8	6	7	5	1982	7
■ Logan County / Gregory K. Snyder / Greta J. Snyder
178 7/8	24 3/8	28	21 7/8	24 3/8	5 3/8	5 3/8	6	6	2 4/8	1958	8
■ Monroe County / Roger E. Schumacher / Roger E. Schumacher
178 2/8	27 4/8	27	19 6/8	21 7/8	4 3/8	4 4/8	5	5	0	1983	9
■ Tuscarawas County / Raymond D. Gerber, Jr. / Raymond D. Gerber, Jr.
177 5/8	29	28 3/8	22	23 1/8	4 4/8	4 4/8	7	8	4 7/8	1984	10
■ Harrison County / Mark Dulkoski / Mark Dulkoski
176 7/8	29 2/8	28 3/8	23	26 1/8	5 7/8	5 4/8	5	6	1 7/8	1975	11
■ Logan County / David Sutherly / David Sutherly
176 2/8	30	28 2/8	23	26 6/8	6 1/8	6 1/8	7	6	8 2/8	1976	12
■ Coshocton County / James R. Gardner / James R. Gardner
175 3/8	24	22 2/8	19 4/8	21 2/8	4 7/8	4 7/8	6	8	1 5/8	1976	13
■ Monroe County / David Mancano / David Mancano

OHIO TYPICAL WHITETAILS (continued)

Score	Length of Main Beam R	L	Inside Spread	Greatest Spread	Circumference at Smallest Place Between Burr and First Point R	L	Number of Points R	L	Total of Lengths Abnormal Points	Date Killed	Rank
\ul{Locality Killed / By Whom Killed / Owner}											
175 3/8	25 2/8	25 4/8	20 1/8	22 6/8	5 3/8	5 3/8	5	5	0	1969	13
■ Gallia County / Jack Auxier / Jack Auxier											
173	28	28 7/8	20 4/8	22 6/8	4 6/8	4 5/8	5	5	0	1975	15
■ Sandusky County / Harold M. Chalfin / Harold M. Chalfin											
172 5/8	26 3/8	26 4/8	21 3/8	23 4/8	4 7/8	4 7/8	5	7	4 2/8	1979	16
■ Highland County / Wilbur D. Rhoads / Wilbur D. Rhoads											
172 5/8	24 1/8	23	18 1/8	20 2/8	4 3/8	4 3/8	5	6	0	1972	16
■ Tuscarawas County / Charles Kerns / Charles Kerns											
172 4/8	26 4/8	26 2/8	21 7/8	24 5/8	5 2/8	5 2/8	6	6	9 1/8	1982	18
■ Muskingum County / Michael Wilson / Michael Wilson											
172 1/8	28 5/8	28 3/8	19 2/8	21 6/8	4 6/8	5	6	7	5 7/8	1972	19
■ Coshocton County / Virgil E. Carpenter / Virgil E. Carpenter											
172	26	25 6/8	22 3/8	24	4 4/8	4 3/8	6	7	1 5/8	1980	20
■ Muskingkum County / David R. Hatfield / David R. Hatfield											
171 7/8	25	24 4/8	20	22	5	5	5	6	1 3/8	1982	21
■ Washington County / Thomas E. Burnette / Thomas E. Burnette											
171 7/8	25 5/8	24 5/8	25 6/8	27 6/8	5 1/8	5 4/8	5	6	1 1/8	1976	21
■ Perry County / Bill Pargeon / Bill Pargeon											
170 7/8	26 7/8	27 1/8	21 3/8	25 3/8	5 2/8	5 2/8	7	7	11 7/8	1975	23
■ Holmes County / Ken Taylor / Ken Taylor											
170 3/8	29 4/8	28 7/8	17 3/8	20 6/8	4 2/8	4 3/8	8	8	6 2/8	1976	24
■ Muskingnum County / John H. O'Flaherty / John H. O'Flaherty											
170 2/8	27 4/8	27 5/8	19 7/8	22 3/8	4 6/8	4 4/8	7	6	2 7/8	1977	25
■ Jefferson County / James S. Pratt / James S. Pratt											
170 1/8	27 6/8	24 7/8	20 7/8	23 3/8	4 7/8	4 7/8	6	6	0	1967	26
■ Jackson County / Theodore R. Yates / Theodore R. Yates											

Photo by Wm. H. Nesbitt

Ken W. Koenig found hunting success in 1976 with this fine typical 187-5/8 from Winona County, Minnesota. Koenig's buck received the Second Place Award in the typical category at the 17th Awards (1977-1979) at Kansas City, Missouri.

Photo by Wm. H. Nesbitt

OHIO STATE RECORD
NON-TYPICAL ANTLERS
SCORE: 328 2/8

Locality: Portage Co.   Date: Picked Up in 1940
Owner: Dick Idol

OHIO

NON-TYPICAL WHITETAILS

Score	Length of Main Beam R	L	Inside Spread	Greatest Spread	Circumference at Smallest Place Between Burr and First Point R	L	Number of Points R	L	Total of Lengths Abnormal Points	Date Killed	Rank
328 2/8	25 5/8	24 4/8	24 3/8	33	6 2/8	5 6/8	23	22	192 7/8	1940	1
■ Portage County / Picked Up / Dick Idol											
261 6/8	29	25 6/8	24 6/8	34	6 7/8	6 7/8	14	17	84 6/8	1975	2
■ Holmes County / Picked Up / Ohio Dept. Nat. Res.											
261 4/8	25	25 2/8	25 3/8	26 4/8	6	6	12	14	72 7/8	1971	3
■ Pike County / Chester T. Veach / Chester T. Veach											
235 4/8	29 2/8	27 1/8	22 7/8	38 1/8	5 7/8	5 6/8	11	13	55 7/8	1957	4
■ Ashtabula County / James L. Clark / James L. Clark											
231 3/8	29 3/8	27 6/8	23 1/8	28 3/8	4 3/8	4 3/8	9	10	44 6/8	1964	5
■ Licking County / Norman L. Myers / Norman L. Myers											
226 4/8	21 3/8	22 2/8	19 2/8	24	4 6/8	4 5/8	13	11	51 2/8	1981	6
■ Muskingum County / Rex Allen Thompson / Rex Allen Thompson											
226 1/8	25 5/8	26 3/8	20 3/8	24 6/8	4 7/8	4 7/8	10	10	33 2/8	1948	7
■ Trumbull County / Paul E. Lehman / Paul E. Lehman											
210 2/8	26 4/8	25 2/8	21 4/8	24	5 3/8	5 3/8	8	9	38 4/8	1981	8
■ Columbiana County / Harold L. Hawkins / Harold L. Hawkins											
204 4/8	30	28 6/8	21 1/8	26 3/8	4 7/8	5 2/8	10	12	41 3/8	1960	9
■ Jackson County / Bernard Tennant / Bernard Tennant											
203 5/8	23	30 6/8	15	26 1/8	6 6/8	6 6/8	8	14	70 5/8	1970	10
■ Meigs County / Wesley Gilkey / Wesley Gilkey											
201 7/8	28 3/8	28 5/8	23 1/8	25 2/8	4 6/8	4 7/8	11	10	28 7/8	1979	11
■ Coshocton County / Lou L. Rogers / Lou L. Rogers											
200 5/8	28	27 6/8	22 1/8	28	5 3/8	5 2/8	8	7	27 6/8	1970	12
■ Jackson County / Glenn McCall / Glenn McCall											
200 4/8	24 5/8	24 7/8	19 3/8	24 3/8	5 4/8	5 4/8	12	10	26 7/8	1969	13
■ Geauga County / Rudy C. Grecar / Rudy C. Grecar											

OHIO NON-TYPICAL WHITETAILS *(continued)*

Score	Length of Main Beam R	Length of Main Beam L	Inside Spread	Greatest Spread	Circumference at Smallest Place Between Burr and First Point R	Circumference at Smallest Place Between Burr and First Point L	Number of Points R	Number of Points L	Total of Lengths Abnormal Points	Date Killed	Rank
* Locality Killed / By Whom Killed / Owner												
200 3/8	27	23 1/8	24 5/8	27 2/8	5 2/8	5	8	7	16 6/8	1983	14
■ Knox County / Albert Hall / Albert Hall												
200 3/8	25 4/8	27	19 1/8	22	6 4/8	5 4/8	10	10	19	1978	14
■ Tuscarawas County / Michael D. Korns, Sr. / Michael D. Korns, Sr.												
199 6/8	28 6/8	29 2/8	19 3/8	22 5/8	6 4/8	6	7	8	16 4/8	1970	16
■ Meigs County / Cody R. Boothe / Cody R. Boothe												
198 5/8	26 2/8	26 6/8	17 4/8	22 4/8	5 2/8	5 4/8	9	6	16 3/8	1962	17
■ Jackson County / Stanley Elam / Stanley Elam												
198 1/8	27	26 3/8	20 7/8	28 5/8	5	5 1/8	10	7	26 1/8	1964	18
■ Hocking County / Hugh Cox / Hugh Cox												
198 1/8	27 6/8	28 3/8	22 4/8	26 3/8	4 6/8	4 6/8	7	9	12 3/8	1959	18
■ Harrison County / Roy Hines / Roy Hines												
197 5/8	31 5/8	32 3/8	25 2/8	28	5 1/8	5 1/2	5	6	15 1/8	1956	20
■ Geauga County / Edward Dooner / Edward Dooner												
195 7/8	29 1/8	21 7/8	21 5/8	30	4 7/8	5	8	8	25 3/8	1976	21
■ Perry County / Pearl R. Wiseman / Pearl R. Wiseman												
242 3/8	27 1/8	30 5/8	18 1/8	24 1/8	5 1/8	5	12	9	42 4/8	1980	*
■ Mahoning County / David L. Klemm / Dick Idol Safaries												

142

Photo Courtesy of Thelma Martens

Thelma Martens with the non-typical 198-4/8 that she took near Cow Creek, Wyoming, in 1951. Mrs. Martens' buck took the First Place Award in the non-typical category at the 5th Competition (1951).

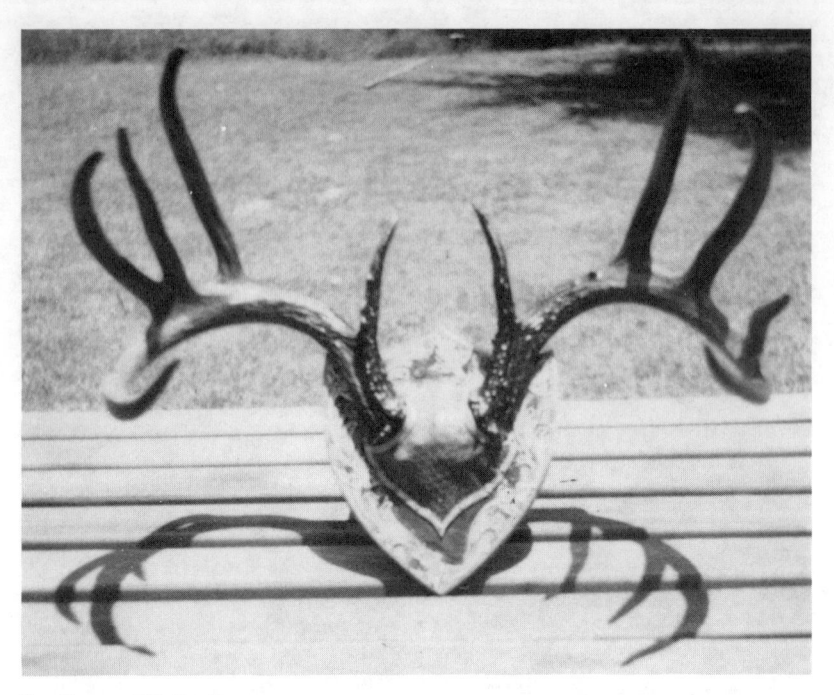

Photo Courtesy of Skip Rowell

OKLAHOMA STATE RECORD
TYPICAL ANTLERS
SCORE: 177 6/8

Locality: Atoka Co.   Date: November 1972
Hunter: Skip Rowell

OKLAHOMA

TYPICAL WHITETAILS

Score	Length of Main Beam R	L	Inside Spread	Greatest Spread	Circumference at Smallest Place Between Burr and First Point R	L	Number of Points R	L	Total of Lengths Abnormal Points	Date Killed	Rank
177 6/8	26 6/8	25 4/8	22 6/8	25	5	5	5	5	0	1972	1
■ Atoka County / Skip Rowell / Skip Rowell											
173 5/8	27 5/8	28 1/8	22 6/8	26 6/8	5 3/8	5 3/8	4	7	6 3/8	1983	2
■ Woods County / Jack Clover / Jack Clover											

Photo by Wm. H. Nesbitt

OKLAHOMA STATE RECORD
NON-TYPICAL ANTLERS
SCORE: 247 2/8

Locality: Johnston Co.   Date: November 1970
Hunter: Bill M. Foster

OKLAHOMA

NON-TYPICAL WHITETAILS

Score	Length of Main Beam R	L	Inside Spread	Greatest Spread	Circumference at Smallest Place Between Burr and First Point R	L	Number of Points R	L	Total of Lengths Abnormal Points	Date Killed	Rank
247 2/8	25 4/8	25 3/8	24 6/8	27	5 5/8	6 1/8	16	14	64	1970	1
■ Johnston County / Bill M. Foster / Bill M. Foster											
234 2/8	27 3/8	26 5/8	20 1/8	25	7	7 1/8	10	12	39 5/8	1984	2
■ Alfalfa County / Loren Tarrant / Loren Tarrant											
216 3/8	26 2/8	24 4/8	18 6/8	26 3/8	5 3/8	5 6/8	14	17	68 5/8	1962	3
■ Comanche County / Dwight O. Allen / Dwight O. Allen											
204 4/8	22 2/8	21 6/8	16 3/8	19 4/8	5 1/8	5	10	11	41 3/8	1970	4
■ Love County / William B. Heller / William B. Heller											
203 6/8	25	26 2/8	17 6/8	0	4 4/8	4 4/8	9	8	30	1981	5
■ McCurtain County / Gary L. Birge / Gary L. Birge											
197 4/8	25 7/8	25 6/8	20 1/8	22 4/8	6 1/8	6 1/8	11	10	19 3/8	1980	6
■ Garfield County / Derald D. Crissup / Derald D. Crissup											
197 1/8	23	22 7/8	17 7/8	0	5 1/8	4 6/8	10	9	18	1982	7
■ Noble County / Kenneth R. Bright / Kenneth R. Bright											

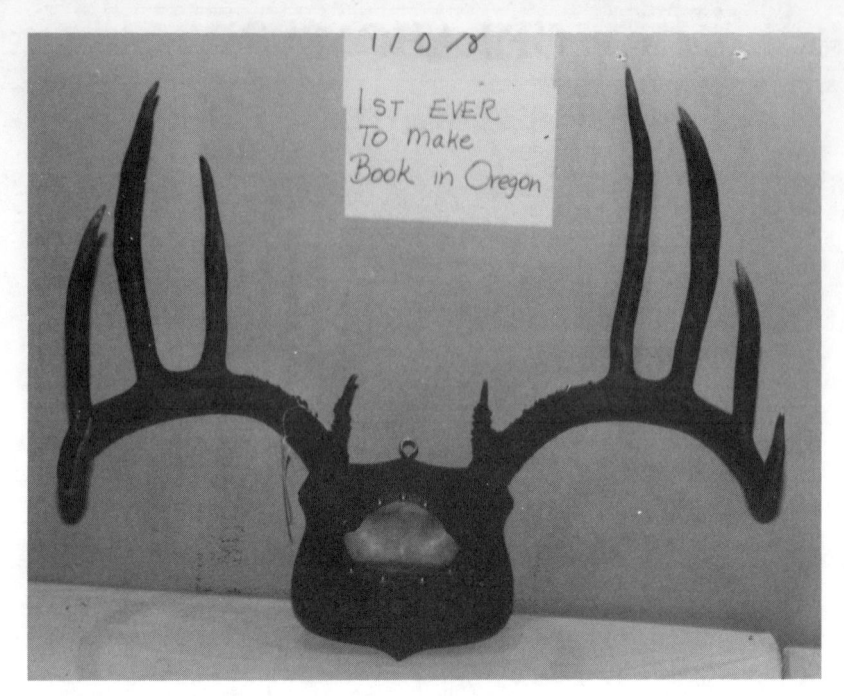

Photo Courtesy of Sterling K. Shaver

OREGON STATE RECORD
TYPICAL ANTLERS
SCORE: 178 2/8

Locality: Wallowa Co.　　Date: October 1982
Hunter: Sterling K. Shaver

OREGON

TYPICAL WHITETAILS

Score	Length of Main Beam R	L	Inside Spread	Greatest Spread	Circumference at Smallest Place Between Burr and First Point R	L	Number of Points R	L	Total of Lengths Abnormal Points	Date Killed	Rank
178 2/8	27 6/8	27 3/8	24 6/8	26 2/8	4 3/8	4 3/8	6	6	2 7/8	1982	1
■ Wallowa County / Sterling K. Shaver / Sterling K. Shaver												

Photo Courtesy of Ivan Parry

PENNSYLVANIA STATE RECORD TYPICAL ANTLERS SCORE: 184 6/8

Locality: Greene Co.   Date: December 1974
Hunter: Ivan Parry

PENNSYLVANIA

TYPICAL WHITETAILS

Score	Length of Main Beam R	L	Inside Spread	Greatest Spread	Circumference at Smallest Place Between Burr and First Point R	L	Number of Points R	L	Total of Lengths Abnormal Points	Date Killed	Rank
* Locality Killed / By Whom Killed / Owner											
184⁶/₈	26⁷/₈	26⁴/₈	20⁶/₈	23³/₈	4⁵/₈	4⁴/₈	5	6	3²/₈	1974	1
■ Greene County / Ivan Parry / Ivan Parry											
182²/₈	27³/₈	27	20⁴/₈	23	4⁷/₈	5	7	5	1²/₈	1930	2
■ Sullivan County / Floyd Reibson / Maynard Reibson											
177⁴/₈	26¹/₈	26	21	23⁵/₈	4	4¹/₈	5	5	0	1957	3
■ Bedford County / Raymond Miller / Raymond Miller											
176⁵/₈	30	28	21⁵/₈	24⁴/₈	4⁶/₈	4⁴/₈	6	7	7⁴/₈	1936	4
■ Mifflin County / John Zerba / Kenneth Zerba											
176	24⁴/₈	24⁷/₈	17⁴/₈	20¹/₈	3⁷/₈	4	8	6	0	1944	5
■ Bradford County / Clyde H. Rinehuls / Clyde H. Rinehuls											
175⁴/₈	25⁵/₈	25	21²/₈	23¹/₈	5	5²/₈	6	6	0	1830	6
■ McKean County / Arthur Young / C. R. Studholme											
173³/₈	25⁶/₈	26²/₈	17⁵/₈	20¹/₈	4⁴/₈	4⁴/₈	5	5	0	1954	7
■ Clarion County / Picked Up / Fred Gallagher											
173³/₈	27⁶/₈	28¹/₈	20¹/₈	23¹/₈	4⁵/₈	4⁵/₈	5	6	0	1947	7
■ Clarion County / Mead Kiefer / Mead Kiefer											
172²/₈	28⁶/₈	26⁴/₈	21⁵/₈	24³/₈	4¹/₈	4³/₈	6	6	3¹/₈	1942	9
■ Bedford County / John F. Sharpe / John F. Sharpe											
170²/₈	25³/₈	25⁶/₈	20	23²/₈	4⁵/₈	4⁶/₈	5	6	0	1945	10
■ Clarion County / Meade R. Kifer / Meade R. Kifer											
170	25⁵/₈	24¹/₈	21⁶/₈	23²/₈	4⁴/₈	4⁶/₈	10	10	15	1943	11
■ Blair County / Claude Feathers / Claude Feathers											

Photo Courtesy of C. Ralph Landis

PENNSYLVANIA STATE RECORD
NON-TYPICAL ANTLERS
SCORE: 207 7/8
Locality: Port Royal   Date: December 1951
Hunter: C. Ralph Landis

PENNSYLVANIA

NON-TYPICAL WHITETAILS

Score	Length of Main Beam R	Length of Main Beam L	Inside Spread	Greatest Spread	Circumference at Smallest Place Between Burr and First Point R	Circumference at Smallest Place Between Burr and First Point L	Number of Points R	Number of Points L	Total of Lengths Abnormal Points	Date Killed	Rank
* Locality Killed / By Whom Killed / Owner											
207 7/8	29 5/8	31 1/8	24 4/8	28	5 5/8	5 5/8	11	7	26 5/8	1951	1
■ Port Royal / C. Ralph Landis / C. Ralph Landis											
207	26	25 6/8	26	32 4/8	5 6/8	5 6/8	11	13	20	1949	2
■ Lycoming County / Al Prouty / Al Prouty											
201 1/8	23	22 5/8	14 5/8	20 1/8	4 6/8	5 1/8	13	16	60 6/8	1966	3
■ Westmoreland County / Richard K. Mellon / Richard K. Mellon											
196 6/8	26 2/8	25 5/8	18 2/8	20 3/8	5 6/8	5 5/8	9	8	39 6/8	1949	4
■ Perry County / Kenneth Reisinger / Kenneth Reisinger											
196	25 5/8	25 1/8	16 1/8	19 3/8	5 1/8	5 4/8	7	12	19 3/8	1956	5
■ Westmoreland County / Edward G. Ligus / Edward G. Ligus											

Photo Courtesy of John M. Wood

SOUTH CAROLINA STATE RECORD
NON-TYPICAL ANTLERS
SCORE: 208 5/8
Locality: Beaufort Co.   Date: October 1971
Hunter: John M. Wood

SOUTH CAROLINA

NON-TYPICAL WHITETAILS

Score	Length of Main Beam R	L	Inside Spread	Greatest Spread	Circumference at Smallest Place Between Burr and First Point R	L	Number of Points R	L	Total of Lengths Abnormal Points	Date Killed	Rank
208 5/8	19 6/8	23 4/8	18 4/8	21 7/8	5	5	11	10	54 1/8	1971	1

■ *Locality Killed / By Whom Killed / Owner*

■ *Beaufort County / John M. Wood / John M. Wood*

155

Photo Courtesy of Eugene J. Lodermeier

SOUTH DAKOTA STATE RECORD
TYPICAL ANTLERS
SCORE: 193
Locality: South Dakota   Date: November 1964
Hunter: Unknown
Owner: Eugene J. Lodermeier

SOUTH DAKOTA
TYPICAL WHITETAILS

Score	Length of Main Beam R	L	Inside Spread	Greatest Spread	Circumference at Smallest Place Between Burr and First Point R	L	Number of Points R	L	Total of Lengths Abnormal Points	Date Killed	Rank
■ Locality Killed / By Whom Killed / Owner
193	25⁶/₈	26	25	27⁵/₈	5³/₈	5⁵/₈	6	6	0	1964	1
■ South Dakota / Unknown / Eugene J. Lodermeier
192	27⁴/₈	28	19²/₈	21²/₈	4⁶/₈	4⁶/₈	8	9	9⁶/₈	1957	2
■ Lyman County / Bob Weidner / E. N. Eichler
189⁵/₈	29²/₈	29²/₈	21⁴/₈	24³/₈	4⁷/₈	4⁶/₈	5	6	2³/₈	1954	3
■ Tabor / Duane Graber / Sam Peterson
184³/₈	28⁴/₈	29	25⁵/₈	31²/₈	5⁶/₈	5⁷/₈	5	7	8⁴/₈	1960	4
■ Kingsbury County / Rudy F. Weigel / Rudy F. Weigel
180⁴/₈	26⁷/₈	25⁵/₈	19	22	5¹/₈	5¹/₈	6	6	4	1975	5
■ Clay County / James E. Olson / James E. Olson
176⁷/₈	28	26⁷/₈	16²/₈	18¹/₈	3⁷/₈	3⁶/₈	5	7	1¹/₈	1959	6
■ Day County / William B. Davis / William B. Davis
176⁵/₈	25	25	23²/₈	24⁷/₈	5	5	6	5	1⁵/₈	1964	7
■ Roberts County / Fred Kuehl / J. D. Andrews
176	26	26³/₈	20	22²/₈	5³/₈	5⁴/₈	5	5	0	1966	8
■ Veblen / John W. Cimburek / John W. Cimburek
175⁶/₈	21⁶/₈	23³/₈	18	19³/₈	4⁴/₈	4⁵/₈	6	6	0	1957	9
■ St. Onge / Don Ridley / Don Ridley
173²/₈	25³/₈	25³/₈	21⁶/₈	25¹/₈	4³/₈	4⁴/₈	5	5	0	1972	10
■ Lyman County / William G. Psychos / William G. Psychos
172³/₈	27⁴/₈	27²/₈	20⁴/₈	23²/₈	6	6¹/₈	5	6	2⁷/₈	1967	11
■ Brookings / Paul W. Back / Paul W. Back
172²/₈	25⁶/₈	24²/₈	20	23⁵/₈	4⁵/₈	4⁵/₈	6	8	2⁴/₈	1979	12
■ Perkins County / Randy G. Swenson / Randy G. Swenson
172¹/₈	27	27³/₈	23²/₈	26	4⁶/₈	4⁴/₈	8	7	8³/₈	1971	13
■ Hughes County / Mark Lilevjen / Mark Lilevjen

SOUTH DAKOTA TYPICAL WHITETAILS *(continued)*

Score	Length of Main Beam R	L	Inside Spread	Greatest Spread	Circumference at Smallest Place Between Burr and First Point R	L	Number of Points R	L	Total of Lengths Abnormal Points	Date Killed	Rank
171	28 5/8	27 7/8	20 4/8	24 2/8	5 2/8	5 1/8	7	7	3 4/8	1963	14
■ Perkins / Ethel Schrader / Ethel Schrader											
170 4/8	24	24 2/8	19 2/8	21 1/8	4 5/8	4 6/8	5	5	0	1982	15
■ Day County / Credan Ewalt / Credan Ewalt											
170 3/8	28 5/8	28 4/8	23 4/8	26 4/8	5 1/8	5	8	8	14 5/8	1969	16
■ Kingsbury County / Jerry Ellingson / Jerry Ellingson											
170 3/8	25 2/8	25 4/8	23 3/8	25 1/8	5 2/8	5 2/8	6	5	1 1/8	1965	16
■ Grant County / James Boerger / James Boerger											

Photo Courtesy of Rudy C. Grecar

Rudy C. Grecar took this non-typical buck that scores 200-4/8 points with a 75 lb. bow at 35 yards in Geauga County, Ohio, during the 1969 archery season. Grecar's buck was an entry in the 14th Competition (1968-1970).

159

Photo Courtesy of J. D. Andrews

SOUTH DAKOTA STATE RECORD
NON-TYPICAL ANTLERS
SCORE: 249 1/8

Locality: Lily   Date: November 1965
Hunter: Jerry Roitsch
Owner: J. D. Andrews

SOUTH DAKOTA

NON-TYPICAL WHITETAILS

Score	Length of Main Beam R	L	Inside Spread	Greatest Spread	Circumference at Smallest Place Between Burr and First Point R	L	Number of Points R	L	Total of Lengths Abnormal Points	Date Killed	Rank
249 1/8	26 2/8	26 7/8	19 2/8	28 2/8	6 4/8	6 2/8	12	20	47 7/8	1965	1
■ Lily / Jerry Roitsch / J. D. Andrews
216 7/8	19 1/8	21 1/8	13 7/8	25 1/8	7	6 5/8	12	15	78 2/8	1960	2
■ Brown County / Francis Shattuck / Sand Lake N.W.R.
210	23 4/8	23 5/8	20 3/8	28 3/8	5 7/8	6 2/8	9	8	26 1/8	1982	3
■ Gregory County / Richard C. Berte / Richard C. Berte
207 7/8	24 4/8	25 2/8	19	27	5 7/8	5 5/8	11	14	34 7/8	1957	4
■ Perkins County / W. E. Brown / J. D. Andrews
207 3/8	28 3/8	27 5/8	21 7/8	24 2/8	5 5/8	5 7/8	10	11	28 1/8	1975	5
■ Roberts County / Delbert Lackey / Delbert Lackey
206 4/8	25 1/8	24 7/8	17 7/8	23 5/8	6 5/8	6 4/8	12	9	42 5/8	1973	6
■ Yankton County / William Sees / William Sees
203 4/8	23 4/8	22 1/8	18 5/8	21 7/8	5 3/8	5 2/8	9	10	24 1/8	1957	7
■ Lawrence County / Ernest C. Larive / Ernest C. Larive
202 1/8	26 1/8	26 4/8	19 3/8	24 4/8	6 1/8	6 2/8	8	9	26 4/8	1960	8
■ Gary / Dennis Cole / Dennis Cole
201 5/8	27 5/8	22 2/8	20 5/8	24 1/8	5 5/8	5 5/8	8	12	32 2/8	1967	9
■ Sisseton / Truman M. Nelson / Truman M. Nelson
201 4/8	22 3/8	23 3/8	16 5/8	21	4 1/8	4 2/8	9	8	28 3/8	1957	10
■ Campbell County / Edward J. Torigian / J. D. Andrews
200 4/8	25 2/8	25 2/8	23	25 4/8	6 1/8	6 1/8	9	6	20	1948	11
■ Brentford / S. C. Mitchell / S. C. Mitchell
196 7/8	24 5/8	24 6/8	19	22 4/8	5	5	10	8	25 3/8	1983	12
■ Edmunds County / Melvin Borkirchert / Melvin Borkirchert

Photo Courtesy of W. A. Foster

TENNESSEE STATE RECORD
TYPICAL ANTLERS
SCORE: 186 1/8
Locality: Roane Co.   Date: 1959
Hunter: W. A. Foster

TENNESSEE

TYPICAL WHITETAILS

Score	Length of Main Beam R	L	Inside Spread	Greatest Spread	Circumference at Smallest Place Between Burr and First Point R	L	Number of Points R	L	Total of Lengths Abnormal Points	Date Killed	Rank
186 1/8	25 1/8	26 2/8	20 1/8	22 1/8	4 6/8	4 7/8	6	5	3	1959	1
■ Roane County / W. A. Foster / W. A. Foster
184 4/8	23 4/8	23 4/8	17	19 2/8	4 6/8	4 6/8	6	6	0	1979	2
■ Fayette County / Benny M. Johnson / Benny M. Johnson
178 5/8	27	26 4/8	21 1/8	23	5 3/8	5 3/8	5	5	0	1978	3
■ Scott County / Charles H. Smith / Charles H. Smith
173 4/8	23 6/8	23 7/8	18 6/8	21 4/8	4 6/8	4 6/8	6	6	0	1962	4
■ Shelby County / John J. Heirigs / John J. Heirigs
173 2/8	27 3/8	25 3/8	18 4/8	20 6/8	4	4 1/8	6	6	0	1972	5
■ Decatur County / Glen D. Odle / Glen D. Odle
173 1/8	26	26 6/8	18 5/8	22	4 1/8	3 7/8	6	6	10	1980	6
■ White County / Sam H. Langford / Sam H. Langford
173	25 4/8	25 1/8	19 4/8	21 1/8	4 5/8	4 5/8	4	4	0	1984	7
■ Sullivan County / C. Alan Altizer / C. Alan Altizer
172 3/8	27 6/8	28 2/8	17 2/8	19 6/8	4 6/8	4 5/8	6	5	2 1/8	1982	8
■ Decatur County / Danny Pope / Danny Pope
172 2/8	26 2/8	25	18 7/8	20 6/8	5	5	6	6	2 1/8	1984	9
■ Stewart County / Joe K. Sanders / Joe K. Sanders

Photo Courtesy of Luther E. Fuller

TENNESSEE STATE RECORD
NON-TYPICAL ANTLERS
SCORE: 223
Locality: Hawkins Co.   Date: November 1984
Hunter: Luther E. Fuller

TENNESSEE

NON-TYPICAL WHITETAILS

Score	Length of Main Beam R	L	Inside Spread	Greatest Spread	Circumference at Smallest Place Between Burr and First Point R	L	Number of Points R	L	Total of Lengths Abnormal Points	Date Killed	Rank
223	21 3/8	23	23 4/8	27 2/8	4 1/8	4 2/8	19	11	61	1984	1
■ Hawkins County / Luther E. Fuller / Luther E. Fuller											
209 7/8	20 6/8	19 7/8	19 6/8	26 3/8	4 7/8	4 6/8	13	11	66 1/8	1982	2
■ Hawkins County / Johnny W. Byington / Johnny W. Byington											
198 3/8	26 2/8	26 1/8	17 5/8	21 4/8	4 2/8	4 2/8	8	10	30 2/8	1978	3
■ Montgomery County / Clarence McElhaney / Clarence McElhaney											
196 6/8	25	25	19 1/8	24	4 6/8	5	9	10	29 1/8	1972	4
■ Unicoi County / Elmer Payne / Elmer Payne											

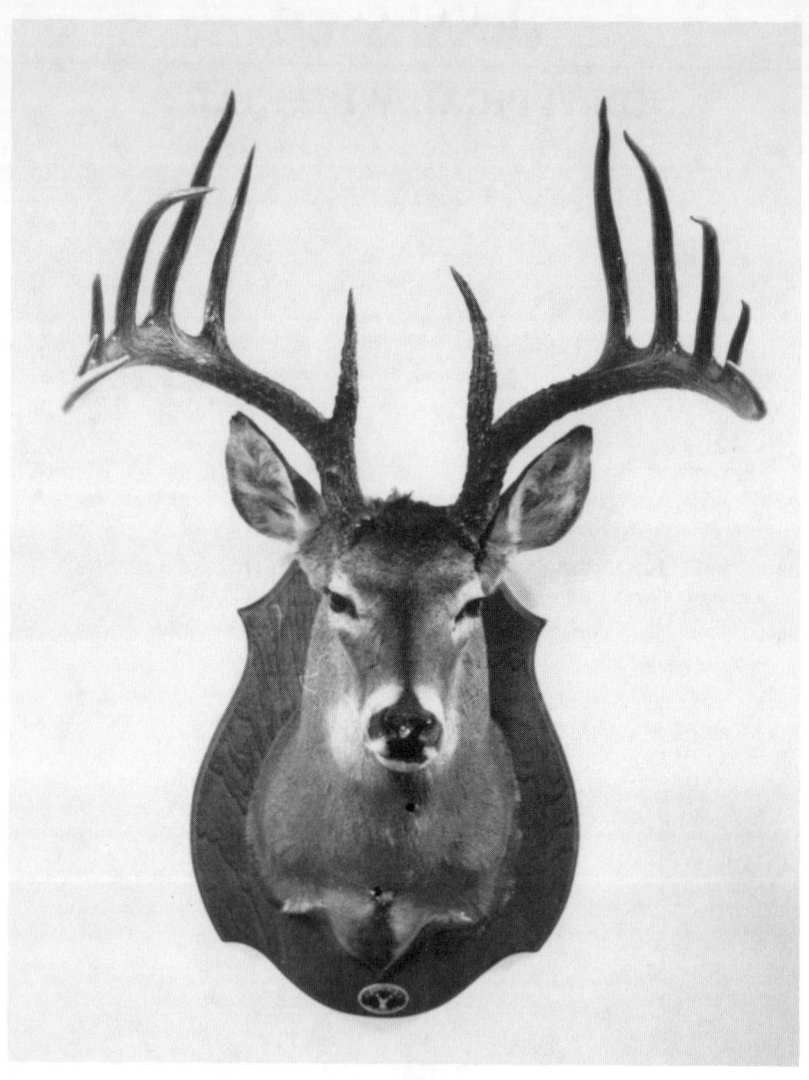

Photo by Wm. H. Nesbitt

TEXAS STATE RECORD
TYPICAL ANTLERS
SCORE: 196 4/8

Locality: Maverick Co.   Date: December 1963
Hunter: Tom McCulloch
Owner: McLean Bowman

TEXAS

TYPICAL WHITETAILS

Score	Length of Main Beam R	L	Inside Spread	Greatest Spread	Circumference at Smallest Place Between Burr and First Point R	L	Number of Points R	L	Total of Lengths Abnormal Points	Date Killed	Rank
196 4/8	28 6/8	27 5/8	24 2/8	25 5/8	4 6/8	4 6/8	8	6	1 4/8	1963	1
■ Maverick County / Tom McCulloch / McLean Bowman										
194 4/8	24 4/8	25	24	26	4 6/8	4 6/8	6	6	0	1973	2
■ Kenedy County / Alexander M. D. Guest / Alexander M. D. Guest										
192 2/8	27 7/8	27 3/8	22 6/8	27 1/8	4 2/8	4 4/8	8	7	7 4/8	1903	3
■ Frio County / Basil Dailey / David M. Dailey										
190	24 2/8	25 2/8	20 6/8	23	5	5	7	6	0	1950	4
■ Dimmit County / C. P. Howard / C. P. Howard										
188 7/8	27 5/8	26 7/8	18 4/8	21 2/8	4 6/8	4 5/8	8	7	4 1/8	1932	5
■ Dimmit County / William Henry Pease / Jeff Vick Pease										
187 5/8	28 2/8	27 6/8	19 6/8	23 4/8	5	5	6	8	5 7/8	1945	6
■ Starr County / Picked Up / Jack F. Quist										
186 2/8	27 4/8	27 4/8	18	20 3/8	4 6/8	4 6/8	8	10	5 6/8	1972	7
■ Kenedy County / Jack Van Cleve III / McGill Estate										
186 2/8	25 2/8	25 6/8	21	23	4 6/8	4 6/8	6	6	0	1967	7
■ La Salle County / Herman C. Schliesing / Herman C. Schliesing										
186 1/8	29 4/8	29 2/8	21	23 3/8	4 6/8	4 5/8	8	9	6 5/8	1965	9
■ Zavala County / Picked Up / Paul W. Sanders, Jr.										
183 7/8	25 6/8	25 3/8	27	30 2/8	5	4 6/8	7	6	1 3/8	1949	10
■ Webb County / Henderson Coquat / Henderson Coquat										
183 1/8	27 7/8	28 2/8	20 5/8	22 4/8	5	5	6	6	0	1973	11
■ Duval County / Charles Drennan / Bill Carter										
181 7/8	24 4/8	24 4/8	15 5/8	17 5/8	4 3/8	4 4/8	6	6	0	1971	12
■ McMullen County / Oscar Hasette / Bill Carter										
180 6/8	26 6/8	26	25	26 6/8	5	4 4/8	6	9	5 6/8	1937	13
■ Dimmit County / Edward Gardner / Edward Gardner										

TEXAS TYPICAL WHITETAILS (continued)

Score	Length of Main Beam R	L	Inside Spread	Greatest Spread	Circumference at Smallest Place Between Burr and First Point R	L	Number of Points R	L	Total of Lengths Abnormal Points	Date Killed	Rank
\■ Locality Killed / By Whom Killed / Owner											
180 5/8	25	23 4/8	19 2/8	20 4/8	4 4/8	4 4/8	7	7	1 1/8	1912	14
■ Maverick County / Jim Webb / Richard H. Bennett											
180 4/8	28	26 2/8	26 6/8	26 6/8	4 4/8	5 2/8	7	7	3 4/8	1958	15
■ Jim Hogg County / Roy Lee Henry / Roy Lee Henry											
180	26	25 7/8	19	24 1/8	4 7/8	4 7/8	10	7	12 2/8	1966	16
■ Zavala County / Mrs. Richard King III / Mrs. Richard King III											
179 6/8	26 3/8	26 2/8	19 6/8	22	4 4/8	4 4/8	6	6	0	1979	17
■ Jim Hogg County / William B. Van Fleet / William B. Van Fleet											
179 2/8	24 2/8	24 2/8	19 4/8	23 7/8	4 4/8	4 5/8	6	6	0	1982	18
■ Dimmit County / William M. Knolle / William M. Knolle											
178 4/8	25 2/8	25	23 2/8	25	5 4/8	5 4/8	5	5	0	1964	19
■ McMullen County / D. H. Waldron / D. H. Waldron											
177 6/8	23 4/8	24	24	26	4 4/8	4 4/8	6	6	0	1974	20
■ Duval County / Harry Heimer / Harry Heimer											
177 6/8	24	24	22	24	4 4/8	4 4/8	6	6	3 6/8	1972	20
■ Kleberg County / Elaine A. O'Brien / Patrick O'Brien											
177 4/8	26	26 4/8	24	26	5	5	6	6	1 2/8	1983	22
■ McMullen County / Unknown / Ken Mamatz											
177 4/8	24 6/8	23 3/8	24 7/8	26 4/8	5 1/8	5 2/8	7	6	3 7/8	1963	22
■ Dimmit County / Carter Younts / Carter Younts											
177 4/8	27 6/8	27 4/8	23 4/8	27 2/8	5	5	6	5	0	1926	22
■ Dimmit County / Tom Brady / McLean Bowman											
177 2/8	26 6/8	25 3/8	26 2/8	28 1/8	5 1/8	5 1/8	7	7	2 6/8	1924	25
■ Webb County / Unknown / Eugene Roberts											
176 4/8	23	23	16 4/8	19 2/8	4 2/8	4 2/8	9	7	5 4/8	1966	26
■ Carrizo Springs / Lin F. Nowotny / Lin F. Nowotny											
176 4/8	25 2/8	24 2/8	19	21 4/8	3 7/8	4 1/8	6	6	0	1964	26
■ Shackelford County / H. V. Stroud / H. V. Stroud											
175 6/8	25 4/8	26 4/8	20	22	5 3/8	5 2/8	6	6	0	1979	28
■ Dimmit County / George E. Light III / George E. Light III											
175 6/8	27 2/8	26 7/8	22 6/8	24 7/8	5 4/8	5	7	6	3 4/8	1978	28
■ Webb County / Norman Frede / Norman Frede											
175 6/8	25 6/8	26	20 2/8	21 6/8	4	4	6	6	0	1915	28
■ Webb County / William Bretthauer, Sr. / George H. Glass											
175 5/8	24 6/8	26 2/8	27 2/8	29	4 4/8	5	4	4	2 1/8	1925	31
■ Hayes County / Bill Kuykendall / Bill Kuykendall											

TEXAS TYPICAL WHITETAILS (continued)

Score	Length of Main Beam R	L	Inside Spread	Greatest Spread	Circumference at Smallest Place Between Burr and First Point R	L	Number of Points R	L	Total of Lengths Abnormal Points	Date Killed	Rank
175 3/8	25	25	18 1/8	20	4 2/8	4 1/8	6	6	0	1978	32
■ Dimmit County / Betsy Campbell / Betsy Campbell
175 2/8	22 7/8	22 7/8	19	22	4 4/8	4 5/8	6	6	0	1928	33
■ Encinal / W. S. Benson, Sr. / W. S. Benson III
175	26	27 4/8	21	23	5 1/8	5 1/8	5	6	0	1984	34
■ Jim Hogg County / Carl D. Ellis / Lee H. Lytton, Jr.
175	24 3/8	22 2/8	18 6/8	21	4 7/8	4 7/8	7	7	0	1972	34
■ La Salle County / Leonard Wolf Bouldin / Leonard Wolf Bouldin
174 5/8	25	25 2/8	24 3/8	26 5/8	4 3/8	4 2/8	7	7	2 2/8	1959	36
■ Kleberg County / C. T. Burris / Darrell Pitts
174 2/8	21 1/8	22	17	18 6/8	4 4/8	4 5/8	6	6	0	1963	37
■ Cass County / R. J. Perkins / John D. Small
174 2/8	23 3/8	23 6/8	15 5/8	18	4 4/8	4 5/8	10	9	4	1979	37
■ La Salle County / Walter L. Taylor / Walter L. Taylor
174 2/8	25 4/8	26	20	21 6/8	4 4/8	4 4/8	6	8	4 2/8	1908	37
■ Zavala County / Ernest Holdsworth / E. M. Holdsworth
174 2/8	24 6/8	24 2/8	22	24	4 6/8	4 6/8	6	5	0	1958	37
■ Dimmit County / Red Tollet / McLean Bowman
173 7/8	25 4/8	26	19 3/8	21 1/8	5	5	6	6	0	1965	41
■ Starr County / Leonard A. Schwarz / Leonard A. Schwarz
173 6/8	23 3/8	24	19 6/8	22 4/8	4 4/8	4 4/8	6	6	0	1970	42
■ Dimmit County / Booth W. Petry / Booth W. Petry
173	24 1/8	25 5/8	16 7/8	19 5/8	3 7/8	3 5/8	6	7	1 1/8	1983	43
■ Trinity County / Don Knight / Don Knight
173	25 2/8	24 2/8	21 7/8	24	4 5/8	4 6/8	9	6	5 3/8	1979	43
■ Hidalgo County / William L. Turk / William L. Turk
172 6/8	28 6/8	29	22 4/8	24 4/8	4 4/8	4 4/8	5	6	0	1964	45
■ Webb County / B. A. Vineyard / B. A. Vineyard
172 5/8	24 2/8	24 4/8	21 1/8	23	5 1/8	5	6	6	0	PR1940	46
■ Frio County / Unknown / Roy Hindes
172 4/8	24 4/8	24 4/8	18 4/8	20 6/8	4 4/8	4 4/8	6	7	0	1961	47
■ Webb County / A. M. Russell / A. M. Russell
172 4/8	25 6/8	27	20 2/8	21 5/8	5 2/8	5	6	6	0	1959	47
■ Cotulla / George E. Light III / George E. Light III
171 6/8	25	24 6/8	22	23 3/8	4 6/8	4 6/8	6	6	0	1962	49
■ Maverick County / Harry Garner / Harry Garner

TEXAS TYPICAL WHITETAILS (continued)

Score	Length of Main Beam R	Length of Main Beam L	Inside Spread	Greatest Spread	Circumference at Smallest Place Between Burr and First Point R	Circumference at Smallest Place Between Burr and First Point L	Number of Points R	Number of Points L	Total of Lengths Abnormal Points	Date Killed	Rank
171 3/8	26	24 5/8	15 1/8	16 7/8	4 3/8	4	5	6	1 1/8	1964	50
■ La Salle County / Charles D. Johnson / Charles D. Johnson											
171 3/8	31 1/8	29	16	19 2/8	5	5	7	9	11 3/8	1962	50
■ Frio County / Leonard Van Horn / Leonard Van Horn											
171 2/8	25 4/8	25 3/8	19 4/8	21 1/8	4 5/8	5	5	6	0	1970	52
■ Webb County / Ernie Pavlas / Ernie Pavlas											
170 7/8	26 4/8	25 7/8	17 5/8	19 6/8	5	5	7	6	1 3/8	1930	53
■ Frio County / Lex Stewart / Lex Stewart											
170 6/8	25 5/8	26	21	23 3/8	5 1/8	5 2/8	5	5	0	1958	54
■ Dimmit County / J. H. Hixon / J. H. Hixon											
170 6/8	28 4/8	28 1/8	24 5/8	27 7/8	4 2/8	4 1/8	6	8	12	1926	54
■ Zapata County / G. O. Elliff / Michael Elliff											
170 4/8	27	27 4/8	23 4/8	27	4 2/8	4 2/8	5	6	0	1979	56
■ Webb County / R. W. Mann / R. W. Mann											
170 4/8	24 2/8	25 2/8	19	20 5/8	4 2/8	4 4/8	6	6	0	1974	56
■ La Salle County / Jerome Knebel / Jerome Knebel											
170 3/8	24 4/8	23 4/8	22	24	5 2/8	5	8	7	12 5/8	1968	58
■ Duval County / R. L. Kruger / R. L. Kruger											
170 3/8	25 5/8	25 1/8	22 2/8	22 7/8	3 7/8	3 7/8	6	6	6 7/8	1922	58
■ Travis County / W. A. Brown / W. A. Brown											
170 2/8	24 6/8	24 3/8	19 5/8	21 5/8	4 5/8	4 5/8	8	7	3 3/8	1968	60
■ Jim Hogg County / Tom P. Hayes / Tom P. Hayes											
170 2/8	24 4/8	24	19 4/8	21	4 6/8	4 6/8	6	5	0	1964	60
■ McMullen County / Earl Welch / Earl Welch											
170	27 5/8	26 5/8	24 1/8	25 4/8	4 1/8	4	6	8	7 5/8	1961	62
■ Atascosa County / Ben H. Moore, Jr. / Ben H. Moore, Jr.											
170	27	28	22 5/8	25	4 5/8	4 4/8	6	5	1 4/8	1957	62
■ Webb County / Herbert Zieschang / Herbert Zieschang											
170	24 2/8	24 2/8	18 4/8	19 5/8	4 1/8	4 1/8	6	7	0	1941	62
■ Oiltown / L. D. Roberts / L. D. Roberts											

Photo Courtesy of Ralph Klimek

Ralph Klimek with the massive non-typical 204-7/8 that he took in Trempealeau County, Wisconsin, in 1960. Klimek's buck was an entry in the 10th Competition (1960-1961).

Photo by Grancel Fitz

TEXAS STATE RECORD
NON-TYPICAL ANTLERS
SCORE: 286

Locality: Brady   Date: 1892
Hunter: Jeff Benson
Owner: Lone Star Brewing Co.

TEXAS

NON-TYPICAL WHITETAILS

Score	Length of Main Beam R	L	Inside Spread	Greatest Spread	Circumference at Smallest Place Between Burr and First Point R	L	Number of Points R	L	Total of Lengths Abnormal Points	Date Killed	Rank
286	23 1/8	18 7/8	15 5/8	27 3/8	4 2/8	4 2/8	23	26	137	1892	1
■ Brady / Jeff Benson / Lone Star Brewing Co.
272	23 7/8	25	17 5/8	22 7/8	6 2/8	5 6/8	23	16	104 7/8	1925	2
■ Junction / Picked Up / Fred Mudge
247 7/8	26 1/8	26	19 5/8	25 4/8	5 5/8	5 4/8	13	17	64 4/8	1966	3
■ Frio County / Raul Rodriquez II / Raul Rodriquez II
240	26 4/8	26	21 5/8	26 6/8	5 4/8	5 4/8	15	11	52 3/8	1905	4
■ Kerr County / Walter R. Schreiner / Charles Schreiner III
235 1/8	24	23 7/8	21 3/8	27	5	4 7/8	14	15	64 5/8	1919	5
■ Frio County / C. J. Stolle / John F. Stolle
220 2/8	28 2/8	28 4/8	21	27 5/8	5	5	9	8	43 6/8	1930	6
■ Zavala County / J. D. Jarratt / J. D. Jarratt
219 3/8	27 4/8	27 4/8	20	24	5 2/8	5 2/8	11	10	27 3/8	1972	7
■ Webb County / Richard O. Rivera / Richard O. Rivera
213	24 4/8	24	17 5/8	19	4 7/8	4 5/8	10	10	39 5/8	1960	8
■ Kinney County / Rankin F. O'Neill / John L. Stein
212 2/8	21	19	24	27 6/8	4	4	9	16	84	1982	9
■ Parker County / Pleasant Mitchell / Pleasant Mitchell
212 2/8	25	25 4/8	19 4/8	21	5 2/8	5 2/8	11	13	32 2/8	1949	9
■ Webb County / Claude W. King / Claude W. King
211	23 6/8	23 4/8	16 3/8	21 4/8	6	6	12	13	48 7/8	PR1973	11
■ Zavala County / Unknown / McLean Bowman
209 3/8	26 1/8	26 1/8	21	26 2/8	5 1/8	5 1/8	13	9	23 1/8	1931	12
■ La Salle County / Unknown / E. T. Reilly
208 2/8	27	26 2/8	18 2/8	20 2/8	5 4/8	5 6/8	10	7	26 4/8	PR1950	13
■ Frio County / Unknown / Roy Hindes

TEXAS NON-TYPICAL WHITETAILS *(continued)*

Score	Length of Main Beam R	L	Inside Spread	Greatest Spread	Circumference at Smallest Place Between Burr and First Point R	L	Number of Points R	L	Total of Lengths Abnormal Points	Date Killed	Rank
206 4/8	22 1/8	22 2/8	19 1/8	23 7/8	5	5	10	13	33 4/8	1947	14
■ Brooks County / John E. Wilson / James Martin Hancock, Jr.
206 3/8	22 7/8	23 2/8	19	0	4 7/8	4 5/8	11	11	40 5/8	1942	15
■ Webb County / Willard V. Brenizer / Gerry Elliff
206 2/8	25 4/8	25	16 6/8	18 6/8	5	5	7	9	35 4/8	1950	16
■ Cotulla / George E. Light III / George E. Light III
205 7/8	25 5/8	25 4/8	20 6/8	28	4 4/8	4 3/8	10	10	36 5/8	1969	17
■ Houston County / Gary Rogers / Gary Rogers
203 7/8	27 4/8	27 4/8	17 4/8	22 2/8	4 6/8	4 6/8	11	8	21 5/8	1920	18
■ Eastland County / Picked Up / William B. Wright, Jr.
203 6/8	24 2/8	25 3/8	16 5/8	22	4	3 7/8	8	8	16 3/8	1941	19
■ Maverick County / Picked Up / Richard H. Bennett
203 4/8	25	25 1/8	22	29 3/8	4 6/8	4 5/8	13	12	36 2/8	1916	20
■ Live Oak County / Alec Coker / Henderson Coquat
202 5/8	23	24	14 7/8	17	5 5/8	5 4/8	9	9	33	1984	21
■ McMullen County / Picked Up / Patrick L. Seals
200 7/8	23 4/8	24 3/8	21	27	4 4/8	4 5/8	11	10	40 5/8	1982	22
■ Kleberg County / Picked Up / John A. Larkin
198 5/8	26 1/8	25 7/8	22 4/8	24 3/8	5	4 7/8	8	7	21 3/8	1962	23
■ Webb County / Larry Bickham / Larry Bickham
198 4/8	25	26 2/8	23 5/8	25 5/8	4 6/8	4 6/8	7	8	23 2/8	1983	24
■ Webb County / Alvin C. Santleben, Jr. / Alvin C. Santleben, Jr.
195 7/8	24 6/8	25	23 1/8	0	3 5/8	3 5/8	8	6	16 5/8	1930	25
■ Webb County / Charles J. Schelper, Sr. / Vernon L. Watson
195 4/8	24 5/8	24 1/8	17 5/8	21 1/8	4 4/8	4 2/8	9	9	34 4/8	1971	26
■ Maverick County / Ronald K. Hudson / Ronald K. Hudson
195 3/8	25 4/8	25 4/8	22 4/8	25	5	4 6/8	9	12	22 7/8	1983	27
■ Webb County / Sidney A. Lindsay, Jr. / Sidney A. Lindsay, Jr.
195 2/8	24 4/8	22	17 3/8	19 1/8	4 3/8	4 2/8	12	10	21 1/8	1975	28
■ Kenedy County / Don E. Harrison / Don E. Harrison
195 1/8	26	25 7/8	21	23 7/8	4 4/8	4 6/8	9	9	17 7/8	1966	29
■ Zapata County / Corando Mirelez / Corando Mirelez

Photo from Boone and Crockett Club Archives

John Batten, a long-time Official Measurer and Awards Judge, checks the inside spread of a trophy at the Final Judging of the 11th Competition (1962-1963). This trophy was taken by Arlee McCullough in Licking County, Ohio, in 1962. Scoring 181-4/8, it received the Second Place Award.

Photo Courtesy of Edward W. Fielder

VIRGINIA STATE RECORD
TYPICAL ANTLERS
SCORE: 178 3/8

Locality: Goochland Co.   Date: December 1981
Hunter: Edward W. Fielder

VIRGINIA

TYPICAL WHITETAILS

Score	Length of Main Beam R	L	Inside Spread	Greatest Spread	Circumference at Smallest Place Between Burr and First Point R	L	Number of Points R	L	Total of Lengths Abnormal Points	Date Killed	Rank
178 3/8	27 2/8	26 4/8	18 5/8	22 4/8	4 6/8	4 6/8	6	6	4 6/8	1981	1
■ Goochland County / Edward W. Fielder / Edward W. Fielder
177 2/8	28 1/8	28	20 6/8	22 4/8	4 6/8	4 6/8	5	5	0	1963	2
■ Augusta County / Donald W. Houser / Donald W. Houser
176 2/8	25 6/8	25 7/8	20 3/8	23 3/8	5 4/8	5 4/8	7	6	5 3/8	1959	3
■ Rappahannock County / George W. Beahm / George W. Beahm
174 4/8	26 3/8	26 2/8	19 1/8	21 5/8	5 2/8	5 5/8	5	7	1 5/8	1977	4
■ Charlotte County / Jerry C. Claybrook / Jerry C. Claybrook
173 4/8	26 4/8	27	20 6/8	24 7/8	4 4/8	4 6/8	7	8	5 2/8	1957	5
■ Augusta County / David H. Wolfe / David H. Wolfe
170 7/8	26 2/8	25 7/8	19 1/8	20 7/8	4 6/8	4 7/8	5	5	0	1953	6
■ Bath County / Maurice Smith / Maurice Smith
170 1/8	26 5/8	27	19 3/8	21 4/8	5 7/8	5 7/8	8	9	8 6/8	1955	7
■ Massanutton Mts. / Lloyd Lam / Lloyd Lam

Photo Courtesy of Peter F. Crocker, Jr.

VIRGINIA STATE RECORD
NON-TYPICAL ANTLERS
SCORE: 216 5/8

Locality: Isle of Wight Co.   Date: January 1963
Hunter: Peter F. Crocker, Jr.

VIRGINIA

NON-TYPICAL WHITETAILS

Score	Length of Main Beam R	L	Inside Spread	Greatest Spread	Circumference at Smallest Place Between Burr and First Point R	L	Number of Points R	L	Total of Lengths Abnormal Points	Date Killed	Rank
\- Locality Killed / By Whom Killed / Owner											
216 5/8	23	25 4/8	25 7/8	30 1/8	5 7/8	5 6/8	11	11	39 6/8	1963	1
■ Isle of Wight County / Peter F. Crocker, Jr. / Peter F. Crocker, Jr.											
216 3/8	26 6/8	26 3/8	20 3/8	34 2/8	4 7/8	5	9	10	45 6/8	1970	2
■ Powhatan County / William E. Schaefer / William E. Schaefer											
211 7/8	25	25 4/8	20 2/8	23 3/8	4 6/8	4 6/8	10	12	35 5/8	1966	3
■ Rockingham County / Dorsey O. Breeden / Dorsey O. Breeden											

Photo Courtesy of George A. Cook III

WASHINGTON STATE RECORD
TYPICAL ANTLERS
SCORE: 181 7/8
Locality: Whitman Co.   Date: October 1985
Hunter: George A. Cook III

WASHINGTON

TYPICAL WHITETAILS

Score	Length of Main Beam R	L	Inside Spread	Greatest Spread	Circumference at Smallest Place Between Burr and First Point R	L	Number of Points R	L	Total of Lengths Abnormal Points	Date Killed	Rank
181 7/8	27 1/8	27 5/8	20 5/8	23 2/8	4 1/8	4 1/8	5	6	0	1985	1
■ Whitman County / George A. Cook III / George A. Cook III											
180 4/8	30	29 1/8	24 5/8	26 5/8	4 1/8	4 7/8	8	8	9 7/8	1983	2
■ Okanogan County / Joe Peone / Joe Peone											
179 4/8	24 1/8	24 2/8	19 2/8	21 6/8	5 2/8	5 1/8	7	6	2 4/8	1972	3
■ Spokane County / Bert E. Smith / Bert E. Smith											
178 4/8	23 7/8	24 6/8	21 3/8	23 1/8	4 3/8	4 3/8	7	7	4 1/8	1957	4
■ Addy / Irving Naff / Irving Naff											
176 5/8	24 1/8	24 2/8	17 6/8	21 3/8	5	5 1/8	8	8	8 1/8	PR1953	5
■ Washington / Unknown / Jonas Bros. of Seattle											
172 6/8	25 4/8	25 5/8	22 4/8	25 5/8	4 5/8	4 4/8	5	6	0	1968	6
■ Spokane County / Maurice Robinette / Maurice Robinette											
171 3/8	22 3/8	23 1/8	14 5/8	16 6/8	5	5	7	6	1 6/8	1970	7
■ Metaline Falls County / Scott Hicks / Scott Hicks											
170 2/8	23 7/8	24 2/8	15	16 6/8	4 4/8	4 4/8	8	7	1	1970	8
■ Spokane County / Edward A. Floch, Jr. / Edward A. Floch, Jr.											
170	22 7/8	22 4/8	18 4/8	20 5/8	4 6/8	4 7/8	5	6	0	1966	9
■ Stevens County / Clair Kelso / Clair Kelso											

Photo Courtesy of Larry G. Gardner

WASHINGTON STATE RECORD
NON-TYPICAL ANTLERS
SCORE: 234 4/8

Locality: Stevens Co.   Date: November 1953
Hunter: Larry G. Gardner

WASHINGTON

NON-TYPICAL WHITETAILS

Score	Length of Main Beam R	L	Inside Spread	Greatest Spread	Circumference at Smallest Place Between Burr and First Point R	L	Number of Points R	L	Total of Lengths Abnormal Points	Date Killed	Rank
234 4/8	29	28 2/8	20 7/8	24 6/8	5 3/8	5 6/8	14	16	42 7/8	1953	1
■ Stevens County / Larry G. Gardner / Larry G. Gardner
233 6/8	26 2/8	26	22	31 6/8	4 7/8	4 6/8	13	13	67 6/8	1964	2
■ Thompson Creek / George Sly, Jr. / George Sly, Jr.
231	26	25 7/8	18	22 6/8	5	5	12	12	43 6/8	1946	3
■ Stevens County / Joe Bussano / Joe Bussano
227 4/8	27 1/8	26 2/8	20 2/8	28	5 2/8	5 2/8	12	9	44	1965	4
■ Pullman / Glenn C. Paulson / Glenn C. Paulson
210 7/8	24 2/8	24 1/8	18 1/8	21 6/8	5 2/8	5 2/8	11	9	32 4/8	1966	5
■ Stevens County / Charles Tucker / Charles Tucker
208	25 4/8	25	19 6/8	22	4 5/8	4 5/8	9	10	16 4/8	1967	6
■ Chesaw / Charles Eder / Charles Eder
207 2/8	24 4/8	19 5/8	11 7/8	25 6/8	5 6/8	5 6/8	11	17	84 3/8	1967	7
■ Oroville / Victor E. Moss / Victor E. Moss
206 1/8	22	20 6/8	20 7/8	27 2/8	4 5/8	4 6/8	10	10	39 6/8	1955	8
■ Loon Lake / Bill Quirt / Bill Quirt
204 3/8	26	24 4/8	18 3/8	23 4/8	4 7/8	5 2/8	11	12	35 6/8	1960	9
■ Newport / David R. Buchite / David R. Buchite
203 3/8	25 2/8	25 2/8	21 5/8	23 6/8	5	5	10	8	28	1961	10
■ Okanogan County / Michael A. Anderson / Michael A. Anderson
201 4/8	25 2/8	23 1/8	16 5/8	18 4/8	4 5/8	5 2/8	14	13	69 3/8	1963	11
■ Stevens County / Robert W. Newell / Robert W. Newell
197 6/8	23 5/8	26 2/8	20 2/8	26	5 2/8	5	10	8	35 2/8	1961	12
■ Hunters / Rachel Mally / Rachel Mally
197 3/8	25	26	17 4/8	24 7/8	5 5/8	5 5/8	9	10	19 1/8	1948	13
■ Stevens County / Coulston W. Drummond / Coulston W. Drummond

WASHINGTON NON-TYPICAL WHITETAILS *(continued)*

Score	Length of Main Beam R	L	Inside Spread	Greatest Spread	Circumference at Smallest Place Between Burr and First Point R	L	Number of Points R	L	Total of Lengths Abnormal Points	Date Killed	Rank
\> Locality Killed / By Whom Killed / Owner											
195 2/8	25 3/8	25 5/8	22 2/8	24	5 3/8	5 3/8	12	13	31 4/8	1981	14
■ Stevens County / Floyd E. Newell / Floyd E. Newell											
195 1/8	24 2/8	23 4/8	23 7/8	25 6/8	5 2/8	5 2/8	10	9	19 3/8	1975	15
■ Whitman County / R. M. & R. M. Boyer / R. M. & R. M. Boyer											

Photo Courtesy of Dorsey O. Breeden

Dorsey O. Breeden with the non-typical 211-7/8 that he took in Rockingham County, Virginia, in 1966. Breeden's buck is one of only three non-typical whitetails listed from Virginia. It was an entry in the 13th Competition (1966-1967).

Photo Courtesy of William D. Given

WEST VIRGINIA STATE RECORD
TYPICAL ANTLERS
SCORE: 182 3/8

Locality: Braxton Co.   Date: November 1976
Hunter: William D. Given

WEST VIRGINIA

TYPICAL WHITETAILS

Score	Length of Main Beam R	L	Inside Spread	Greatest Spread	Circumference at Smallest Place Between Burr and First Point R	L	Number of Points R	L	Total of Lengths Abnormal Points	Date Killed	Rank
182³⁄₈	28¹⁄₈	27¹⁄₈	21⁵⁄₈	23⁶⁄₈	4⁴⁄₈	4⁵⁄₈	6	6	0	1976	1
■ Braxton County / William D. Given / William D. Given
180⁵⁄₈	25	23⁶⁄₈	23³⁄₈	24⁶⁄₈	5³⁄₈	5³⁄₈	7	6	10⁴⁄₈	1969	2
■ Cheat Mt. / Joseph V. Volitis / Joseph V. Volitis
175¹⁄₈	27³⁄₈	27¹⁄₈	21²⁄₈	23⁶⁄₈	5⁷⁄₈	6	6	5	1¹⁄₈	1984	3
■ Wetzel County / Matthew Scheibelhood / Matthew Scheibelhood
171	27¹⁄₈	26³⁄₈	19⁴⁄₈	21⁶⁄₈	4⁴⁄₈	4⁴⁄₈	5	5	0	1958	4
■ Hampshire County / Conda L. Shanholtz / Conda L. Shanholtz

Photo Courtesy of Ed Bailey

WEST VIRGINIA STATE RECORD
NON-TYPICAL ANTLERS
SCORE: 205 6/8
Locality: Ritchie Co.   Date: November 1979
Hunter: Ed Bailey

WEST VIRGINIA

NON-TYPICAL WHITETAILS

Score	Length of Main Beam R	L	Inside Spread	Greatest Spread	Circumference at Smallest Place Between Burr and First Point R	L	Number of Points R	L	Total of Lengths Abnormal Points	Date Killed	Rank
\■ Locality Killed / By Whom Killed / Owner											
205 6/8	24 3/8	24	21	23	5	5 2/8	9	9	27	1979	1
■ Ritchie County / Ed Bailey / Ed Bailey											
204 6/8	28 4/8	26 5/8	21 7/8	25 1/8	5 7/8	5 7/8	10	12	22 3/8	1960	2
■ Gilmer County / Brooks Reed / Brooks Reed											
203 1/8	23 7/8	24 4/8	19 6/8	24 4/8	5 4/8	5 7/8	10	12	26 1/8	1981	3
■ Wetzel County / Tom Kirkhart / Tom Kirkhart											

Photo Courtesy of Charles T. Arnold

WISCONSIN STATE RECORD
TYPICAL ANTLERS
SCORE: 206 1/8

Locality: Burnett Co.   Date: November 1914
Hunter: James Jordan
Owner: Charles T. Arnold

WISCONSIN

TYPICAL WHITETAILS

Score	Length of Main Beam R	L	Inside Spread	Greatest Spread	Circumference at Smallest Place Between Burr and First Point R	L	Number of Points R	L	Total of Lengths Abnormal Points	Date Killed	Rank
206 1/8	30	30	20 1/8	23 5/8	6 7/8	6 1/8	5	5	0	1914	1
■ Burnett County / James Jordan / Charles T. Arnold											
191 3/8	31 5/8	31 1/8	27 5/8	30 2/8	6 1/8	6 1/8	5	6	0	1910	2
■ Vilas County / Robert Hunter / May Docken											
186 1/8	28	26 2/8	21 4/8	25 2/8	6 1/8	6	8	5	2 5/8	1963	3
■ Waupaca County / Fred Penny / Dale Trinrud											
185	29 1/8	28 5/8	18 5/8	20 7/8	4 4/8	4 3/8	5	5	0	1968	4
■ Vernon County / Harold Christianson / Harold Christianson											
184	24 5/8	24 4/8	18 5/8	22	5 1/8	5 2/8	7	6	1 1/8	1969	5
■ Menominee County / Keith Miller / Charles Loberg											
183 7/8	28	27 1/8	19 6/8	22	5	4 7/8	7	5	2 7/8	1980	6
■ Forest County / James M. Thayer / James M. Thayer											
183 6/8	26 7/8	25 1/8	18 5/8	21	5 4/8	5 4/8	7	7	1 2/8	1965	7
■ Pepin County / LaVerne Anibas / LaVerne Anibas											
183 5/8	27 1/8	26	23 2/8	25	4 6/8	4 6/8	7	6	4 5/8	1953	8
■ Buffalo County / Lee F. Spittler / Mrs. Lee F. Spittler											
183 2/8	26 7/8	26 7/8	16	20	5	5	7	7	5 4/8	1900	9
■ Ashland County / Unknown / Martin Bonack											
182 6/8	28 2/8	28	22 6/8	25 2/8	4 6/8	4 5/8	6	5	0	1942	10
■ Vilas County / George Sparks / Mac's Taxidermy											
182 4/8	24 2/8	23 6/8	18	22 2/8	5 1/8	5 1/8	6	6	0	PR1985	11
■ Menominee County / Unknown / John L. Stein											
182 3/8	28 3/8	27 3/8	19 1/8	22 4/8	4 3/8	4 4/8	5	6	0	1984	12
■ Buffalo County / Anthony F. Wolfe / Anthony F. Wolfe											
181 7/8	25	25 2/8	21	23 2/8	4 3/8	4 3/8	6	6	0	1982	13
■ Lafayette County / Michael Morrissey / Michael Morrissey											

WISCONSIN TYPICAL WHITETAILS (continued)

Score	Length of Main Beam R	L	Inside Spread	Greatest Spread	Circumference at Smallest Place Between Burr and First Point R	L	Number of Points R	L	Total of Lengths Abnormal Points	Date Killed	Rank
181	28 3/8	28 1/8	20	22	4 1/8	4 1/8	5	5	0	1977	14
■ Wood County / James D. Wyman / James D. Wyman											
181	25 5/8	26 5/8	19	21	5 5/8	5	5	5	0	1959	14
■ Langlade County / Elroy W. Timm / Elroy W. Timm											
180 3/8	26 1/8	27	20 1/8	22 1/8	4 3/8	4 1/8	7	8	3 3/8	1955	16
■ Sheboygan County / Unknown / James K. Lawton											
180 2/8	26 3/8	26 3/8	18 1/8	20 1/8	4 5/8	4 5/8	6	6	0	1979	17
■ Eau Claire County / Dennis B. Bryan / Dennis B. Bryan											
180 1/8	25 1/8	26 5/8	17 3/8	20 1/8	4 7/8	4 5/8	7	6	5 1/8	1961	18
■ Ashland County / Audrey Kundinger / Audrey Kundinger											
180	27 1/8	27 5/8	20	22	4 1/8	5	5	6	4 2/8	1938	19
■ Oneida County / Milo K. Fields / Milo K. Fields											
179 3/8	26 1/8	26 2/8	17 1/8	22 5/8	4 1/8	4 5/8	6	6	0	1966	20
■ Vernon County / Alois V. Schendel / Alois V. Schendel											
179 2/8	23 5/8	25 1/8	19 1/8	21 2/8	5 5/8	5 5/8	7	7	1	1984	21
■ Buffalo County / Jerome Kulig / Jerome Kulig											
179 2/8	26 7/8	28	16	18 2/8	4 1/8	4 3/8	6	5	0	1981	21
■ Ashland County / Jack D. Hultman / Jack D. Hultman											
179	25	23 7/8	18 2/8	21 2/8	5 5/8	5 3/8	5	6	0	1931	23
■ Chippewa County / John F. Kukuska / John F. Kukuska											
178 1/8	27 1/8	27 1/8	21 1/8	23 3/8	5 5/8	5 1/8	5	5	0	1983	24
■ Price County / Terry Staroba / Terry Staroba											
178 1/8	27 5/8	27 1/8	17 1/8	20 1/8	4 1/8	4 1/8	8	7	7 3/8	1957	24
■ Iron County / DuWayne A. Weichel / Robert G. Steidtmann											
178	27 5/8	27 2/8	20	22	5 1/8	5 2/8	7	7	4 2/8	1981	26
■ Price County / John E. Martinson / John E. Martinson											
178	27	27 2/8	17 1/8	19 5/8	4 5/8	5	7	6	3 1/8	1949	26
■ Price County / Emery Swan / Emery Swan											
177 5/8	25 5/8	25 5/8	19 5/8	21 3/8	5 5/8	5 3/8	5	5	0	1984	28
■ Washburn County / Patrick Henk / Patrick Henk											
177 1/8	26	26 1/8	21 5/8	24	4 5/8	4 1/8	8	6	1 3/8	1926	29
■ Oneida County / Elmer Ahlborn / Gene Ahlborn											
177 3/8	26	26	20 2/8	22 5/8	5 3/8	5 2/8	6	5	1 5/8	1981	30
■ Rusk County / David A. Reichel / David A. Reichel											
177 3/8	27	26 2/8	23 1/8	26 2/8	5	5 1/8	5	5	0	1981	30
■ Menominee County / William Matchapatow, Sr. / William Matchapatow, Sr.											

WISCONSIN TYPICAL WHITETAILS (continued)

Score	Length of Main Beam R	L	Inside Spread	Greatest Spread	Circumference at Smallest Place Between Burr and First Point R	L	Number of Points R	L	Total of Lengths Abnormal Points	Date Killed	Rank
177²⁄₈	25⁵⁄₈	25⁷⁄₈	18²⁄₈	20⁵⁄₈	4⁶⁄₈	4⁶⁄₈	6	6	0	1982	32
■ Richland County / Dewitt S. Pulham / Dewitt S. Pulham											
177¹⁄₈	27²⁄₈	27	21⁷⁄₈	24⁵⁄₈	4⁴⁄₈	4⁴⁄₈	5	5	0	1984	33
■ Walworth County / Daniel J. Brede / Daniel J. Brede											
177	28¹⁄₈	28	17⁷⁄₈	20	4⁶⁄₈	4⁶⁄₈	6	7	4⁶⁄₈	1932	34
■ Bayfield County / Elof E. Sjostrom / Mrs. Elof E. Sjostrom											
176⁷⁄₈	27³⁄₈	27⁷⁄₈	20³⁄₈	22⁴⁄₈	4⁵⁄₈	4⁵⁄₈	5	5	0	1984	35
■ Pierce County / John M. Oelke / John M. Oelke											
176⁶⁄₈	26³⁄₈	25	19	21⁷⁄₈	5³⁄₈	5⁴⁄₈	5	6	0	1950	36
■ Langlade County / Jack Ryan / LaVern Emerich											
176⁶⁄₈	27¹⁄₈	26	20⁷⁄₈	23	5²⁄₈	5²⁄₈	5	6	2⁵⁄₈	1938	36
■ Vilas County / Porter Dean / Safari North Tax.											
176⁴⁄₈	25	25	19⁴⁄₈	23	4⁴⁄₈	4³⁄₈	7	6	2²⁄₈	1969	38
■ Crawford County / Louis Franks / Louis Franks											
176¹⁄₈	28	27⁴⁄₈	21²⁄₈	23⁵⁄₈	5⁴⁄₈	5⁴⁄₈	6	5	1³⁄₈	1943	39
■ Florence County / Theron A. Meyer, Sr. / Theron A. Meyer, Sr.											
176	28⁵⁄₈	29⁶⁄₈	17⁵⁄₈	20⁶⁄₈	5³⁄₈	5³⁄₈	8	7	10³⁄₈	1936	40
■ Florence County / John G. Kozicki / Vernon J. Kozicki											
175⁵⁄₈	25⁶⁄₈	27	21²⁄₈	24⁶⁄₈	5¹⁄₈	5¹⁄₈	6	5	0	1954	41
■ Pepin County / Carl E. Frick / Carl E. Frick											
175¹⁄₈	22¹⁄₈	22⁷⁄₈	20⁵⁄₈	22⁵⁄₈	5	5²⁄₈	6	6	0	1983	42
■ Marinette County / John Nielson / John Nielson											
175¹⁄₈	25⁵⁄₈	27	20²⁄₈	22⁶⁄₈	5	5	8	7	3⁷⁄₈	1968	42
■ Menominee County / Gerald Ponfil / Gerald Ponfil											
174⁷⁄₈	28¹⁄₈	28¹⁄₈	21³⁄₈	23⁷⁄₈	5	5	4	4	0	1977	44
■ Burnett County / Myles Keller / Myles Keller											
174⁴⁄₈	26²⁄₈	27⁴⁄₈	21	25⁵⁄₈	5⁶⁄₈	5⁶⁄₈	8	6	10²⁄₈	1924	45
■ Hayward / Bill Metcalf / John Metcalf											
174	26⁴⁄₈	26	17⁵⁄₈	20	4⁴⁄₈	4⁵⁄₈	7	5	3¹⁄₈	1970	46
■ Jefferson County / Gary A. Coates / Gary A. Coates											
173⁵⁄₈	26⁶⁄₈	26⁶⁄₈	17⁵⁄₈	19⁶⁄₈	4⁴⁄₈	4⁴⁄₈	5	5	0	1940	47
■ Sawyer County / Maurice Peterson / Mac's Taxidermy											
173⁴⁄₈	26	26	21	23	5³⁄₈	5¹⁄₈	5	5	0	1967	48
■ Vilas County / Unknown / Donald Krueger											
173²⁄₈	25⁶⁄₈	24²⁄₈	25²⁄₈	26⁴⁄₈	5⁴⁄₈	5¹⁄₈	7	6	1¹⁄₈	1959	49
■ Price County / Clarence Parmelee / J. D. Andrews											

WISCONSIN TYPICAL WHITETAILS (continued)

Score	Length of Main Beam R	L	Inside Spread	Greatest Spread	Circumference at Smallest Place Between Burr and First Point R	L	Number of Points R	L	Total of Lengths Abnormal Points	Date Killed	Rank
	■ Locality Killed / By Whom Killed / Owner										
172 7/8	24 5/8	24 3/8	20 1/8	23 1/8	5 1/8	5 3/8	5	5	0	1965	50
	■ Ashland County / Einar Sein / Rick Iacono										
172 6/8	25 1/8	25 1/8	18 6/8	21	4 5/8	4 5/8	5	6	1 2/8	1918	51
	■ Woodruff / Unknown / Mac's Taxidermy										
172 3/8	24 5/8	24 3/8	18	21 3/8	4 6/8	4 7/8	8	7	7 5/8	1984	52
	■ Rusk County / Randy A. Jochem / Randy A. Jochem										
172 2/8	23	23	19	22 4/8	5	5 1/8	6	7	5 4/8	1965	53
	■ Adams County / W. R. Ingraham / W. R. Ingraham										
172 2/8	24 6/8	24 3/8	18	20 2/8	4 4/8	4 5/8	6	6	0	1936	53
	■ Vilas County / Ray Hermanson / J. James Froelich										
172 2/8	27 1/8	28	20	22 2/8	4 6/8	4 5/8	5	6	0	1928	53
	■ Lincoln County / Alfred Theilig / Philip Schlegel										
172 1/8	25 6/8	25 5/8	19 3/8	22	5 4/8	5 2/8	5	5	0	1949	56
	■ Juneau County / Unknown / Clark G. Gallup										
172	25 7/8	25 2/8	19	21 3/8	4 5/8	4 5/8	5	5	0	1983	57
	■ Waukesha County / Donald R. Friedlein / Donald R. Friedlein										
172	26 2/8	23	21 1/8	24	4 6/8	4 6/8	5	6	0	1960	57
	■ Buffalo County / Ralph Duellman / Ralph Duellman										
172	26 4/8	25 2/8	19 1/8	21 1/8	5 2/8	5 3/8	5	6	3 7/8	1939	57
	■ Oconto County / Henry J. Bredael / Henry J. Bredael										
171 6/8	28 1/8	27 2/8	19 3/8	22	5 3/8	5 3/8	4	6	1 1/8	1973	60
	■ Buffalo County / Richard Schultz / Richard Schultz										
171 6/8	26 5/8	26 4/8	18	20	4 6/8	4 5/8	5	5	0	1945	60
	■ Niagara / Francis H. Van Ginkel / David Watson										
171 4/8	25	24 5/8	20 1/8	22 5/8	4 3/8	4 4/8	6	6	0	1983	62
	■ Rusk County / Luke Dernovsek III / Luke Dernovsek III										
171 3/8	25 3/8	26 5/8	18 5/8	21	5 3/8	5 2/8	5	5	0	1969	63
	■ Forest County / Chester Cox, Jr. / Chester Cox, Jr.										
171 3/8	26 5/8	26 6/8	21 5/8	24	4 4/8	4 4/8	9	7	7 6/8	1938	63
	■ Juneau County / Fay Hammersley / Fay Hammersley										
171 2/8	25 6/8	25 7/8	19 2/8	21 2/8	5	5	5	6	0	1956	65
	■ Bayfield County / Lawrence Stumo / Lawrence Stumo										
171 1/8	23 5/8	23 5/8	18 3/8	20	7 2/8	6 3/8	5	5	0	1979	66
	■ Bayfield County / James A. Peters / James A. Peters										
171	26 2/8	25 5/8	20 5/8	22 4/8	4 1/8	4 1/8	6	6	1 5/8	1964	67
	■ Buffalo County / Clarence H. Castleberg, Jr. / Clarence H. Castleberg, Jr.										

WISCONSIN TYPICAL WHITETAILS (continued)

Score	Length of Main Beam R	L	Inside Spread	Greatest Spread	Circumference at Smallest Place Between Burr and First Point R	L	Number of Points R	L	Total of Lengths Abnormal Points	Date Killed	Rank
170 5/8	26 6/8	27 2/8	18 3/8	23	5 4/8	5 4/8	6	8	6 6/8	1970	68

■ Price County / Nyle H. Rodman / Nyle H. Rodman

| 170 5/8 | 27 5/8 | 26 5/8 | 19 3/8 | 22 | 4 6/8 | 4 6/8 | 7 | 7 | 1 2/8 | 1963 | 68 |

■ Douglas County / George Pettingill / George Pettingill

| 170 4/8 | 25 2/8 | 24 2/8 | 16 4/8 | 19 1/8 | 5 | 5 | 7 | 7 | 3 | 1981 | 70 |

■ Oneida County / Leonard E. Westberg / Leonard E. Westberg

| 170 3/8 | 25 5/8 | 25 1/8 | 16 4/8 | 18 4/8 | 4 7/8 | 5 | 9 | 9 | 11 7/8 | 1905 | 71 |

■ Price County / N. J. Groelle / Melvin Guenther

| 170 1/8 | 23 6/8 | 25 6/8 | 20 5/8 | 23 4/8 | 4 2/8 | 4 3/8 | 6 | 6 | 0 | 1968 | 72 |

■ Marinette County / Leonard Schartner / Leonard Schartner

| 191 7/8 | 27 5/8 | 26 5/8 | 19 3/8 | 22 | 4 6/8 | 4 7/8 | 6 | 6 | 0 | 1979 | * |

■ Waukesha County / Kenneth Lange / Kenneth Lange

Photo Courtesy of Elmer F. Gotz

WISCONSIN STATE RECORD
NON-TYPICAL ANTLERS
SCORE: 245

Locality: Buffalo Co. Date: November 1973
Hunter: Elmer F. Gotz

WISCONSIN

NON-TYPICAL WHITETAILS

Score	Length of Main Beam R	L	Inside Spread	Greatest Spread	Circumference at Smallest Place Between Burr and First Point R	L	Number of Points R	L	Total of Lengths Abnormal Points	Date Killed	Rank
■ Locality Killed / By Whom Killed / Owner												
245	27 4/8	27	20 6/8	27 5/8	5 3/8	5 4/8	15	15	57 1/8	1973	1
■ Buffalo County / Elmer F. Gotz / Elmer F. Gotz												
241 3/8	29 2/8	25 7/8	19 3/8	22 5/8	5 2/8	5	9	11	43 6/8	1940	2
■ Wisconsin / Unknown / Robert Kietzman												
233 7/8	23 6/8	22 4/8	16 5/8	30 1/8	6	5 7/8	16	15	62 6/8	1937	3
■ Loraine / Homer Pearson / McLean Bowman												
233	26	27 4/8	20 4/8	27	5 7/8	6	14	11	68 2/8	1949	4
■ Burnett County / Victor Rammer / Jerry C. Ganske												
232	25 6/8	25	17	21 4/8	6	6	18	11	47	1955	5
■ Waukesha County / John Herr, Sr. / Mac's Taxidermy												
231 5/8	28 1/8	26 5/8	19 2/8	26	5 1/8	5 1/8	11	11	39 5/8	1979	6
■ Dane County / Dennis D. Shanks / Dennis D. Shanks												
231 2/8	25 6/8	26 3/8	18 4/8	24 4/8	5	4 7/8	17	13	65 6/8	1958	7
■ Forest County / Robert Jacobson / Robert Jacobson												
228 2/8	26 6/8	29 2/8	21	34 2/8	5 2/8	5 2/8	13	10	45 2/8	1910	8
■ Cable / Charles Berg / Eva Mae Fisher												
227 4/8	25 3/8	25 2/8	18 1/8	25 4/8	6 4/8	6 4/8	16	17	65 2/8	1934	9
■ Bayfield County / Earl Holt / Mrs. Earl Holt												
226 6/8	25 5/8	27 4/8	15 5/8	20 4/8	4 7/8	5 2/8	22	25	64 3/8	1911	10
■ Rusk County / Joe Michalets / John R. Michalets												
222 6/8	24 4/8	23 4/8	17 1/8	22	5 4/8	5 6/8	8	8	25 1/8	1936	11
■ Rusk County / Raymond Charlevois / Philip Schlegel												
222 4/8	25 4/8	23 6/8	21 1/8	27 7/8	5 3/8	5 2/8	14	11	55 1/8	1983	12
■ Richland County / Janice K. Beranek / Janice K. Beranek												
219 2/8	26	30 5/8	19 2/8	22 4/8	6 2/8	6 2/8	13	11	32	1958	13
■ Buffalo County / Glenn Lehman / Glenn Lehman												

WISCONSIN NON-TYPICAL WHITETAILS *(continued)*

Score	Length of Main Beam R	Length of Main Beam L	Inside Spread	Greatest Spread	Circumference at Smallest Place Between Burr and First Point R	Circumference at Smallest Place Between Burr and First Point L	Number of Points R	Number of Points L	Total of Lengths Abnormal Points	Date Killed	Rank
■ *Locality Killed / By Whom Killed / Owner*											
218⅞	28⅛	27⅞	20	22⅛	5²⁄₈	4⅞	12	11	43³⁄₈	1914	14
■ *Florence County / W. C. Gotstein / J. D. Andrews*											
218⁴⁄₈	27	26³⁄₈	18⅞	24	5²⁄₈	5³⁄₈	12	12	27⅞	1920	15
■ *Sawyer County / Walter Kittleson / Walter Kittleson*											
218³⁄₈	27	24³⁄₈	17	20	5⅞	5⅝	9	11	36³⁄₈	1951	16
■ *La Crosse County / Daniel P. Cavadini / J. D. Andrews*											
215³⁄₈	29⁴⁄₈	28⁶⁄₈	23⅞	28	5⁶⁄₈	5⁶⁄₈	8	8	37	1969	17
■ *Lafayette County / Roger Vickers / Roger Vickers*											
214³⁄₈	27³⁄₈	26	17⅝	25⅝	5	5	11	11	50⁴⁄₈	1963	18
■ *Bayfield County / Clarence Lauer / Mrs. Clarence Lauer*											
214³⁄₈	25	25⅛	15³⁄₈	17⁴⁄₈	5²⁄₈	5³⁄₈	11	10	21²⁄₈	1926	18
■ *Price County / Henry J. Copt / James A. Copt*											
213⅞	25	25³⁄₈	18	24	5⅝	5⅞	17	12	52⅞	1949	20
■ *Sawyer County / Charles Ross / Charles Ross*											
213⅝	23	23⅞	16²⁄₈	27⁶⁄₈	6	6⅛	10	12	67⅝	1968	21
■ *Buffalo County / Norman C. Ratz / Ed Klink*											
212⅞	30	23³⁄₈	21⅛	26⁴⁄₈	5²⁄₈	5	7	12	30	1976	22
■ *Waukesha County / Max Mollgaard / Max Mollgaard*											
211⁴⁄₈	23²⁄₈	23²⁄₈	13⁶⁄₈	21⅝	6²⁄₈	5⁶⁄₈	12	10	47⁶⁄₈	1984	23
■ *Dodge County / Michael A. Koehler / Michael A. Koehler*											
210⁴⁄₈	26⅞	25⁶⁄₈	20	23	5⅛	5⅛	12	11	29⁴⁄₈	1970	24
■ *Dane County / LaVerne W. Marten / LaVerne W. Marten*											
210³⁄₈	28⁴⁄₈	27⁴⁄₈	21⁴⁄₈	24⅛	5	5⅛	9	10	18⅛	1947	25
■ *Marinette County / George E. Bierstaker / Mrs. George E. Bierstaker*											
209³⁄₈	23⅝	21⁶⁄₈	16⁶⁄₈	21⅛	4³⁄₈	4⁴⁄₈	11	10	39⅛	1982	26
■ *Grant County / Tim Yanna / Tim Yanna*											
208⅝	27⁴⁄₈	28	22	31	6	5⅞	10	8	34⅝	PR1945	27
■ *Taylor County / Unknown / Mac's Taxidermy*											
207⅝	24	23⁶⁄₈	23⁶⁄₈	25⁴⁄₈	6³⁄₈	6²⁄₈	10	8	34³⁄₈	1984	28
■ *Buffalo County / Dennis M. Eberhart / Dennis M. Eberhart*											
207⁴⁄₈	25²⁄₈	24⁶⁄₈	16²⁄₈	20⁴⁄₈	5²⁄₈	5²⁄₈	12	11	54	1938	29
■ *Burnett County / Harold Miller / Mac's Taxidermy*											
207	23⁴⁄₈	23⅛	18⁴⁄₈	26	5⁶⁄₈	6⁴⁄₈	16	13	69	1954	30
■ *Bayfield County / Francis F. Zifko / Francis F. Zifko*											
206⅞	23⁴⁄₈	25⅝	18⁴⁄₈	24⁶⁄₈	5⅛	4⅞	14	12	61⅝	1966	31
■ *Horicon Marsh / Picked Up / Ronald A. Lillge*											

Score	Length of Main Beam R	Length of Main Beam L	Inside Spread	Greatest Spread	Circumference at Smallest Place Between Burr and First Point R	Circumference at Smallest Place Between Burr and First Point L	Number of Points R	Number of Points L	Total of Lengths Abnormal Points	Date Killed	Rank
	■ *Locality Killed / By Whom Killed / Owner*										
206 7/8	24 3/8	25	16 5/8	22 4/8	5 5/8	5 3/8	14	9	32 4/8	1942	31
	■ *Oneida County / Clarence Staudenmayer / Clarence Staudenmayer*										
206 1/8	23 2/8	22 5/8	22	29 1/8	5 4/8	5 4/8	10	9	43 5/8	PR1974	33
	■ *Lincoln County / Picked Up / Louis Pond*										
205 3/8	25 3/8	27 1/8	22 2/8	23 6/8	4 1/8	4 1/8	10	9	28 1/8	1968	34
	■ *Trempealeau County / Dennis L. Ulberg / Dennis L. Ulberg*										
204 7/8	26 3/8	26 4/8	21 4/8	26 6/8	4 5/8	4 6/8	6	8	18 5/8	1960	35
	■ *Trempealeau County / Ralph Klimek / Ralph Klimek*										
204 3/8	23 4/8	24	20 4/8	28 7/8	5 5/8	5 6/8	10	12	44 1/8	PR1975	36
	■ *Waukesha County / Unknown / Mac's Taxidermy*										
202 7/8	25 1/8	24 2/8	23 7/8	26 4/8	5	5	7	10	38	1932	37
	■ *Marinette County / Theodore Maes / Theodore Maes*										
202 5/8	29	29 3/8	20 6/8	22 7/8	4 7/8	4 7/8	10	9	16 1/8	1964	38
	■ *Dane County / Ray S. Outhouse / Ray S. Outhouse*										
202	26 3/8	27	22 5/8	25	6 1/8	6 1/8	6	9	21 3/8	1960	39
	■ *Bayfield County / Indian / Richard Wanasek*										
200 7/8	23	23 7/8	19	26	4 7/8	4 6/8	11	9	33 1/8	1963	40
	■ *Rusk County / Gerald Cleven / Gerald Cleven*										
200 6/8	24 1/8	24 3/8	17 6/8	21 1/8	5	5	11	9	45	1946	41
	■ *Juneau County / Anchor Nelson / J. D. Andrews*										
199 5/8	29	27 7/8	19 4/8	22	6 3/8	6 1/8	8	6	15 7/8	1968	42
	■ *Jefferson County / Jerome Stockheimer / Jerome Stockheimer*										
199	22 7/8	21	17 7/8	22	5 3/8	5	13	7	64 7/8	1946	43
	■ *Clark County / George Mashin / Douglas Wampole*										
198 5/8	24 2/8	24 2/8	17 7/8	20 4/8	5 4/8	6 4/8	9	15	27	PR1920	44
	■ *Hayward / Unknown / Harold Burrows*										
198 5/8	25 3/8	25 2/8	23 2/8	25 4/8	5	5	10	10	33 7/8	1977	44
	■ *Oconto County / Paul M. Krueger / Paul M. Krueger*										
197 5/8	24 4/8	24 1/8	20 3/8	24	6 2/8	5 1/8	7	11	41	1945	46
	■ *Sawyer County / James Borman / James Borman*										
196 6/8	22 2/8	22 5/8	17 5/8	21 6/8	5	5	8	8	18 1/8	1934	47
	■ *Vilas County / Joe Wilfer / Rick Iacono*										
196	26 4/8	25 6/8	18 7/8	21 2/8	5	5 2/8	6	7	22 3/8	1970	48
	■ *Buffalo County / William A. Gatzlaff / William A. Gatzlaff*										
195 7/8	27 1/8	25 2/8	20 2/8	23 2/8	5 2/8	5 2/8	11	10	18 7/8	1973	49
	■ *Grant County / Roger Derrickson / Roger Derrickson*										

WISCONSIN NON-TYPICAL WHITETAILS *(continued)*

Score	Length of Main Beam R	L	Inside Spread	Greatest Spread	Circumference at Smallest Place Between Burr and First Point R	L	Number of Points R	L	Total of Lengths Abnormal Points	Date Killed	Rank
	■ *Locality Killed / By Whom Killed / Owner*										
195 2/8	28 4/8	27 2/8	20 5/8	24 4/8	4 7/8	4 6/8	11	8	15 3/8	1959	50
	■ *Du Charme Coulee / Eugene E. Morovitz / Eugene E. Morovitz*										
195 2/8	26	24 6/8	19 2/8	21 4/8	6 2/8	6 3/8	9	9	19 4/8	1890	50
	■ *Rusk County / Alexander King / Roger King*										
237 5/8	25 3/8	25 1/8	18 2/8	24 4/8	5 1/8	5	15	12	44 1/8	1980	*
	■ *Sawyer County / David D. Sprangers / David D. Sprangers*										

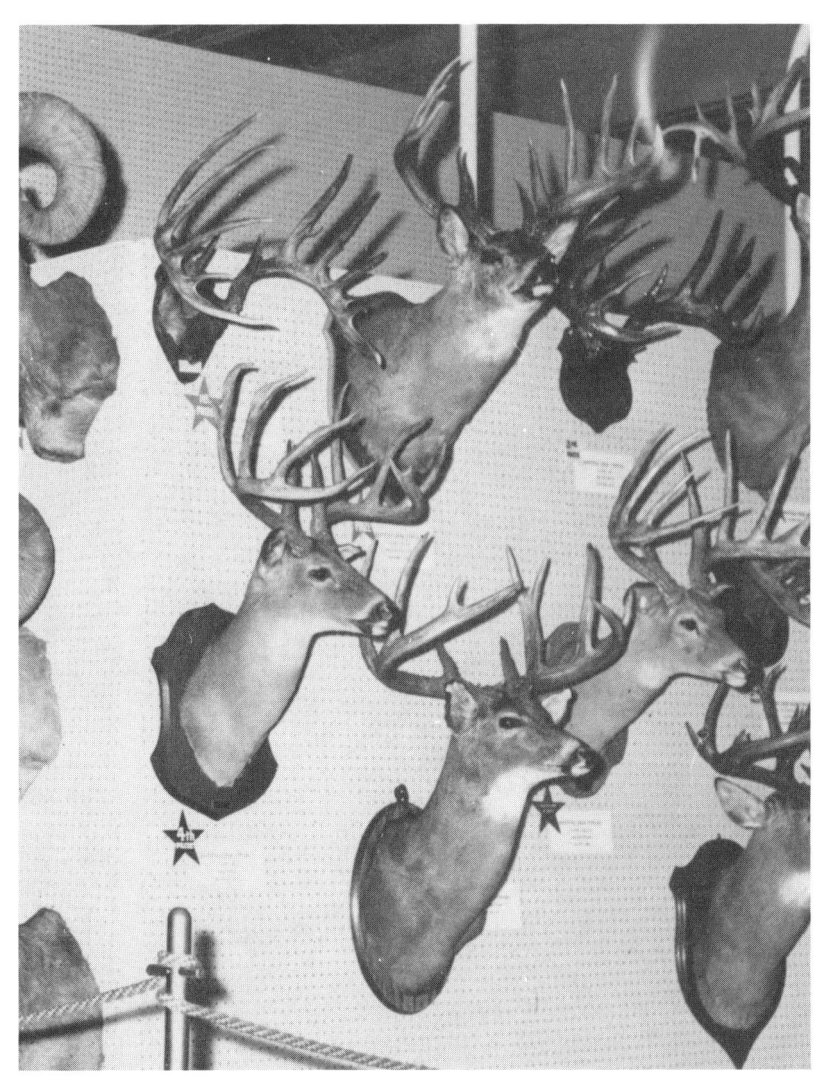

Photo from Boone and Crockett Club Archives

A portion of the trophy display at the 11th Competition (1962-1963). Whitetails displayed include: (from top, l-r) E. McMaster's typical 191-5/8 taken in Flathead County, Montana, in 1963; A. McCullough's typical 181-4/8 taken in Licking County, Ohio, in 1962; A. Smith's typical 181 taken near Stettler, Alberta, in 1962; T. Neal's typical 180 taken in Desha County, Arkansas, in 1962; J. O. Engebretson's typical 175-4/8 taken in Jo Daviess County, Illinois, in 1963.

Photo Courtesy of H. W. Julien

WYOMING STATE RECORD
TYPICAL ANTLERS
SCORE: 177 1/8

Locality: Newcastle   Date: November 1954
Hunter: H. W. Julien

WYOMING

TYPICAL WHITETAILS

Score	Length of Main Beam R	Length of Main Beam L	Inside Spread	Greatest Spread	Circumference at Smallest Place Between Burr and First Point R	Circumference at Smallest Place Between Burr and First Point L	Number of Points R	Number of Points L	Total of Lengths Abnormal Points	Date Killed	Rank
177 1/8	25 5/8	26 1/8	19	21 5/8	5 1/8	5 2/8	7	10	9 1/8	1954	1
■ Newcastle / H. W. Julien / H. W. Julien											
174 3/8	25 2/8	25 3/8	20 1/8	23 1/8	4 5/8	4 6/8	5	5	0	1984	2
■ Goshen County / Casey L. Hunter / Casey L. Hunter											
170 3/8	23 1/8	23 2/8	19 5/8	21 2/8	4 6/8	4 5/8	6	6	0	1985	3
■ Niobrara County / Joseph A. Perry III / Joseph A. Perry III											

Photo Courtesy of J. D. Andrews

WYOMING STATE RECORD
NON-TYPICAL ANTLERS
SCORE: 238 7/8

Locality: Crook Co.   Date: November 1962
Hunter: Unknown
Owner: J. D. Andrews

WYOMING

NON-TYPICAL WHITETAILS

Score	Length of Main Beam R	L	Inside Spread	Greatest Spread	Circumference at Smallest Place Between Burr and First Point R	L	Number of Points R	L	Total of Lengths Abnormal Points	Date Killed	Rank
238 7/8	22 4/8	21 6/8	18 1/8	21 4/8	5	5 2/8	17	15	68	1962	1
■ Crook County / Unknown / J. D. Andrews											
224 1/8	25	24 7/8	19 6/8	28 2/8	4 5/8	4 3/8	12	13	37 5/8	1947	2
■ Crook County / John S. Mahoney / John S. Mahoney											
214 2/8	24 6/8	25 3/8	20 4/8	22 7/8	6 4/8	6 2/8	8	8	33 6/8	1953	3
■ Crook County / Clinton Berry / Clinton Berry											
211 7/8	22	23 2/8	21 4/8	24 6/8	4 4/8	4 4/8	15	15	45 1/8	1971	4
■ Crook County / Curtis U. Nelson / Curtis U. Nelson											
204 2/8	23	23	17 2/8	23 4/8	4 6/8	4 4/8	11	15	44	1956	5
■ Crook County / David Sipe / David Sipe											
202 3/8	23 5/8	25 3/8	16 5/8	19 2/8	4 5/8	4 5/8	11	6	19	1968	6
■ Crook County / Marshall Miller / Marshall Miller											
200 3/8	24 6/8	22 4/8	18	20 3/8	4 3/8	4 4/8	8	10	24 3/8	1967	7
■ Crook County / Paul L. Wolz / Paul L. Wolz											
197 7/8	25	23 2/8	16 5/8	23 6/8	5 1/8	5 1/8	11	11	42 2/8	1973	8
■ Weston County / G. Huls & B. L. Arfmann / Chester S. Jones											
198 4/8	24 2/8	23 1/8	18	20 1/8	5 2/8	5 4/8	13	12	31 6/8	1951	9
■ Cow Creek / Thelma Martens / Thelma Martens											

Photo by Wm. H. Nesbitt

ALBERTA PROVINCE RECORD
TYPICAL ANTLERS
SCORE: 204 2/8

Locality: Beaverdam Creek   Date: October 1967
Hunter: Stephen Jansen

ALBERTA

TYPICAL WHITETAILS

Score	Length of Main Beam R	L	Inside Spread	Greatest Spread	Circumference at Smallest Place Between Burr and First Point R	L	Number of Points R	L	Total of Lengths Abnormal Points	Date Killed	Rank
204 2/8	26 1/8	22 6/8	25 1/8	26 6/8	5 1/8	5 1/8	7	10	6 7/8	1967	1
■ Beaverdam Creek / Stephen Jansen / Stephen Jansen											
190 5/8	22 4/8	23 5/8	19 5/8	22 4/8	4 4/8	4 4/8	7	6	0	1969	2
■ Buffalo Lake / Eugene L. Boll / Eugene L. Boll											
188 4/8	27 2/8	24 5/8	22 2/8	25 2/8	5 6/8	5 5/8	5	5	0	1977	3
■ Metiskow / Norman T. Salminen / Norman T. Salminen											
183	25 6/8	26	21	23	4 6/8	4 5/8	5	5	0	1966	4
■ Red Deer River / Picked Up / Ovar Uggen											
181 7/8	26 4/8	26 2/8	21 3/8	24 1/8	4 6/8	4 6/8	5	5	0	1984	5
■ Hotchkiss / Andy G. Petkus / Andy G. Petkus											
181 4/8	25 4/8	27	22 6/8	25 1/8	5 6/8	5 6/8	6	7	3 6/8	1977	6
■ Pine Lake / Robert Crosby / Robert Crosby											
181	27	26 5/8	20	22 6/8	5 7/8	5 7/8	5	6	1 1/8	1962	7
■ Stettler / Archie Smith / Archie Smith											
180 7/8	25 7/8	25 3/8	17 7/8	21	5 1/8	5 1/8	6	7	9	1981	8
■ Castor / Norman D. Stienwand / Norman D. Stienwand											
180 3/8	27 5/8	26	21 5/8	24 4/8	4 5/8	4 5/8	5	5	0	1964	9
■ Antler Lake / German Wagenseil / German Wagenseil											
180 1/8	24	24 4/8	19 1/8	21 6/8	4 7/8	5	5	7	6	1 2/8	1975	10
■ Vermillion / Ralph M. McDonald / Ralph M. McDonald											
180	26 7/8	26 1/8	20 4/8	23	5 7/8	5 7/8	5	7	1 2/8	1969	11
■ Castor / Kenneth Larson / Kenneth Larson											
179 6/8	29 1/8	28	21	23 5/8	5 6/8	5 5/8	7	6	10 6/8	1977	12
■ Longview / Eldred Umbach / Eldred Umbach											
179 5/8	25 4/8	25 7/8	19 5/8	23	6	6	5	6	1 1/8	1969	13
■ Rumsey / Arley Harder / Arley Harder											

ALBERTA TYPICAL WHITETAILS *(continued)*

Score	Length of Main Beam R	L	Inside Spread	Greatest Spread	Circumference at Smallest Place Between Burr and First Point R	L	Number of Points R	L	Total of Lengths Abnormal Points	Date Killed	Rank
* *Locality Killed / By Whom Killed / Owner*											
179 4/8	23 1/8	23 5/8	19 2/8	22	4 5/8	4 5/8	6	6	0	1969	14
■ *Coronation / Harold McKnight / Harold McKnight*											
178 6/8	27	24 4/8	22 1/8	24 4/8	5 7/8	5 7/8	7	7	4 7/8	1981	15
■ *Breton / George Clark / George Clark*											
178 5/8	24 1/8	24 7/8	20 4/8	23 7/8	4 7/8	5 1/8	6	7	6 5/8	1973	16
■ *Pincher Creek / Unknown / H. Bruce Freeman*											
178 3/8	25 1/8	24 4/8	26 7/8	28 7/8	5 6/8	5 4/8	6	7	2 6/8	1977	17
■ *Hardisty / George R. Walker / George R. Walker*											
177	28 1/8	26 1/8	20 7/8	23 7/8	5 4/8	5 6/8	7	6	5 1/8	1984	18
■ *Innisfree / Donald M. Baranec / Donald M. Baranec*											
176 5/8	26 1/8	25 7/8	21 1/8	25 2/8	6 1/8	6 1/8	6	5	3	1978	19
■ *Buffalo / Bob Fraleigh / Bob Fraleigh*											
175 7/8	27	26 6/8	22 5/8	24 7/8	4 4/8	4 4/8	5	5	0	1984	20
■ *Sundre / Russell D. Holmes / Russell D. Holmes*											
175 1/8	23 5/8	22 7/8	22 3/8	26	5 6/8	5 5/8	5	5	0	1963	21
■ *Chedderville / Larry Trimble / Larry Trimble*											
173 6/8	26 6/8	26 6/8	19 1/8	21 4/8	4 7/8	4 7/8	5	7	3 5/8	1981	22
■ *Minburn / Joseph R. McGillis / Joseph R. McGillis*											
173 5/8	26 2/8	26 4/8	22 5/8	24 5/8	5 2/8	5 2/8	6	7	2 2/8	1952	23
■ *Alberta / Frank Lind / Frank Lind*											
173	24 5/8	24 7/8	16 4/8	19 3/8	5 3/8	5 2/8	5	5	0	1983	24
■ *Bonnyville / Lionel P. Tercier / Lionel P. Tercier*											
173	23 2/8	25 5/8	19 5/8	22 2/8	4 6/8	4 6/8	7	8	6 3/8	1983	24
■ *Bunder Lake / Steve Swinhoe / Steve Swinhoe*											
172 6/8	24 3/8	23 4/8	16 5/8	19 1/8	5	5	7	6	9 7/8	1980	26
■ *Edgerton / Richard T. Abbott / Richard T. Abbott*											
172 4/8	24 4/8	24 3/8	20	22 4/8	5	5	6	6	0	1971	27
■ *Chauvin / Ron D. Jakimchuk / Ron D. Jakimchuk*											
171 4/8	24 5/8	21 7/8	21 3/8	24 7/8	5	4 7/8	8	6	2 5/8	1984	28
■ *Crooked Lake / Bruce J. Ferguson / Bruce J. Ferguson*											
171 4/8	24 6/8	26 1/8	19 2/8	21 5/8	5 2/8	5 1/8	5	5	0	1953	28
■ *Hayter / H. D. L. Loucks / H. D. L. Loucks*											
171 3/8	24 6/8	23 6/8	21 5/8	24 1/8	4 4/8	4 4/8	5	5	0	1977	30
■ *Athabasca River / Ron J. Holm / Ron J. Holm*											
171 1/8	22 6/8	21	18 5/8	20 3/8	5 1/8	5 2/8	6	6	0	1958	31
■ *Medicine Hat / Frank Chevalier / Marcel Houle*											

ALBERTA TYPICAL WHITETAILS (continued)

Score	Length of Main Beam R	L	Inside Spread	Greatest Spread	Circumference at Smallest Place Between Burr and First Point R	L	Number of Points R	L	Total of Lengths Abnormal Points	Date Killed	Rank
171	24 5/8	23 6/8	21	24 6/8	5	5	5	5	0	1968	32
■ Seven Persons / Haven Lane / Haven Lane
170 7/8	26 4/8	27 4/8	21 1/8	23 7/8	5 6/8	5 2/8	5	5	0	1971	33
■ Kingman / Robert D. Kozack / Robert D. Kozack
170 2/8	25 1/8	26	20 4/8	22 5/8	6 1/8	6 7/8	5	5	0	1984	34
■ Ribstone Creek / David H. Crum / David H. Crum
170 1/8	20 6/8	21 4/8	16 7/8	19 5/8	4 5/8	4 5/8	6	5	0	1980	35
■ Smoky River / Bernie Reiswig / Bernie Reiswig
170 1/8	24 3/8	24 2/8	18 1/8	20 3/8	4 4/8	4 2/8	5	5	0	1971	35
■ Pincher Creek / Dave Simpson / Dave Simpson

Photo by Wm. H. Nesbitt

ALBERTA PROVINCE RECORD
NON-TYPICAL ANTLERS
SCORE: 277 5/8
Locality: Hardisty   Date: November 1976
Hunter: Doug Klinger

ALBERTA

NON-TYPICAL WHITETAILS

Score	Length of Main Beam R	Length of Main Beam L	Inside Spread	Greatest Spread	Circumference at Smallest Place Between Burr and First Point R	Circumference at Smallest Place Between Burr and First Point L	Number of Points R	Number of Points L	Total of Lengths Abnormal Points	Date Killed	Rank
277 5/8	27 5/8	28 4/8	24 6/8	30	6	6 1/8	17	16	93 1/8	1976	1

■ Hardisty / Doug Klinger / Doug Klinger

| 255 4/8 | 23 2/8 | 22 7/8 | 18 1/8 | 27 2/8 | 5 6/8 | 5 5/8 | 18 | 15 | 61 7/8 | 1973 | 2 |

■ Pigeon Lake / Leo Eklund / Leo Eklund

| 241 1/8 | 26 4/8 | 26 1/8 | 18 1/8 | 25 4/8 | 6 1/8 | 6 | 19 | 18 | 74 | 1984 | 3 |

■ Bighill Creek / Donald D. Dwernychuk / Donald D. Dwernychuk

| 233 2/8 | 26 7/8 | 26 2/8 | 24 6/8 | 28 | 4 3/8 | 4 5/8 | 9 | 9 | 39 4/8 | 1973 | 4 |

■ Acadia Valley / James J. Niwa / James J. Niwa

| 231 6/8 | 26 1/8 | 25 3/8 | 23 2/8 | 26 1/8 | 6 | 6 1/8 | 11 | 13 | 44 | 1978 | 5 |

■ Peace River / Terry Doll / Terry Doll

| 230 6/8 | 27 5/8 | 27 2/8 | 19 3/8 | 29 | 5 7/8 | 6 | 14 | 16 | 52 5/8 | 1973 | 6 |

■ Red Deer / Delmer E. Johnson / Delmer E. Johnson

| 222 5/8 | 24 6/8 | 23 7/8 | 18 5/8 | 24 4/8 | 5 1/8 | 5 5/8 | 9 | 9 | 26 2/8 | 1964 | 7 |

■ Edgerton / Nick Leskow / Russell Thornberry

| 221 6/8 | 23 2/8 | 25 7/8 | 21 5/8 | 25 6/8 | 5 5/8 | 5 5/8 | 13 | 10 | 55 3/8 | 1984 | 8 |

■ Snipe Lake / Robert Dickson, Sr. / Robert Dickson, Sr.

| 213 4/8 | 26 3/8 | 23 3/8 | 18 6/8 | 22 5/8 | 6 1/8 | 6 4/8 | 12 | 11 | 42 | 1973 | 9 |

■ Rochester / Lamar A. Windberg / Lamar A. Windberg

| 211 2/8 | 23 2/8 | 24 4/8 | 16 5/8 | 28 7/8 | 5 7/8 | 5 7/8 | 10 | 9 | 44 2/8 | 1966 | 10 |

■ Hughenden / Morris Sather / Morris Sather

| 208 2/8 | 26 5/8 | 24 | 19 3/8 | 24 1/8 | 5 3/8 | 7 3/8 | 10 | 10 | 41 1/8 | PR1981 | 11 |

■ Chauvin / Picked Up / Shane Hansen

| 207 7/8 | 26 5/8 | 26 | 24 2/8 | 26 6/8 | 5 1/8 | 5 4/8 | 7 | 9 | 26 1/8 | 1979 | 12 |

■ Monitor / Raymond Worobo / Raymond Worobo

| 207 5/8 | 25 4/8 | 25 4/8 | 21 2/8 | 25 7/8 | 6 | 6 | 11 | 7 | 16 5/8 | PR1970 | 13 |

■ Keephills / Unknown / William J. Greenhough

ALBERTA NON-TYPICAL WHITETAILS *(continued)*

Score	Length of Main Beam R	Length of Main Beam L	Inside Spread	Greatest Spread	Circumference at Smallest Place Between Burr and First Point R	Circumference at Smallest Place Between Burr and First Point L	Number of Points R	Number of Points L	Total of Lengths Abnormal Points	Date Killed	Rank
■ *Locality Killed / By Whom Killed / Owner*											
207 2/8	27 1/8	26 5/8	18 3/8	20 6/8	5 2/8	5 1/8	7	10	23 5/8	1977	14
■ *Drayton Valley / Hassib Halabi / Hassib Halabi*											
207 1/8	25 7/8	24 3/8	20 6/8	23 4/8	5 1/8	5 2/8	9	10	40 3/8	1977	15
■ *Provost / Michael D. Kerley / Michael D. Kerley*											
204 6/8	26 7/8	25 7/8	21 1/8	24 2/8	5 1/8	5	6	8	31 3/8	1977	16
■ *Innisfree / Donald Baranec / Donald Baranec*											
204 2/8	25 5/8	23 1/8	17 1/8	23 1/8	5 1/8	5 4/8	7	15	76 3/8	1980	17
■ *Silver Lake / Edwin Nelson / Gary Padleski*											
204	27 2/8	25 2/8	21 7/8	24 3/8	5 2/8	5 3/8	7	12	55 1/8	1966	18
■ *Sheep River / Walter L. Brown / Walter L. Brown*											
201 7/8	24 2/8	23 3/8	23 4/8	26 2/8	5 4/8	5 4/8	9	7	23 3/8	1964	19
■ *Burmis / Joe Tapay / Joe Tapay*											
201 5/8	25	24 7/8	17 1/8	21 2/8	5 2/8	5 1/8	10	8	28	1976	20
■ *Ohaton / Curtis Siegfried / Curtis Siegfried*											
201	25 7/8	26 4/8	20 3/8	24 3/8	4 4/8	4 5/8	9	13	23 7/8	1966	21
■ *Cessford / Russell C. Chapman / Russell C. Chapman*											
200 4/8	25 1/8	22 4/8	19 6/8	25 3/8	6 1/8	6	10	10	29	1968	22
■ *Wainwright / Paul Pryor / Paul Pryor*											
199 6/8	23 2/8	24	17 4/8	20 4/8	5 1/8	5 3/8	8	9	30 2/8	1979	23
■ *Rochester / James Weismantel / James Weismantel*											
199	24 7/8	27 2/8	19 7/8	25	5	5	8	7	23 1/8	1984	24
■ *Westaskiwin / John Miller / John Miller*											
197 4/8	25 5/8	26 4/8	25 5/8	31	5	5	11	7	41 3/8	1967	25
■ *Wainwright / George Bauman / George Bauman*											
195 6/8	24 2/8	24 6/8	18 3/8	20 5/8	5 1/8	5	7	7	18 1/8	1972	26
■ *Wetaskiwin / Lewis D. Callies / Lewis D. Callies*											
195 5/8	25 4/8	25 6/8	19 1/8	21 2/8	5	5 2/8	8	8	21	1980	27
■ *Duffield / Robert A. Schaefer / Robert A. Schaefer*											
195 3/8	25 2/8	26 3/8	20 1/8	25 3/8	5 3/8	5 2/8	11	8	26	1980	28
■ *Grassland / Frederick Neuhmann / Frederick Neuhmann*											
267 7/8	25	24 4/8	22 6/8	29 2/8	6 1/8	6 2/8	20	18	95 3/8	1984	*
■ *Shoal Lake / Jerry Froma / Jerry Froma*											

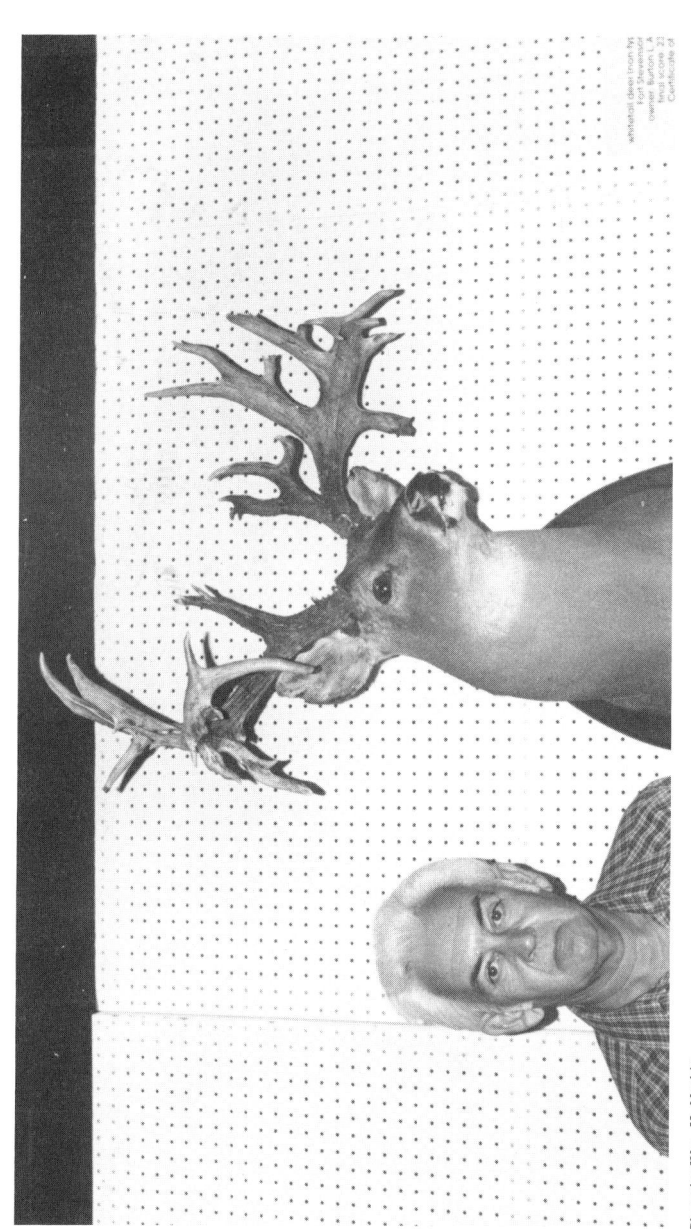

Photo by Wm. H. Nesbitt

Mark T. Hathcock with the 28-pointer that he took in 1978 while hunting in Carroll County, Mississippi. Mark's massive buck, which scores 217-5/8 points, took the Second Place Award in the non-typical category at the 17th Awards (1977-1979).

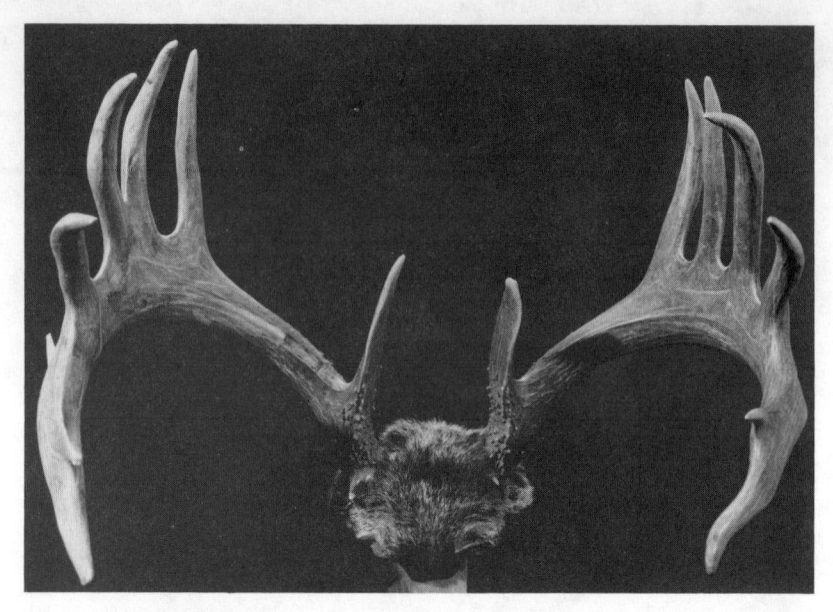

Photo Courtesy of Frank Gowing

BRITISH COLUMBIA PROVINCE RECORD
TYPICAL ANTLERS
SCORE: 177 7/8

Locality: Ymir   Date: November 1961
Hunter: Frank Gowing

BRITISH COLUMBIA
TYPICAL WHITETAILS

Score	Length of Main Beam R	L	Inside Spread	Greatest Spread	Circumference at Smallest Place Between Burr and First Point R	L	Number of Points R	L	Total of Lengths Abnormal Points	Date Killed	Rank
\> Locality Killed / By Whom Killed / Owner											
177 7/8	24 2/8	23 7/8	19 3/8	22 1/8	4 6/8	4 4/8	7	7	0	1961	1
■ Ymir / Frank Gowing / Frank Gowing											
174 5/8	26	26 2/8	21 1/8	23 3/8	5 3/8	5 3/8	5	6	2	1978	2
■ Baldonnel / D. Ian Williams / D. Ian Williams											
174 4/8	22 5/8	24 1/8	16 6/8	19 1/8	4 5/8	4 6/8	5	5	0	1958	3
■ Fort Steele / John Lum / John Lum											
174 1/8	26 4/8	26 3/8	20	23 6/8	5 1/8	5	6	6	2 7/8	1980	4
■ Anarchist Mt. / George Urban / George Urban											
173 6/8	24 5/8	24 4/8	23 1/8	27 2/8	5 2/8	5 4/8	5	5	0	1984	5
■ Hart Creek / Greg Lamontange / Greg Lamontange											
171 6/8	24 4/8	23 2/8	19 4/8	21 5/8	4 5/8	4 5/8	10	8	8 4/8	1982	6
■ Gray Creek / Ross Oliver / Ross Oliver											
171	25 2/8	25 4/8	19 2/8	22 4/8	4 7/8	4 7/8	5	6	1 6/8	1984	7
■ Okanagan Range / Picked Up / Dennis A. Dorholt											
170 3/8	25 3/8	25 3/8	26 3/8	28 3/8	5 1/8	5 2/8	5	6	0	1957	8
■ Whatshan Lake / Ernest Roberts / Ernest Roberts											

Photo Courtesy of Karl H. Kast

BRITISH COLUMBIA SECOND PLACE
NON-TYPICAL ANTLERS
SCORE: 218

Locality: West Kootenay   Date: 1940
Hunter: Karl H. Kast

BRITISH COLUMBIA

NON-TYPICAL WHITETAILS

Score	Length of Main Beam R	L	Inside Spread	Greatest Spread	Circumference at Smallest Place Between Burr and First Point R	L	Number of Points R	L	Total of Lengths Abnormal Points	Date Killed	Rank
* Locality Killed / By Whom Killed / Owner												
245 7/8	31 2/8	27 6/8	25 3/8	35 6/8	5 5/8	5 6/8	11	14	54 2/8	1905	1
■ Elk River / James I. Brewster / James I. Brewster												
218	25	27 1/8	19 3/8	24	5 2/8	5	11	12	45 1/8	1940	2
■ West Kootenay / Karl H. Kast / Karl H. Kast												
205 5/8	25 4/8	26 1/8	22 5/8	24 7/8	5	5	10	12	33 2/8	1980	3
■ Midway / Gordon Kamigochi / Gordon Kamigochi												
202 2/8	25 1/8	24 7/8	19 2/8	24 2/8	4 6/8	4 7/8	9	9	25 2/8	1956	4
■ East Kooteney / Andrew W. Rosicky / Andrew W. Rosicky												
198 1/8	21 7/8	21 2/8	17	21	4 7/8	5	13	12	43 3/8	1935	5
■ Nelway / Edward John / Edward John												

Photo Courtesy of Arnold W. Poole

MANITOBA PROVINCE RECORD
TYPICAL ANTLERS
SCORE: 179 3/8

Locality: Oberon   Date: November 1968
Hunter: Arnold W. Poole

MANITOBA

TYPICAL WHITETAILS

Score	Length of Main Beam R	L	Inside Spread	Greatest Spread	Circumference at Smallest Place Between Burr and First Point R	L	Number of Points R	L	Total of Lengths Abnormal Points	Date Killed	Rank
179 3/8	26	26 2/8	17 3/8	22	6	5 5/8	6	6	7	1968	1
■ Oberon / Arnold W. Poole / Arnold W. Poole
179	25 6/8	25 6/8	19 3/8	21 6/8	5	5 1/8	5	6	2 1/8	1959	2
■ Waldersee / Wm. Wutke / Wm. Wutke
178 6/8	26	25	22 7/8	25 1/8	5 2/8	5 1/8	6	6	2 3/8	1959	3
■ Elkhorn / Jerry May / Jerry May
176 7/8	25 4/8	26	19 7/8	0	5 5/8	5 4/8	5	5	0	1960	4
■ Pierson / Bud Smith / Bud Smith
176 3/8	25	25 1/8	17 5/8	21	4 5/8	5 1/8	6	5	0	1977	5
■ Stockton / Robert R. Blain / Robert R. Blain
176 1/8	25 1/8	23 7/8	24 1/8	25 6/8	5 5/8	5 5/8	5	6	0	1984	6
■ Assiniboine River / G. G. Graham / G. G. Graham
174 7/8	26 5/8	25	22 6/8	25 3/8	5 3/8	5 4/8	6	9	9 3/8	1954	7
■ Rivers / N. Manchur / N. Manchur
173 6/8	25	25 3/8	22 4/8	25	5 1/8	5	5	5	0	1967	8
■ McAuley / Alex D. Vallance / Alex D. Vallance
173 4/8	24 7/8	23 6/8	17	19 4/8	5 6/8	5 7/8	7	6	5 2/8	1962	9
■ Clover Leaf / Walter Lucko / Walter Lucko
172 5/8	25 1/8	24 5/8	19 1/8	22 1/8	5 7/8	5 6/8	7	5	6 2/8	1967	10
■ Shoal Lake / Gary Phillips / Gary Phillips
172	24 4/8	23 6/8	17	20 2/8	5 2/8	5 4/8	5	5	0	1947	11
■ Neepawa / Jim Sinclair / Jim Sinclair
171 6/8	24 6/8	24 6/8	19	21 4/8	5 2/8	5 1/8	5	5	0	1963	12
■ Turtle Mt. / Roy Hainsworth / Roy Hainsworth
171 1/8	26	26 3/8	21 6/8	23 7/8	5	4 7/8	11	6	16 2/8	1961	13
■ Woodlands District / Bill Rutherford / Bill Rutherford

MANITOBA TYPICAL WHITETAILS *(continued)*

Score	Length of Main Beam R	L	Inside Spread	Greatest Spread	Circumference at Smallest Place Between Burr and First Point R	L	Number of Points R	L	Total of Lengths Abnormal Points	Date Killed	Rank
* Locality Killed / By Whom Killed / Owner												
170 6/8	24	24	21 2/8	24	5	5 1/8	6	6	0	1963	14
■ *Arnes / T. Litwin / T. Litwin*												
170 3/8	26 3/8	26	20 3/8	23 3/8	5 2/8	5	5	5	0	1967	15
■ *Portage La Prairie / Robert Boyachek / Robert Boyachek*												
170	26 4/8	27	23	25 1/8	6 1/8	6 1/8	5	5	0	1951	16
■ *Virden / Jessie Byer / Jessie Byer*												

Photo Courtesy of Gary E. Landry

Gary E. Landry poses with a very fine typical he took with a bow in Wayne County, Ohio, in 1975. Scoring 182-7/8 points, this buck was an entry in the 16th Awards (1974-1976).

Photo by Wm. H. Nesbitt

MANITOBA PROVINCE RECORD
NON-TYPICAL ANTLERS
SCORE: 257 3/8

Locality: Elkhorn   Date: November 1973
Hunter: Harvey Olsen

MANITOBA

NON-TYPICAL WHITETAILS

Score	Length of Main Beam R	Length of Main Beam L	Inside Spread	Greatest Spread	Circumference at Smallest Place Between Burr and First Point R	Circumference at Smallest Place Between Burr and First Point L	Number of Points R	Number of Points L	Total of Lengths Abnormal Points	Date Killed	Rank
▪ *Locality Killed / By Whom Killed / Owner*											
257 3/8	25 5/8	23 5/8	16 2/8	27 4/8	4 6/8	4 4/8	21	17	73 7/8	1973	1
▪ *Elkhorn / Harvey Olsen / Harvey Olsen*											
237 3/8	24 2/8	23 7/8	20 2/8	25 5/8	5 4/8	5 4/8	12	16	59 1/8	1925	2
▪ *Whiteshell / Angus McVicar / Angus McVicar*											
231 3/8	28	28 4/8	26 1/8	29 7/8	6 6/8	6 3/8	9	9	47 4/8	1968	3
▪ *Holland / Wm. Ireland / J. D. Andrews*											
214 7/8	25 2/8	24 4/8	24 3/8	29 2/8	4 6/8	4 6/8	9	12	35 2/8	1954	4
▪ *Aweme / Criddle Bros. / Criddle Bros.*											
208 1/8	25 7/8	24 5/8	19 6/8	21 7/8	4 6/8	4 4/8	8	8	46 3/8	1946	5
▪ *Griswold / J. V. Parker / J. V. Parker*											
197	23 4/8	24 2/8	19 4/8	24	5	5	11	9	44 4/8	1946	6
▪ *Oak River / Sam Henry / J. J. Henry*											

Photo Courtesy of Bill Hanson

NEW BRUNSWICK SECOND PLACE
TYPICAL ANTLERS
SCORE: 178 3/8

Locality: Queens Co.   Date: November 1970
Hunter: Bert Bourque

NEW BRUNSWICK

TYPICAL WHITETAILS

Score	Length of Main Beam R	L	Inside Spread	Greatest Spread	Circumference at Smallest Place Between Burr and First Point R	L	Number of Points R	L	Total of Lengths Abnormal Points	Date Killed	Rank
* Locality Killed / By Whom Killed / Owner												
180 6/8	31 6/8	31 2/8	19 4/8	23 2/8	6	5 5/8	6	8	15 6/8	1937	1
■ New Brunswick / Unknown / Acad. Nat. Sci., Phil.												
178 3/8	27	27 3/8	17 5/8	20 2/8	4 3/8	4 4/8	5	7	1 2/8	1970	2
■ Queens County / Bert Bourque / Bert Bourque												
176 4/8	24 6/8	24 5/8	19 4/8	21 2/8	4 5/8	4 5/8	6	7	2 6/8	1960	3
■ Charlotte County / Albert E. Dewar / Albert E. Dewar												
172	27 3/8	28 3/8	18 2/8	20 1/8	5	5 1/8	5	5	0	1983	4
■ Westmoreland County / Edgar Cormier / Edgar Cormier												
171 5/8	25 4/8	26 5/8	19 3/8	21 5/8	5 5/8	5 6/8	7	7	0	1984	5
■ Bonnell Brook / Steve R. McCutcheon / Steve R. McCutcheon												

Photo Courtesy of Charles T. Arnold

NEW BRUNSWICK PROVINCE RECORD
NON-TYPICAL ANTLERS
SCORE: 243 7/8

Locality: Wirral   Date: October 1962
Hunter: H. Glenn Johnston
Owner: Arnold Alward

NEW BRUNSWICK

NON-TYPICAL WHITETAILS

Score	Length of Main Beam R	L	Inside Spread	Greatest Spread	Circumference at Smallest Place Between Burr and First Point R	L	Number of Points R	L	Total of Lengths Abnormal Points	Date Killed	Rank
243 7/8	26 7/8	26 3/8	16 2/8	27 7/8	8 2/8	8 2/8	18	15	67 7/8	1962	1
■ Wirral / H. Glenn Johnston / Arnold Alward												
242 2/8	24 3/8	21 5/8	20 5/8	28 4/8	6 1/8	6 5/8	18	14	83 5/8	1958	2
■ Auburnville / John L. MacKenzie / Arnold Alward												
239 1/8	24 2/8	24 1/8	18 6/8	24 5/8	6 1/8	5 6/8	20	14	68 1/8		3
■ New Brunswick / Unknown / Johnny M. Hollier												
224 2/8	26 4/8	27 6/8	20 5/8	27 7/8	5	5 1/8	11	11	40 1/8	1966	4
■ Salmon River / Ford Fulton / McLean Bowman												
204 1/8	28 5/8	25 7/8	22 2/8	31 4/8	5 7/8	6 1/8	12	9	32 5/8	1984	5
■ Charlotte County / Gary L. Lister / Gary L. Lister												
203 6/8	28	27 3/8	20	29 4/8	5 1/8	5 3/8	7	10	21 6/8	1903	6
■ George Lake / Henry Kirk / Ron Kirk												
196 4/8	25 1/8	25 4/8	17 7/8	23 7/8	4 7/8	5 1/8	9	12	53 5/8	1959	7
■ Charlotte County / Clayton Tatton / J. D. Andrews												

Photo Courtesy of Charles T. Arnold

NOVA SCOTIA PROVINCE RECORD
NON-TYPICAL ANTLERS
SCORE: 253

Locality: Goldenville   Date: November 1945
Hunter: Neil MacDonald
Owner: Dick Idol

NOVA SCOTIA

NON-TYPICAL WHITETAILS

Score	Length of Main Beam R	Length of Main Beam L	Inside Spread	Greatest Spread	Circumference at Smallest Place Between Burr and First Point R	Circumference at Smallest Place Between Burr and First Point L	Number of Points R	Number of Points L	Total of Lengths Abnormal Points	Date Killed	Rank
* Locality Killed / By Whom Killed / Owner
253	28	28	21 4/8	27 4/8	5 5/8	5 6/8	14	26	69 4/8	1945	1
■ Goldenville / Neil MacDonald / Dick Idol
222 1/8	24 2/8	25 6/8	20 6/8	32 7/8	5 6/8	5 3/8	16	10	49 6/8	1949	2
■ Ostrea Lake / Verden M. Baker / C. L. Gage
200 1/8	26	24 2/8	23	25 2/8	6	6	11	12	56 3/8	1960	3
■ Parrsboro / Allison Smith / Edward B. Shaw
196	28 7/8	30 4/8	25 1/8	28 3/8	5 4/8	5 2/8	12	10	29 5/8	1984	4
■ Annapolis Valley / David Cabral / David Cabral

Photo Courtesy of Richard Kouhi

ONTARIO PROVINCE RECORD
TYPICAL ANTLERS
SCORE: 171 2/8
Locality: Macintosh Date: November 1967
Hunter: Richard Kouhi

ONTARIO

TYPICAL WHITETAILS

Score	Length of Main Beam R	L	Inside Spread	Greatest Spread	Circumference at Smallest Place Between Burr and First Point R	L	Number of Points R	L	Total of Lengths Abnormal Points	Date Killed	Rank
171 2/8	26 2/8	25	22 4/8	25 3/8	5 6/8	5 6/8	5	5	0	1967	1

■ *Locality Killed / By Whom Killed / Owner*

■ Macintosh / Richard Kouhi / Richard Kouhi

Photo by Wm. H. Nesbitt

SASKATCHEWAN PROVINCE RECORD
TYPICAL ANTLERS
SCORE: 200 2/8

Locality: Whitkow   Date: November 1983
Hunter: Peter J. Swistun

SASKATCHEWAN

TYPICAL WHITETAILS

Score	Length of Main Beam R	L	Inside Spread	Greatest Spread	Circumference at Smallest Place Between Burr and First Point R	L	Number of Points R	L	Total of Lengths Abnormal Points	Date Killed	Rank
200 2/8	26 3/8	27 1/8	24	26 5/8	5	4 7/8	6	7	2 2/8	1983	1
■ Whitkow / Peter J. Swistun / Peter J. Swistun												
193 6/8	24 5/8	24 4/8	18 1/8	20 3/8	5	5	7	7	4 1/8	1959	2
■ Christopher Lake / Jerry Thorson / Jerry Thorson												
191 6/8	27	26	19 6/8	21 7/8	4 5/8	4 6/8	5	6	0	1973	3
■ Hudson Bay / George Chalus / George Chalus												
188 4/8	25	26 3/8	22 5/8	24 6/8	4 7/8	4 6/8	5	6	1 1/8	1957	4
■ Burstall / W. P. Rolick / W. P. Rolick												
185 3/8	27 6/8	28	20 5/8	22 6/8	4 7/8	4 7/8	5	5	0	1984	5
■ Canwood / Clark Heimbechner / Clark Heimbechner												
184 6/8	24 1/8	26 1/8	21 2/8	24 1/8	5 3/8	5 4/8	6	6	0	1971	6
■ Dore Lake / Garvis C. Coker / Garvis C. Coker												
182 1/8	25 6/8	25 2/8	22 7/8	25 3/8	5 6/8	5 5/8	5	5	0	1984	7
■ Round Lake / Jesse Bates / Jesse Bates												
181 3/8	25 2/8	24 3/8	21 2/8	23 3/8	5 6/8	5 6/8	7	6	1 1/8	1955	8
■ Southey / A. K. Flaman / Sam Peterson												
181 1/8	27 3/8	27 6/8	20 7/8	23 7/8	6 2/8	5 6/8	10	7	12 2/8	1960	9
■ Empress / Don Leach / Don Leach												
180 3/8	25 6/8	26 3/8	21 5/8	24 5/8	5	5 1/8	7	6	1	1961	10
■ Stoughton / Joe Zbeetnoff / Joe Zbeetnoff												
180 2/8	26 1/8	25	22 5/8	24 4/8	5 4/8	5 2/8	7	7	2 7/8	1959	11
■ Lumsden / Mike Lukas / E. M. Gazda												
180 1/8	23 3/8	23 5/8	17 5/8	20	5 2/8	5 2/8	5	5	0	1956	12
■ Maryfield / Donald Cook / Richard Christoforo												
179 3/8	28 5/8	28	20 7/8	23 2/8	5 6/8	5 6/8	5	5	0	1958	13
■ Parkman / Harold Larsen / Sam Peterson												

SASKATCHEWAN TYPICAL WHITETAILS *(continued)*

Score	Length of Main Beam R	L	Inside Spread	Greatest Spread	Circumference at Smallest Place Between Burr and First Point R	L	Number of Points R	L	Total of Lengths Abnormal Points	Date Killed	Rank
179²⁄₈	27⁵⁄₈	27	20	25¹⁄₈	5⁴⁄₈	5⁶⁄₈	9	9	14	1964	14
■ Cypress Hills / Raymond McCrea / Raymond McCrea											
178⁶⁄₈	27⁵⁄₈	27⁵⁄₈	25⁴⁄₈	27⁵⁄₈	5³⁄₈	5⁴⁄₈	6	5	0	1965	15
■ Windthorst / Clarence E. Genest / Clarence E. Genest											
178⁵⁄₈	27⁷⁄₈	29²⁄₈	26³⁄₈	28⁵⁄₈	5²⁄₈	5²⁄₈	6	7	3²⁄₈	1966	16
■ Debden / Henry Rydde / Henry Rydde											
178⁵⁄₈	28⁷⁄₈	27	24	26⁵⁄₈	5¹⁄₈	5¹⁄₈	7	7	2⁷⁄₈	1957	16
■ Beechy / Archie D. McRae / Archie D. McRae											
177⁶⁄₈	26⁴⁄₈	26⁴⁄₈	18³⁄₈	22⁶⁄₈	5	5¹⁄₈	9	7	11²⁄₈	1979	18
■ Shaunavon / Stan J. Crawford / Stan J. Crawford											
177⁵⁄₈	25⁵⁄₈	26²⁄₈	19¹⁄₈	23²⁄₈	5⁴⁄₈	5³⁄₈	5	5	0	1971	19
■ Endeavour / Terry L. Halgrimson / Terry L. Halgrimson											
177⁴⁄₈	25	24⁴⁄₈	21¹⁄₈	23²⁄₈	5²⁄₈	5⁴⁄₈	5	6	1¹⁄₈	1956	20
■ Dundurn / L. B. Galbraith / L. B. Galbraith											
176⁴⁄₈	23³⁄₈	23⁴⁄₈	22	23⁷⁄₈	5³⁄₈	5⁵⁄₈	6	5	1²⁄₈	1960	21
■ Esterhazy / Albert Kristoff / Albert Kristoff											
176²⁄₈	23	25⁵⁄₈	18⁶⁄₈	21	5	4⁷⁄₈	5	5	0	1959	22
■ Swanson / L. S. Wood / L. S. Wood											
175⁷⁄₈	23	23¹⁄₈	16⁶⁄₈	19²⁄₈	5¹⁄₈	5¹⁄₈	5	5	0	1964	23
■ Hanley / G. Koyl & Wm. King / Gavin Koyl											
175⁶⁄₈	25³⁄₈	26¹⁄₈	19⁶⁄₈	22⁵⁄₈	5³⁄₈	5³⁄₈	5	5	0	1958	24
■ Southey / J. A. Maier / J. A. Maier											
175³⁄₈	26¹⁄₈	25⁴⁄₈	23³⁄₈	26¹⁄₈	5¹⁄₈	5²⁄₈	5	5	0	1958	25
■ Bridgeford / Elgin T. Gates / Elgin T. Gates											
175²⁄₈	28¹⁄₈	28⁶⁄₈	17⁶⁄₈	20⁷⁄₈	5²⁄₈	5²⁄₈	5	6	1	1977	26
■ Val Marie / Leon Perrault / Leon Perrault											
175²⁄₈	24	23⁶⁄₈	19⁶⁄₈	23²⁄₈	5⁴⁄₈	5⁵⁄₈	6	5	2²⁄₈	1965	26
■ Qu'Appelle / Douglas Garden / Douglas Garden											
175¹⁄₈	25⁴⁄₈	24⁵⁄₈	19⁷⁄₈	22⁴⁄₈	5²⁄₈	5¹⁄₈	6	5	0	1981	28
■ Shaunavon / Richard Klink / Richard Klink											
175¹⁄₈	25⁵⁄₈	26⁵⁄₈	22¹⁄₈	25³⁄₈	4⁵⁄₈	4⁵⁄₈	5	5	0	1964	28
■ Gerald / Ken Cherewka / Ken Cherewka											
174	26¹⁄₈	26²⁄₈	20⁴⁄₈	34	5	4⁶⁄₈	7	7	10	1961	30
■ Bulyea / W. H. Dodsworth / E. B. Shaw											
173⁷⁄₈	24⁵⁄₈	23⁷⁄₈	23³⁄₈	25²⁄₈	5¹⁄₈	4⁷⁄₈	8	7	8	1960	31
■ Dundurn / Herb Wilson / Herb Wilson											

SASKATCHEWAN TYPICAL WHITETAILS *(continued)*

Score	Length of Main Beam R	L	Inside Spread	Greatest Spread	Circumference at Smallest Place Between Burr and First Point R	L	Number of Points R	L	Total of Lengths Abnormal Points	Date Killed	Rank
173 6/8	24 1/8	24 1/8	17 6/8	21 1/8	4 6/8	4 6/8	6	6	0	1982	32
■ Regina / Don Wolk / Don Wolk
173 4/8	24 3/8	25	20 1/8	22 6/8	5 2/8	5 3/8	5	6	2 5/8	1964	33
■ Tuffnell / Ed Mattson / Ed Mattson
173 2/8	26 7/8	24 3/8	20 6/8	22 7/8	5 2/8	5	5	5	0	1966	34
■ Antler / Elmer Lowry / Elmer Lowry
173 2/8	25 5/8	25 6/8	21	24	6	5 6/8	8	5	4 6/8	1964	34
■ Whitewood / L. Reichel / L. Reichel
173 2/8	24 3/8	25 3/8	20 6/8	23 7/8	4 5/8	4 6/8	5	5	0	1959	34
■ Bemersyde / R. L. McCullough / R. L. McCullough
173 1/8	24 4/8	25 3/8	16 3/8	19 7/8	4 3/8	4 3/8	5	5	0	1984	37
■ Big Muddy Valley / Lyndon T. Ross / Lyndon T. Ross
173 1/8	25 5/8	24 7/8	19 2/8	22 6/8	5	5	7	7	8 5/8	1962	37
■ Estuary / Melvin J. Anderson / Melvin J. Anderson
173 1/8	23 6/8	24 1/8	20 3/8	24 2/8	5	5	6	5	4	1957	37
■ Marie / King Trew / King Trew
172 7/8	25 6/8	25 5/8	22 5/8	25 6/8	4 7/8	5	6	6	3 4/8	1951	40
■ Windthorst / Jack Glover / Jack Glover
172 5/8	25 4/8	26	22 6/8	25	4 3/8	4 4/8	6	5	1 1/8	1960	41
■ Esterhazy / J. Weise / J. Weise
172 4/8	27 3/8	26 7/8	22 5/8	25 1/8	4 6/8	5 1/8	5	4	2 7/8	1963	42
■ Laird / A. E. Nikkel / A. E. Nikkel
172 3/8	30 1/8	30 3/8	22 3/8	26 4/8	5 4/8	5 4/8	9	9	13 4/8	1985	43
■ Porcupine Plain / Kim Mikkonen / Kim Mikkonen
172 2/8	27 4/8	26 4/8	19 4/8	24 3/8	4 5/8	4 6/8	6	8	15 2/8	1962	44
■ Manor / Albert McConnell / Albert McConnell
172 2/8	26 4/8	25 6/8	20	27 5/8	6	5 6/8	7	7	9 4/8	1958	44
■ Weyburn / Wilfred LaValley / Wilfred LaValley
172	25	26 4/8	21 4/8	23 4/8	5 1/8	5 2/8	5	5	0	1963	46
■ Parkman / A. T. Mair / A. T. Mair
172	24 3/8	24	17 7/8	19 6/8	5 2/8	5 2/8	5	6	1 5/8	1962	46
■ N. Battleford / Dick Napastuk / Dick Napastuk
172	26 2/8	27 1/8	18 5/8	23 3/8	5 5/8	5 5/8	9	8	10 1/8	1959	46
■ Wadena / Edgar Smale / Edgar Smale
171 6/8	25 6/8	25 6/8	18 2/8	20 3/8	4 4/8	4 5/8	5	5	0	1967	49
■ Maple Creek / G. J. Burch / G. J. Burch

235

SASKATCHEWAN TYPICAL WHITETAILS *(continued)*

Score	Length of Main Beam R	Length of Main Beam L	Inside Spread	Greatest Spread	Circumference at Smallest Place Between Burr and First Point R	Circumference at Smallest Place Between Burr and First Point L	Number of Points R	Number of Points L	Total of Lengths Abnormal Points	Date Killed	Rank
■ *Locality Killed / By Whom Killed / Owner*											
171 6/8	27 1/8	26 5/8	21 5/8	25 4/8	4 6/8	5 2/8	6	9	15 1/8	1963	49
■ *Asquith / M. S. Vanin / M. S. Vanin*											
171 5/8	26	25 3/8	24 4/8	25 6/8	4 6/8	4 7/8	7	8	16 5/8	1968	51
■ *Langbank / Thomas K. Grimm / Thomas K. Grimm*											
171 5/8	25 6/8	26 4/8	20 6/8	23 4/8	5 1/8	5 1/8	7	6	1 3/8	1961	51
■ *Hanley / L. R. Libke / L. R. Libke*											
171 3/8	22 5/8	22 4/8	18	21 1/8	5 3/8	5 3/8	7	6	1 3/8	1965	53
■ *Grenfell / George DeMontigny / George DeMontigny*											
171 1/8	23 2/8	23 1/8	20 6/8	23 4/8	5	5 2/8	5	6	1 1/8	1966	54
■ *Whitewood / Wm. Cook / Wm. Cook*											
171	28 1/8	26 7/8	21	23 4/8	4 6/8	4 6/8	5	5	0	1969	55
■ *Speers / Charles E. Strautman / Charles E. Strautman*											
171	23 5/8	26	19 2/8	21 5/8	5 1/8	5 1/8	5	6	0	1961	55
■ *Windthorst / Thomas Dovell / Thomas Dovell*											
170 6/8	23 3/8	23 3/8	19 5/8	22 7/8	4 6/8	4 5/8	5	6	2 1/8	1984	57
■ *Great Sand Hills / Ralph Cervo / Ralph Cervo*											
170 6/8	25 3/8	25 1/8	19 4/8	22 3/8	5 3/8	5 3/8	7	6	6 6/8	1959	57
■ *Gerald / Jerry Norek / Jerry Norek*											
170 6/8	25 2/8	24 4/8	24 2/8	26	4 5/8	4 6/8	6	5	1	1959	57
■ *Elbow / W. H. Crossman / W. H. Crossman*											
170 4/8	24 2/8	24	20 6/8	23 3/8	5 5/8	5 6/8	5	5	0	1965	60
■ *Preeceville / Vernon Hoffman / Vernon Hoffman*											
170 4/8	25 4/8	24 5/8	19 1/8	21 4/8	4 7/8	4 5/8	8	7	10 7/8	1960	60
■ *Craven / Ted Paterson / Ted Paterson*											
170 3/8	27 3/8	26 2/8	25 6/8	27 6/8	5 4/8	5 5/8	5	5	4 3/8	1962	62
■ *Fort Qu'Appelle / L. A. Magnuson / L. A. Magnuson*											
170 2/8	24 3/8	24 7/8	21 6/8	24	4 3/8	4 3/8	6	6	0	1965	63
■ *Avonlea / Doug English / Doug English*											
170 2/8	26 2/8	25 7/8	22	26	5 1/8	5 2/8	7	6	11 6/8	1965	63
■ *Lestock / Zoltan Blaskovich / Zoltan Blaskovich*											
170 2/8	27 2/8	26 6/8	20	22 3/8	5	5 1/8	5	5	0	1959	63
■ *Dafoe / A. Linder / A. Linder*											
170 1/8	23 7/8	22 7/8	16 1/8	18 4/8	5 5/8	5 5/8	7	6	1 4/8	1966	66
■ *Swift Current / Brian Baumann / Brian Baumann*											
190 6/8	27 7/8	27 5/8	22 4/8	25 2/8	5 3/8	5 6/8	5	5	0	1980	*
■ *Pelly / James R. Strelioff / James R. Strelioff*											

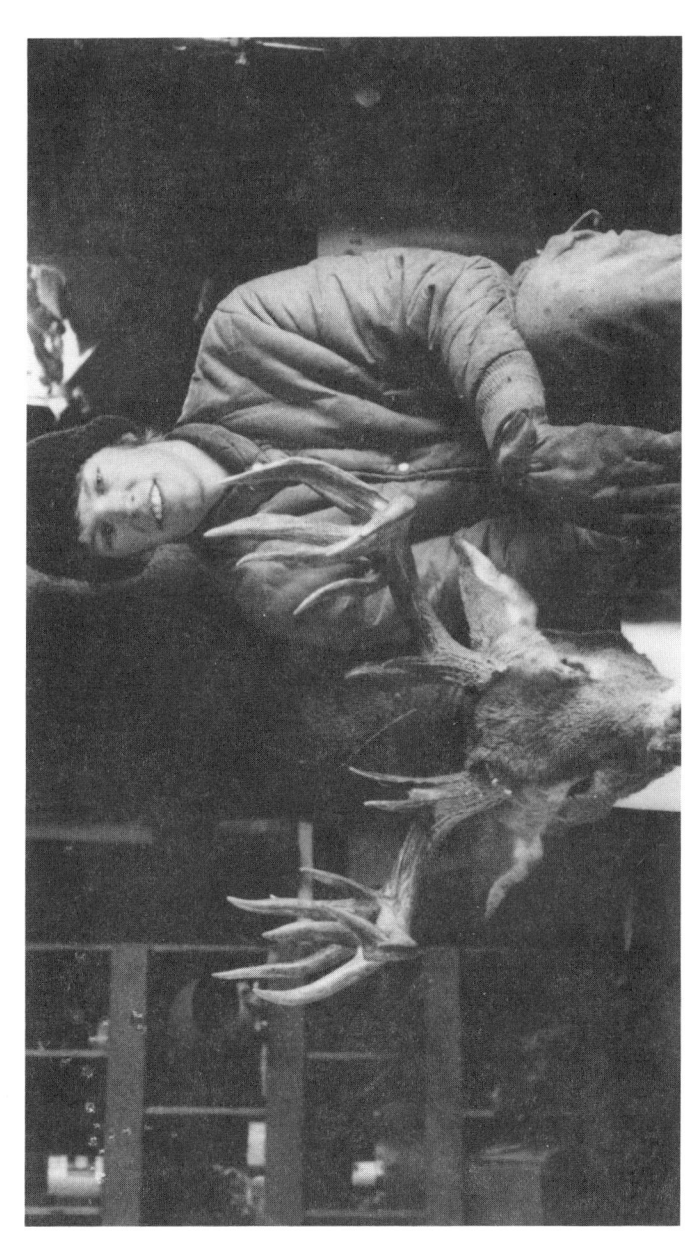

Photo Courtesy of Mark D. Holmes

Mark D. Holmes with the non-typical he took in Rosebud County, Montana, in 1983. Holmes' buck scores 197 points and was an entry in the 19th Awards (1983-1985).

Photo Courtesy of Charles T. Arnold

SASKATCHEWAN PROVINCE RECORD
NON-TYPICAL ANTLERS
SCORE: 265 3/8

Locality: White Fox   Date: November 1957
Hunter: Elburn Kohler
Owner: Charles T. Arnold

SASKATCHEWAN

NON-TYPICAL WHITETAILS

Score	Length of Main Beam R	L	Inside Spread	Greatest Spread	Circumference at Smallest Place Between Burr and First Point R	L	Number of Points R	L	Total of Lengths Abnormal Points	Date Killed	Rank
265 3/8	25 7/8	26	18 3/8	20 4/8	6 6/8	6 5/8	16	17	67 4/8	1957	1
■ White Fox / Elburn Kohler / Charles T. Arnold
248 4/8	22 6/8	24 3/8	22	30 2/8	5 7/8	5 7/8	13	11	87 4/8	1964	2
■ Moose Mtn. Park / Walter Bartko / George Hooey
245 4/8	24 6/8	21 5/8	16 5/8	21 7/8	5 3/8	5	18	12	71 1/8	1962	3
■ Carrot River / Picked Up / Ken Halloway
243 5/8	24 1/8	24 1/8	22 2/8	26	5 1/8	5	11	15	35 3/8	1951	4
■ Govan / A. W. Davis / Sam Peterson
238 1/8	24 2/8	21 7/8	22	25 6/8	5 2/8	5 2/8	13	15	86 1/8	1967	5
■ Whitewood / Jack Davidge / Jack Davidge
236 4/8	24 6/8	25	20 5/8	27 5/8	5 4/8	5	17	12	77 5/8	1959	6
■ Reserve / Harry Nightingale / McLean Bowman
235 4/8	25 4/8	24 5/8	19 6/8	26 6/8	5 4/8	5 7/8	9	20	60 2/8	1958	7
■ Pipestone Valley / E. J. Marshall / E. J. Marshall
233 7/8	27	26 7/8	21 4/8	24	5 5/8	5 3/8	9	14	47 1/8	1961	8
■ Tompkins / Don Stueck / McLean Bowman
233	20 2/8	23 4/8	19 6/8	23	6 4/8	5 2/8	12	7	64 6/8	1968	9
■ Punnichy / Steve Kapay / John L. Stein
231 7/8	24	22 2/8	18	25 3/8	5 5/8	5 4/8	10	20	70 3/8	1954	10
■ Harris / Herman Cox / R. M. Burnett
226 6/8	28 4/8	28 2/8	22 1/8	25 6/8	5 4/8	5 5/8	10	12	23 3/8	1960	11
■ Manor / Stan Balkwill / McLean Bowman
225	25 4/8	25 6/8	21 3/8	23 4/8	5 6/8	6	15	12	48 7/8	1981	12
■ Nipawin / Picked Up / John L. Stein
223 3/8	20 7/8	24 5/8	19	26 3/8	5 5/8	5 3/8	19	12	99 5/8	1960	13
■ Cochin / Vic Pearsall / Vic Pearsall

SASKATCHEWAN NON-TYPICAL WHITETAILS *(continued)*

Score	Length of Main Beam R	L	Inside Spread	Greatest Spread	Circumference at Smallest Place Between Burr and First Point R	L	Number of Points R	L	Total of Lengths Abnormal Points	Date Killed	Rank
222 5/8	27	25 5/8	19 2/8	0	5 3/8	5 7/8	9	12	35 3/8	1952	14
■ Mair / R. A. McGill / Mr. & Mrs. Murray Melom											
218 3/8	20 7/8	24 3/8	19 3/8	28 2/8	4 6/8	5	13	15	80 6/8	1958	15
■ South Goodeve / Fred Bohay / Fred Bohay											
217 7/8	23 3/8	23 1/8	19	26	5 3/8	5 2/8	11	11	45 4/8	1957	16
■ Sprucehome / Tom Pillar / Tom Pillar											
216 2/8	23 5/8	24	18 4/8	23 4/8	4 4/8	4 4/8	10	8	41 4/8	1961	17
■ Buchanan / Mike Spezrivka / Linda Christoforo											
213 7/8	27 3/8	25 3/8	16 5/8	21	5 3/8	5 3/8	12	8	27	1966	18
■ Bresaylor / Barry Braun / Barry Braun											
213	25 7/8	24 1/8	20 6/8	0	5 4/8	5 6/8	5	15	56	1966	19
■ Rush Lake / Jim Runzer / Murray Bromley											
212 5/8	24 6/8	25 2/8	17 5/8	20 4/8	5	5	11	13	32 3/8	1984	20
■ Glentworth / Garnet Fortnum / Garnet Fortnum											
211 7/8	25 6/8	26 3/8	24 1/8	29 1/8	6	5 7/8	14	11	39 4/8	1951	21
■ Raymore / Adolf Wulff / Adolf Wulff											
211 5/8	28 2/8	28 4/8	23	29 4/8	5 7/8	6	11	11	40 3/8	1981	22
■ Glaslyn / Carl R. Frohaug / Carl R. Frohaug											
211 3/8	24 7/8	25 2/8	16 6/8	21 5/8	5 6/8	5 6/8	11	10	24 7/8	1972	23
■ Borden / Leonard Verishine / Leonard Verishine											
210	26	26 1/8	18	22 4/8	5 5/8	5 4/8	10	9	23	1955	24
■ Glenewen / H. Frew / H. Frew											
209 7/8	25 2/8	24 1/8	22 4/8	25	4 6/8	4 5/8	9	9	39 1/8	1967	25
■ Maryfield / W. W. Nichol / W. W. Nichol											
207 5/8	24 2/8	23 6/8	17 5/8	23 3/8	5 6/8	5 4/8	7	8	30 6/8	1961	26
■ Moosomin / Leslie Hanson / Sam Peterson											
206 6/8	25 1/8	25 1/8	24	27	5 4/8	5 4/8	7	11	29	1959	27
■ Beechy / Harold Penner / Spanky Greenville											
206 1/8	22 2/8	22 5/8	18 1/8	21	5 4/8	5 1/8	15	10	44 7/8	1956	28
■ Kisbey / J. Harrison / J. Harrison											
205 3/8	23 3/8	21 7/8	18 7/8	27 1/8	4 7/8	5	6	12	71	1954	29
■ Kelvington / D. Minor / D. Minor											
205 1/8	26 1/8	24 6/8	20 3/8	28 1/8	4 7/8	5	10	9	42 4/8	1961	30
■ Leross / R. Weger / R. Weger											
204 6/8	23 3/8	23 1/8	15 2/8	26 6/8	5 4/8	6 6/8	9	10	32	1958	31
■ Moose Jaw / Earl Sears / Earl Sears											

SASKATCHEWAN NON-TYPICAL WHITETAILS (continued)

Score	Length of Main Beam R	L	Inside Spread	Greatest Spread	Circumference at Smallest Place Between Burr and First Point R	L	Number of Points R	L	Total of Lengths Abnormal Points	Date Killed	Rank
204	23⁵⁄₈	23⁶⁄₈	18³⁄₈	21	5⁷⁄₈	5⁶⁄₈	13	14	39⁷⁄₈	1981	32
■ Holbein / Jesse Bates / Jesse Bates
203³⁄₈	22⁴⁄₈	23²⁄₈	19²⁄₈	22⁶⁄₈	6	6¹⁄₈	8	8	25¹⁄₈	1966	33
■ S. Piapot / Frank Kelly / Frank Kelly
203²⁄₈	23⁷⁄₈	23³⁄₈	17²⁄₈	20¹⁄₈	5¹⁄₈	5³⁄₈	13	13	27²⁄₈	1966	34
■ Esterhazy / Walter Tucker / Walter Tucker
202²⁄₈	24	23⁵⁄₈	27	29⁵⁄₈	5⁴⁄₈	5⁴⁄₈	11	8	50⁶⁄₈	1954	35
■ Hungry Hollow / K. W. Henderson / K. W. Henderson
202¹⁄₈	25¹⁄₈	25²⁄₈	22⁶⁄₈	28³⁄₈	4⁷⁄₈	5	9	9	29³⁄₈	1958	36
■ Zehner / Lee Danison / Lee Danison
200	25¹⁄₈	25⁴⁄₈	18⁴⁄₈	23⁴⁄₈	4⁷⁄₈	4⁵⁄₈	11	10	22²⁄₈	1966	37
■ Outlook / Earl B. Schmitt / Earl B. Schmitt
199²⁄₈	21⁴⁄₈	21⁵⁄₈	20⁶⁄₈	22⁷⁄₈	5⁶⁄₈	5⁶⁄₈	8	8	21⁶⁄₈	1958	38
■ Jasmin / Richard Gill / Richard Gill
197⁶⁄₈	24	24⁴⁄₈	18⁴⁄₈	20⁶⁄₈	5¹⁄₈	5⁴⁄₈	10	7	23⁶⁄₈	1967	39
■ Langham / Leonard Waldner / Leonard Waldner
197²⁄₈	24⁵⁄₈	24³⁄₈	18⁵⁄₈	25⁴⁄₈	4⁴⁄₈	4³⁄₈	9	14	39¹⁄₈	1984	40
■ Redvers / Eugene M. Gazda / Eugene M. Gazda
196³⁄₈	25⁶⁄₈	24⁴⁄₈	22⁷⁄₈	28⁴⁄₈	5	5²⁄₈	7	9	26⁴⁄₈	1959	41
■ Prairie River / Herb Kopperud / Herb Kopperud
195⁶⁄₈	26⁴⁄₈	27⁴⁄₈	19⁶⁄₈	22¹⁄₈	5³⁄₈	5¹⁄₈	11	10	39²⁄₈	1961	42
■ Moosomin / Tom Ryan / Tom Ryan
195⁵⁄₈	25⁴⁄₈	25⁶⁄₈	19	26	6	6¹⁄₈	10	10	27⁷⁄₈	1949	43
■ Parkman / H. E. Kennett / H. E. Kennett

Photo Courtesy of Antonio G. Gonzalez

MEXICO RECORD
TYPICAL ANTLERS
SCORE: 174 2/8

Locality: Cerralvo   Date: 1900
Hunter: Unknown
Owner: Antonio Garcia Gonzalez

MEXICO

TYPICAL WHITETAILS

Score	Length of Main Beam R	L	Inside Spread	Greatest Spread	Circumference at Smallest Place Between Burr and First Point R	L	Number of Points R	L	Total of Lengths Abnormal Points	Date Killed	Rank
174 2/8	28 2/8	27 3/8	25 2/8	27 3/8	5 2/8	5 1/8	4	4	0	1900	1

■ *Cerralvo / Unknown / Antonio G. Gonzalez*

Photo Courtesy of Ron Kolpin

MEXICO RECORD
NON-TYPICAL ANTLERS
SCORE: 223 6/8

Locality: Nuevo Leon   Date: January 1983
Hunter: Ron Kolpin

MEXICO

NON-TYPICAL WHITETAILS

Score	Length of Main Beam R	L	Inside Spread	Greatest Spread	Circumference at Smallest Place Between Burr and First Point R	L	Number of Points R	L	Total of Lengths Abnormal Points	Date Killed	Rank
223 6/8	25 1/8	24 2/8	16 3/8	25 4/8	4 3/8	4 3/8	10	13	53 1/8	1983	1
■ Nuevo Leon / Ron Kolpin / Ron Kolpin												
210 6/8	23 6/8	25 4/8	22	24	5	5	11	8	44 4/8	1981	2
■ Coahuila / Picked Up / Jim Jacob												
208 1/8	25 6/8	24 2/8	18 2/8	23 3/8	4 7/8	5	12	12	38 1/8	1959	3
■ Mexico / Unknown / William M. Day												

This book was:

Compiled with able assistance of:
Lise Boorse Capobianco
Carol D. Eads
Laurie L. Gehrke

Book design and layout by: Wm. H. Nesbitt

Typeset by: Graphic Composition, Inc.
Athens, GA

Printed and bound by: BookCrafters
Fredericksburg, VA